Themes in Social Anthropology
edited by David Turton

Sacrifice in Africa

To the members of the Laboratoire Systèmes de pensée en Afrique noire (Ecole Pratique des Hautes Etudes, 5th Section, associated with the CNRS, Paris)

Luc de Heusch

Translated by Linda O'Brien and Alice Morton

Sacrifice in Africa

A structuralist approach

Manchester University Press

Published by
Manchester University Press,
Oxford Road, Manchester M13 9PL, UK.

British library cataloguing in publication data
Heusch, Luc de
   Sacrifice in Africa.—(Themes in social anthropology)
   1. Sacrifice—Africa   2. Rites and ceremonies
   —Africa
   I. Title   II. Turton, David   III. Series
   291.3'4   BL2400

   ISBN 0-7190-1716-5

Phototypeset in Century Schoolbook by
Saxon Press, Derby
Printed in Great Britain by
Butler & Tanner Ltd, Frome and London

Contents

Km 0 1500

Nile

Niger

Lake Chad

Chari

Congo

Zambezi

Limpopo

Orange

Location of peoples

1	Nuer	12	Venda
2	Dinka	13	Lovedu
3	Lele	14	Tswana
4	Kuba	15	Mofu
5	Tetela	16	Rukuba
6	Hamba	17	Dogon
7	Lega	18	Bambara
8	Rwanda	19	Minyanka
9	Zulu	20	Gourmantche
10	Thonga	21	Diola
11	Swazi	22	Massa

Introduction

In 1975 the Laboratory, Systems of Thought in Black Africa, for which I, along with Michel Cartry, assumed responsibility, decided to explore the problem of sacrifice. We did not know then that we were headed for a long adventure, marked by drifting, changes in mid-course, discouragement and exciting discoveries. We began by examining our own fieldwork, collecting from highly diverse civilisations. We soon discovered that we often paid little attention to barnyard animals, goats, sheep and even dogs. African ethnography seemed uninterested in the minute prescriptions (*a priori* judged insignificant) which regulate sacrificial rites. A few great monographs (*Nuer Religion* by Evans-Pritchard, for example) are the exceptions to the widespread rule. Even then, the interpretation seems inspired by a pre-established schema, neglecting numerous aspects. Hubert and Mauss's theory was naturally at the centre of our ongoing debate. However keen their intuition, their analysis soon appeared to us inadequate in acknowledging the complexity of the sacrificial rites and the systems of thought encircling them, explicitly or implicitly justifying them.

Several of us decided to study more thoroughly in the field this neglected sector of religious anthropology, following the example of Griaule and Dieterlen, who many years earlier had discovered that sacrifice is at the heart of Dogon myth. Naturally, the new material accumulated during the next five years was far from always indicating the same problematic. Varying axes of research soon appeared. Be that as it may, the perspectives opened by Griaule and Dieterlen were proved decisive in many societies, both within and outside Mali (see Chapters VI and VII).

Germaine Dieterlen was with us throughout this collective work; many times her observations, indeed her criticisms, rekindled our lagging enthusiasm. The Laboratory published four 'cahiers' devoted to sacrifice, in 1976, 1978, 1979 and 1981. Several foreign guests (Meyer Fortes, John Middleton, Jack Goody) honoured us with a lecture. Many non-Africanist colleagues periodically participated in our work. It is only fair to recognise

[1]These publications can be obtained from Laboratoire Associé 221 CNRS Paris (Systèmes de pensée en Afrique noire), CNRS, 27 rue Paul Bert, Ivry 94200.

that in this domain, Hellenists and Indianists have made considerable advances. It suffices to evoke here the admirable publications of M. Detienne and J.P. Vernant, M. Biardeau and C. Malamoud.

This book does not pretend to close an ever-open study, and I am certainly not the spokesman for the numerous authors who collaborated in the 'cahiers'. I shall adopt, at my own risk, a structuralist perspective which certain of my colleagues are entitled to challenge. I shall first develop the paper I gave at the laboratory on a few Bantu societies. I am more familiar with them than the others. I shall try to decipher in them a first field of symbolic tranformations which, in certain respects, deserve to be compared with the sacrificial preoccupations of the Mofu of Cameroon, described by J.F. Vincent and, more remotely, with those of the ancient Greeks.

I shall then try to situate within western Africa a second group of transformations by liberally commenting on the analyses and observations made by Marcel Griaule, Germaine Dieterlen, Geneviève Calame-Griaule, Youssouf Cissé (the Dogon and the Bambara), Jean-Paul Colleyn, Philippe Jespers and Danielle Jonckers. Obviously, the great wealth of material does not permit me to include in these essays (each centred on one or several particular cultures) the entirety of the rich documentation gathered by our group.

My efforts to be succinct and to avoid dispersing the readers' attention forced me to make a somewhat arbitrary choice in order to emphasise some principal themes. Nevertheless, my debt of gratitude extends to all my colleagues in the laboratory, to whom this book is dedicated.

It was written in three stages. Max Gluckman honoured me with an invitation to Manchester, as Simon Visiting Professor; unfortunately, he passed away before my visit. I especially dedicate to the memory of this great anthropologist the chapter devoted to the Thonga of southern Africa, which was prepared for the lectures given at Manchester in November 1976. The chapters bearing on the Zulu, Swazi and Rwanda were the subjects of classes given at the University of Western Ontario (Canada), Department of Anthropology, in the winter of 1980. I hope that Jim Freedman, who gave me the free time necessary for reflection, will find here the expression of my gratitude. Finally, the academic year 1980–81 was most auspicious for the completion of this book. I would especially like to thank the Fonds National de le Recherche Scientifique of Belgium, which allowed me to go on leave to the United States of America and the Center for Advanced Study in the Behavioral Sciences, which welcomed me, providing working conditions as agreeable as they were fruitful. I often sorely tried the patience of my two translators, Linda O'Brien and Alice Morton during the successive rewritings of the text. I extend my heartiest thanks to them, as well as to Noal Mellott, who kindly contributed to this difficult undertaking, which consists of rendering French philosophical phraseology into acceptable English.

I

Preliminary readings
From Hubert and Mauss to Evans-Pritchard

The famous 'Essai sur la nature et la fonction du sacrifice' by Henri Hubert and Marcel Mauss, which was published in the *Année sociologique* at the turn of the century, marks the end of an era in the systematic examination of a major religious rite which Christianity has placed at the centre of its symbolic system. Although it is almost entirely devoted to the analysis of Hindu, Semitic and Greco-Roman data, and therefore contains hardly any reference to non-literate societies, this short work has had a profound influence on anthropology. It is surprising, therefore, that the ideas developed in it have not been subjected to a thorough re-examination, and that no theory of comparable importance has been put forward, despite the steady accumulation, since it was published, of excellent ethnographic information in a number of monographs. Evans-Pritchard, in his preface to the belated English translation (*Sacrifice: its Nature and Function*, 1964) attributes this situation to a lack of interest in religious phenomena on the part of the succeeding generation of sociologists and anthropologists. But this is not entirely true. Religion was, for example, the focus of the scientific expeditions conducted by Marcel Griaule among the Dogon. Beginning in 1931, these expeditions led, after the Second World War, to the discovery of the extraordinary complexity of those ancient West African civilisations which had not been penetrated by Islam. Griaule, however, was little inclined to theoretical speculation. He chose, as did his close collaborator, Germaine Dieterlen, to listen to the Dogon themselves. Never has so much time and patience been devoted to the faithful transcription of an African conception of man and his world, a conception which equals in its extent the greatest of metaphysical systems.

It is to Lévi-Strauss, Mauss's disciple, that we owe the renewal of interest in comparative religious anthropology in France.

Two different and opposed views of ritual may be found in his work, one of which is by far the most abundantly illustrated. Thus he gives many pointed examples of the close symbolic links between ritual organisation and mythical elaboration. Yet in the final pages of *L'Homme nu (The Naked Man)*, in discussing the ideas of Victor Turner, he writes that there are grounds for distinguishing between the rite, properly speaking, and the various commentaries that accompany it. He introduces here the very interesting concept of 'implicit mythology', a concept which I intend to make use of in the pages which follow. But he also maintains, curiously, that the very nature of ritual differs radically from that of myth. 'The gestures executed, the objects manipulated, are all means by which rituals avoid speech' (Lévi-Strauss, 1971:600). If so, the function of ritual is not to reinforce mythical thought but to overthrow it. Thus Lévi-Strauss presents ritual to us as a 'bastardisation of thought'—a desperate attempt to affirm the priority of 'living' ('*le vivre*') over that of 'thinking' (*le penser*) (Lévi-Strauss, 1971: 603).

It is in this light that one must view the few pages that Lévi-Strauss devoted to sacrifice, a few years earlier, in *La Pensée sauvage* (1962). Here, he radically opposes sacrifice, an absurd act, to classificatory thought, which builds up totemic representations. The latter constitute a symbolic code which is able to link social groups with the natural order through the careful differentation of animal and vegetable species. Is the sacrificial use of animals and vegetables as 'unreasonable' as Evans-Pritchard's famous cucumber, to which Lévi-Strauss pays so much attention, might lead one to think? According to Evans-Pritchard, the Nuer, when destitute, are quite ready to sacrifice a wild fruit, *Cucumis prophetarum* (Crawford), in place of an ox, and Lévi-Strauss argues that a cucumber can be the real equivalent of an ox in sacrifice only because the principle of substitution is here used to the full, and that this constitutes a direct challenge to the logic of classificatory thought. We shall see later on whether this is really so, but first we must place the theory of Hubert and Mauss in its proper perspective.

Their aim was to elaborate a general model, a 'sacrificial schema', that could be applied to all religious systems. Unlike their evolutionist predecessors, Robertson Smith and Frazer, however, they avoided the question of origins and began by pointing out that it was totally arbitrary to argue, as had Robertson Smith, that, because totemic practices sometimes call for the ritual killing and eating of the forbidden animal, sacrifice originated with these practices. 'Robertson Smith's error was above all one of method. Instead of analysing in its original complexity the Semitic ritual system, he set about classifying the facts genealogically, in accordance with the analogical connections which he believed he saw between them' (Hubert and Mauss, 1964:7). They levelled the same type of criticism at Frazer, who was particularly interested in the ritual execution of the spirits of vegetation and of their human representatives. Recognising the force of these arguments, Lévi-Strauss justly wonders why, for so long, 'it should have been possible to regard totemism as the origin of sacrifice in the history of religion' (Lévi-Strauss, 1966:223). In opposition to the evolution-ary schemes of Robertson Smith and Frazer, Hubert and Mauss proposed a formal, generic definition: 'Sacrifice is a religious act which, through the consecration of a victim, modifies the condition of the moral person who accomplishes it or that of certain objects with which he is concerned' (Hubert and Mauss, 1964:13). They use the words 'sacrifice' and 'consecra-tion' in their etymological sense, 'to make sacred' (Hubert and Mauss, 1964:35). In this they explicitly adopted the sociological perspective that Durkheim was to defend, thirteen years later, in his *Elementary Forms of the Religious Life*. Durkheim, of course, saw the opposition between sacred and profane as the foundation of all societies, the sacred being a set of symbolic figures, radically separated from the world of men, through which the group expresses its own transcendent existence, its moral values. The problem for Hubert and Mauss, then, is the following: how is it that sacrifice is the means, *par excellence*, of establishing communication between the profane world and the sacred world?

The model that came to their minds was that of rites of passage. The 'consecration' of the victim, its passage from one state to another, takes place in an isolated zone, cut off from the rest of the world. In order to discover how this takes place, and to establish a universal sacrificial schema, Hubert and Mauss considered it necessary to choose, as a paradigmatic case, a complex and well described rite that included all the important components of the drama. For this purpose they selected the Vedic sacrifice of ancient India. Here the sacrifier must submit to preliminary purifications that rid his body of the imperfections of his profane nature. He must, in effect, penetrate a sacred zone, separated by a magic circle. The victim must be perfect, as it will become, progressively, divine. In the last phase, the sacredness with which it is invested becomes so great that the sacrifier hesitates to approach it. Nevertheless, he must remain in contact with it, because his personality and that of the animal merge, and he risks sharing its fate. The culminating point is the actual killing. This separates the divine principle, which is present within it, from the body, which continues to belong to the profane world. Death renders the consecration 'definitive and irrevocable' (Hubert and Mauss, 1964:33). The body of the animal, invested with sacred matter, 'serves to procure the useful effects of the sacrifice' (Hubert and Mauss, 1964:35). The remains can be given to the protective gods (or evil demons), or given to men (to whom they communicate their religious efficacity), or they can be shared amongst them. The sacrificer now has only to carry out exit rites in order to re-enter the profane world.

Hubert and Mauss thus invite us to participate in a tragic drama, a kind of criminal act of sacrilege, in which the approach of the sacred sends shivers down the spine. The scenario described by Hubert and Mauss remains generally relevant for Vedic India, but we shall see that it does not suit the

African rites at all. In any event, an essential question has to be answered: was it necessary to postulate the existence of a sacred zone, separate and forbidden, as the very condition for sacrifice?

The universal schema elaborated by Hubert and Mauss seems to me marred by a certain amount of Indo-European ethnocentrism. It is Latin which opposes *sacer* to *profanus*. *Sacer* evokes a distinct ontological domain, attributed to the divine and presenting an ambiguous character (Benveniste, 1969, vol. II:197) *Sacer* means, in fact, 'consecrated to the gods and laden with an indelible stain, majestic and cursed, worthy of veneration and inciting horror' (Benveniste 1969, Vol. II:188). One can understand, then, why Hubert and Mauss assert that the immolation of a victim is a crime, a sacrilege, a dangerous infringement of the realm of the sacred. It is in Latin that *sacrificium*, from which we have 'sacrifice', constitutes a mediatory operation that literally 'renders sacred' the victim. Thus Hubert and Mauss's analysis is relevant for Roman religion, as Benveniste does not fail to emphasise. A *homo sacer*, a veritable bearer of pollution, is, for men, 'that which the sacred animal is for the gods'; they are both separated from human society, from the profane world (Benveniste, 1969:188–9).

We should also note that the slaying of the animal, which Hubert and Mauss see as the culmination of the process of transformation of the victim into a 'sacred' object, is designated, in Latin, by a different term, *mactare*. On analysing this verb, Benveniste explains that it expresses 'a growing, a strengthening of the god, obtained by means of the sacrifice which nourishes him' (Benveniste 1969:225). It will become evident that the alimentary metaphors and the energy circuit flowing through the sacrificial field pose particularly difficult problems, which vary from one civilisation to another.

Let us examine once again, with the help of Benveniste's scholarly analysis, the old vocabulary on which Hubert and Mauss based their work. Now it is most curious that a common term to designate the 'sacred' cannot be found in Indo-European languages, and even more curious that no common root can be found to express 'sacrifice' (Benveniste, 1969:179,223). On the other hand, one frequently finds two distinct terms used to define the structure of the religious world. In Latin, *sacer* is completed by *sanctus*, an adjective which was to be further elaborated under Christianity and which designates 'that which is forbidden by a sanction (*sanctio*) against all transgression, like the *leges sanctae*' (Benveniste, 1969:189). *Sanctire*, continues Benveniste, is 'to delimit the field of application of a rule and to render it inviolable by placing it under the god's protection, by calling divine punishment upon any possible violator' (Benveniste, 1969:190). But is this not what anthropologists usually mean by 'ritual prohibition?' Inevitably, this term turns up in Benveniste's text. '*Sanctus* is the resulting state of a prohibition for which men are responsible, of a prescription backed up by law' (Benveniste, 1969:191). Benveniste comes to the conclusion that the study of these semantic pairs in the Indo-European languages 'leads one to suppose the existence of a dichotomous notion in prehistory: 'positive' (that which is filled with divine presence) and 'negative' (that which is forbidden to men)' (Benveniste 1969, vol. II:179).

There exists in Roman thought, therefore, a category which is embarrassing for the theory of Hubert and Mauss and, in general, for the Durkeimian conception of religious forms. Thus one reads in *Digeste* (I:8) 'one designates as *sancta*, properly speaking, things that are *neither sacred nor profane* [my emphasis] but that are confirmed by a certain sanction, as for example, the laws are *sanctae;* that which is submitted to a sanction is *sanctum*, even if it is not consecrated to the god' (Benveniste, 1969:189).

In Durkheimian sociology the notion of *sacer* was frequently identified with the concept of prohibition, the latter having been confused with the ambiguous notion of pollution that the Romans associated with *sacer*. The so-called 'phenomenology of religions' seized upon this synthesis to establish the ambivalent, mysterious power of the 'sacred.' In the preface to the French edition of Mary Douglas's book, *Purity and Danger*, I tried to show that the system of ritual prohibitions should not be confused with ideas relating to 'pollution', even though Christianity links them in the notion of sin, which is a metaphysical impurity resulting from the transgression of a major prohibition. Africans, however, do not consider the matter in this way. I shall emphasise this important point later, because one common function of sacrificial rites is to restore the normal physical condition of man—his health, or his status—which has been compromised by some 'offence'.

One must not be misled by words which have a precise meaning only in particular symbolic contexts—Roman, in that which concerns the sacred and sacrifice; Christian, in that which concerns the transgression of prohibitions. Benveniste, who is usually so attentive to the semantic variations of historically related terms, affirms with a certain lack of prudence that 'the Latin term *sacer* contains *what is for us* [my emphasis] the most precise and specific idea of "sacred"' (Benveniste, 1969:187).

The sacred/profane opposition is clearly a misleading starting point for the analysis of ritual. This bi-polarity is fundamental to Hubert and Mauss's thesis, to the examination of which I now return. Throughout their third and fourth chapters, Hubert and Mauss endeavour to show that their schema varies according to the general and the specific functions of sacrifice. Here we come to the diverse forms taken by the sacrificial schema seen as a means of communication between the sacred and the profane ... 'According to the end sought, according to the function it is to fill, the parts of which it is composed can be arranged in different proportions and in a different order. Some can assume more importance to the detriment of others; some may even be completely lacking. Hence arise the multiplicity of sacrifices, but without there being specific differences between the various combinations' (Hubert and Mauss, 1964:50).

The authors then introduce a major distinction between 'sacralisation' sacrifice and 'desacralisation' sacrifice. In the first case, the movement is made from profane to sacred and the sacrifier[1] is as closely associated as possible with the consecrated victim. After the departure of the spirit that resides in the victim, an alimentary communion takes place. The entrance rites are strongly developed, but not the exit rites, because 'the sacrifier even when he has returned to the profane world, must retain something of what he has acquired during the course of the sacrifice' (Hubert and Mauss, 1964:51). In desacralisation rites it is more often a matter of ridding the sacrifier of any impurity contracted by the non-observance of a religious prescription or by the contact with impure things. The pollution would itself be likened to a consecration; it projected the sinner, a criminal, into the dangerous zone of the sacred, transforming him into a sacred object. Sickness, death and sin are 'identical from the religious viewpoint'. (Hubert and Mauss, 1964:53). The entrance rites are now reduced and all attention is paid to the exit rites which purify the sacrifier separating him from the dangerous state of sacralisation in which he has been since the start of the procedure. The transference of the sacred now takes place in the opposite direction, from the sacrifier to the victim. The thesis subsequently becomes more complicated, for Hubert and Mauss warn us from the start that we would seek in vain for 'examples of an expiatory sacrifice into which no element of communion is interpolated, or for examples of communion sacrifices which do not in some respect resemble expiatory ones' (Hubert and Mauss, 1964:17). We shall not follow them in their meanderings. It is sufficient for us to note that the basic reason for this complexity is that 'what is pure and what is impure are not mutually exclusive opposites; they are two aspects of religious reality' (Hubert and Mauss, 1964:60).

Once again, it is the ambivalence of the Latin concept designated by the word *sacer* (majestic and cursed) that explains the ambiguity of the matter. If this concept belongs to a particular people, if the semantic zone that it covers does not have the universal reach implicitly attributed to it by Hubert and Mauss's thesis, what then remains of the dialectic between 'sacralisation' and 'desacralisation?'

Hubert and Mauss's Anglo-Saxon heritage

Evans-Pritchard rightly considered that the whole essay was 'an uncon-

---

[1] I follow here John Middleton's usage: 'The sacrificer is he who actually performs the rite. I used the word "sacrifier" for the person on whose behalf the rite is performed, the French *sacrifiant*.' ('Rite and sacrifice among the Lugbara', *Systèmes de pensée en Afrique noire*, cahier 4, Le sacrifice III, 1979, 178.)

vincing masterpiece of metaphysical sociology' (Evans-Pritchard 1965:70–1); but he did admire the attempt to construct what he calls a 'grammar of the sacrificial rite'. In fact, the essay provides neither a 'grammar' nor a correct vocabulary, but merely conveys the authors' own ideology of the sacred. Despite his scepticism, Evans-Pritchard does not hesitate to use the latter in his own analysis (remarkable in so many other respects) of Nuer religion. He considers as desacralising rites all the individual sacrifices aimed at ridding the Nuer of the dangerous presence of the Divinity (God) or the spirit representing him. He qualifies as sacralising rites the collective sacrifices accompanying various social activities and especially the rites of passage (Evans-Pritchard, 1956:198–9) while nevertheless acknowledging that it is impossible to introduce an absolute distinction. In truth, his brilliant description never provides the evidence of these concepts among the Nuer. *Nuer Religion* deals almost exclusively with individual sacrifices. A man who has voluntarily or involuntarily infringed an interdiction is in a state of *nueer, kor* or *rual*, depending upon the circumstances. Evans-Pritchard translated all these cases by 'sin'. Herein lies, I believe, a misconception. Firstly, sin is not provoked by a pathogenic contact with the Divinity but, on the contrary, by a loss of grace. The Christian sinner finds himself abandoned by God; he who has infringed among the Nuer is threatened by the untimely intervention of the Divine. Various linguistic metaphors liken the consequences of sin to a stigma of the soul, which is thought to have lost its purity. The breaking of fundamental moral commandments, which Catholic thought defines as sin, is effectively established in the symbolic areas of 'pollution' (de Heusch, 1971:15). Evans-Pritchard has obviously superimposed this model on Nuer thought, which is far removed from it.

How did Evans-Pritchard manage to assimilate the *nueer* state with 'sin' as we have just defined it? By means of a series of semantic alterations in the translation of the indigenous vocabulary which I shall try to illuminate. In the language of the neighbouring Dinka, the word *nueer* means 'to destroy' or 'to kill' (Evans-Pritchard, 1956:183), and it is this basic meaning which must be retained. Actually, among the Nuer, the term *nueer* designates both a series of specific afflictions and the transgressions of particular prohibitions which have caused them (Evans-Pritchard, 1956: 191). This physical deterioration, not to say this threat of death, is a sanction in the Latin sense (*sanctio*) usually inflicted by a spirit of the air. Healing requires atonement in the form of sacrifice. According to Evans-Pritchard, this is, in the circumstances, addressed directly to God, for whom the air spirits are but hypostases.

In order to understand the procedure, we must begin by examining the very notion of prohibition, which is subsumed by the vocable *thek* (to respect). But the *thek* concept embodies no religious connotation whatever. It constitutes the symbolic armatures for social relationships; it establishes a certain distance in communication. Its area of application is most diverse (Evans-Pritchard, 1956: 177–82). A man should 'respect' (*thek*) his wife's parents, particularly by refraining from taking his meals in their house or appearing nude in their presence. The eldest child 'respects' his parents' spoons and his mother's sleeping hide; 'were he not to do so, he might cause the mother to be barren and injure the father, himself, and the cattle' (Evans-Pritchard, 1956:179). Those who have buried a body 'respect' water (they may not drink any). During her menstrual period a woman must abstain from milking, and *thek* also refers to the permanent ban on the performance of this strictly female activity by men.

There is no need to give more examples here, nor to identify the logic which lies behind this set of prescriptions. I wish only to emphasise, along with Evans-Pritchard himself, that 'they are intended to keep people apart from other people or from creatures or things, either altogether or in certain circumstances or with regard to certain matters, and this is what they achieve' (Evans-Pritchard, 1956:181). The category *thek* functions like an operator, selecting a certain number of relations of symbolic incompatibility. As a classificatory system it constitutes, along with kinship rules, the symbolic foundation of all social structure. The intervention of the religious factor comes later, as a sanction that strikes the person who transgresses the rule, deliberately or not.

The Nuer carefully distinguish the body from the spirit (*tie*) (Evans-Pritchard, 1956:154–5). There is no evidence of any kind that would enable us to understand how the *nueer* state affects the spiritual principle at the same time that it does the body. Thus we must ask ourselves what leads Evans-Pritchard to state, without explanation, that 'uncleanness' is not only physical but that it also alters 'the spiritual state' (Evans-Pritchard, 1956:191). Is it not in fact the very term 'uncleanness', which he has arbitrarily chosen, that leads to this equally arbitrary conclusion? Among another African population, the Dogon of Mali, the breaking of a prohibition effectively brings on a loss of spiritual substance, but this notion, as we shall see, is completely foreign to the concept of 'uncleanness' as it is understood in the Judeo-Christian tradition (see Chapter VI). In any case, *Nuer Religion* provides us with no precise description whatever of the alterations in the human psyche which could validate its author's thesis.

The Western concept of sin is inapplicable to Nuer thought. The *nueer* condition is specifically a disorder in the social body which manifests itself in an attack on the integrity of a physical body either of the guilty person or of his close kin. On the strength of his proposed translation Evans-Pritchard nevertheless undertakes to show that sacrifice fulfils a purifying and expiatory function.

The ideal victim is an ox. The sacrificer (who most often is also the sacrifier) begins by rubbing ashes on the animal's back with his right hand.

This act effects 'not only the consecration of the beast to God, but also an identification of man with ox' (Evans-Pritchard, 1956:208). The life of an animal is thus substituted for that of the sacrificer at the scene of the sacrifice (Evans-Pritchard, 1956:261). But how does the author reach this conclusion? Primarily by invoking a ritual of welcome: when a man returns from a long journey and presents himself to his father, the latter rubs ashes on his son's forehead to show 'unity, solidarity or identification' (Evans-Pritchard, 1956:262). The gradation of the words is not insignificant. From the unity and solidarity of the members of the family group, Evans-Pritchard slides to their identity, which, in view of the rigid division of generations, is, to say the least, surprising. Let us take another example. After the birth of the first child, the mother 'brings the baby to her husband's home and lays him in the ashes of the hearth in the centre of his grandfather's byre' (Evans-Pritchard, 1948:40). In this second case, the contact with the ashes is manifestly a rite of passage introducing the child into the paternal lineage through the intermediary of a sign connoting the domestic hearth. The sacrifice requires a previous rite of the same kind which solemnly marks the ownership link between the animal and its master. But nothing indicates that the latter is exposing himself through the victim to a kind of symbolic suicide. To make his thesis conform to Hubert and Mauss's schema, Evans-Pritchard distorts the elements of his research. Further, in an article published some years before *Nuer Religion*, he admits his embarrassment: 'I must confess that this is not an interpretation that I reached entirely by observation, but one taken over from studies of Hebrew and other sacrifices because it seems to make better sense than any other as an explanation of the Nuer facts' (Evans-Pritchard, 1953:191). One could not state more clearly that the interpretative schema originates elsewhere.

One need only pursue Nuer thought to discover that the sacrificial ox partakes of the 'having' and not of the 'being' of the sacrifier. Let us analyse the verb *kok* which is applied to the sacrificial offering of the ox. Evans-Pritchard himself admits that this term, which is to be found in the vocabulary of a certain number of Nilotic populations, conveys the idea of a special kind of exchange, of a relationship between partners rather than between things (Evans-Pritchard, 1956:221–4). In their contacts with Arab merchants, the Nuer use the word *kok* to designate the recent purchasing procedure which is not clearly understood. In accepting a gift, the merchant enters into a reciprocal relationship; he is obligated to come to the aid of the giver. But Evans-Pritchard makes further semantic slips, fully as indefensible as the preceding ones. In the sacrificial context, two supplementary notions are added to the usual meaning: those of ransom and of redemption (Evans-Pritchard, 1956:224). However, no serious support is provided for this interpretation, which permits the author to cling to the idea that the sacrifice he describes is the purifying expiation of a sin. The Nuer state expressly that the immolated ox protects (*gang*) the threatened person and that the affliction from which he suffers 'will be finished' with the sacrifice (Evans-Pritchard, 1956:220).

The idea of 'uncleanness' itself derives from an abuse of language. Evans-Pritchard claims that the function of the sacrifice is also expressed by the verb *woc*. Used in many prófane concepts, this word means 'getting rid of something, especially by wiping it out' (Evans-Pritchard, 1956:190). But the formulation 'especially by wiping it out' is in itself tendentious. Kiggen's dictionary translates *woc* simply as 'to move, put away, take away anything' (Kiggen, 1948:329). This 'anything' which must be got rid of appears throughout the book to be the destructive mark of a pathogenic spirit, the result of an abusive conjunction between man and the spiritual world. Consequently the role of the sacrifice is disjunctive.

The expression *cuol woc*, 'to wipe out the debt', designates most especially the funeral ceremony performed several months after burial (Evans-Pritchard, 1956:146). One or several animals are sacrificed in honour of the dead person and the meat is divided among the different categories of kin according to strict rules. The verb *col*, from which the substantive *cuol* is derived, means, both in Nuer and in other Nilotic languages, 'to pay compensation for an injury' (Evans-Pritchard, 1956:149). The invocations which accompany the ritual express, like a refrain, 'the request to turn away, made to both God and the ghost of the dead man' (Evans-Pritchard, 1956:228). Clearly this is a separation rite, as is attested by the final sacrifice, which takes place the following morning shortly after sunrise. A goat is cut in two lengthwise, from throat to tail; the left half (the bad part) is thrown into the bush; the right half (the good part) is brought into the hut in front of which the sacrifice took place (Evans-Pritchard, 1956:152). The severing of the links with the dead is again expressed in the rite of hair-cutting imposed on members of the family (*ibid:*152). *Cuol woc*, then, involves paying a debt so as to put a potentially dangerous ancestor at a distance, just as *kok* involves getting rid of a pathogenic spirit by the gift of an ox. In neither case does indigenous language permit us to infer the notion of spiritual uncleanness.

Let us listen to the sacrificer who seeks to rid himself of a *nueer* affliction. He has just rubbed the ashes on the tethered animal's back. He holds his spear in his hand and addresses the divine power directly. He states the purpose of the sacrifice and the motivating circumstances. The incisive nature of the speech (*lam*), enunciated in a loud voice as he comes and goes around the animal, is in its tone quite different to prayer (*pal*) (Evans-Pritchard, 1956: 211–12). The speech pretends to place no importance on the illness, as if it were already cured. There is no discernible intention whatever to transfer it to the animal. The sacrificer gesticulates with assurance, brandishing his spear. He is in the process of paying his debt. He is offering a valorised part of his social being (the ox) to atone for an offence which he may not have committed voluntarily. Apart from his own person, this offence has threatened the very existence of the symbolic code of which God and the spirits are the ultimate guarantors.

The sharing of the victim, which will take place later, clearly manifests the separation of men from the supernatural powers: 'The Nuer say that God takes either the *yiegh*, the life, or the *tie*, the spirit.' They also say that 'what belongs to God in the sacrifice is the *riem*, the blood that soaks into the earth, and the *wau*, the chyme or perhaps a mixture of chyme and chyle' (Evans-Pritchard, 1956:212). Men eat the meat of the victim. What does this sharing mean? Nothing that resembles the expulsion of an uncleanness or of a sin which a 'sacralised' animal would take over. The sacrifice re-establishes the separation of the super-natural world (God, the air spirits) from the human world which had unfortunately been joined together in the person of the sick man. This topological confusion is itself the result of too close a linkage between two people, or between a person and an object, which are symbolically incompatible and are separated by a prohibition. The sacrifice, like the *thek* system which it sanctions, is based on exclusion, and this principle is the very guaranty of established social order to the extent that it institutes significant differences.

Now we shall consider a certain number of specific cases which are likewise classified by Evans-Pritchard in the category of 'sin'. We shall begin with the illness *kor*, which is brought on by adultery. '*Kor* is a condition brought about by a man having congress with his wife after she has been unfaithful to him.' It is a sickness which attacks the kidneys, striking, not the guilty parties, but the innocent husband. But *kor* affects him only if the adultery has been committed under his roof. Then it is a particularly serious offence which threatens the social order—a blow to marital rights.

Nevertheless, it is surprising that the illness affects the victim. Let us try to understand this. There is sexual incompatibility between husband and wife after her adultery. She is separated from her husband; a guilty man has come between them. A prohibition, a distance, has thus been created between the innocent husband and his adulterous wife. Paradoxically, it is *he* who is at fault for approaching her. Evans-Pritchard states very clearly that the *kor* condition is brought about by the imprudent husband.

Note that the sacrifice which enables the husband to rid himself of this specific sickness differs somewhat from the general schema. The wronged man is the sacrificer, but the guilty wife and her accomplice must participate. The rite is usually conducted by a religious functionary (Evans-Pritchard, 1956:186). Thus we are dealing with an extremely serious act, a profound blow to social order—much more serious than the transgression of an ordinary prohibition such as would bring on the *nueer* state, which is only a private matter. That is why *kor*, resulting from adultery, is denoted by a specific term. But the rite is a recent introduction.

Like the term *kor* itself, i comes from the Dinka. It is apparently an attempt to reinforce the social order. Actually the Nuer themselves attach little opprobrium to adultery, 'of which they speak light-heartedly and without disgust or shame' (Evans-Pritchard, 1956:185). We now understand better why it is the victim and not the guilty party who finds himself afflicted.

Consistent with his overall interpretation of offences, Evans-Pritcard nevertheless states that all three of those involved are 'polluted'. What does that mean exactly? We learn that 'the adulterer, the husband and the wife are all dangerous to anyone they come into contact with who has an open sore, for the *kor* may enter him through it' (Evans-Pritchard, 1956:187). Contagion is, thus, limited to those whose corporal integrity is already threatened. Let us translate this into sociological terms. The adultery poses a threat to the social fabric; it is a challenge to one of the fundamental rules of matrimonial alliance. This weakening of the entire society quite naturally threatens those who are already weakened by a sore. One can interpret this as a metaphor and not as decisive proof of the contagion of a 'pollution'; *nueer*, or *kor*, is simply the physical consequence of a rent in the social fabric as defined by prohibitions. Evans-Pritchard himself insists strongly on the Nuer's strict identification of the offence and the resulting sickness. Yet he contrives to introduce into his analysis a complementary mystical term—sin. This desperate attempt to fit Nuer thinking into Judeo-Christian theology is completely without foundation.

The Nuer introduce yet another specific term (*rual*) to designate incest, which is a blow to the system of kinship and alliance. Evans-Pritchard, again, presents the consequence of this infraction as a 'sin' calling for a sacrifice of desacralisation. The Nuer say that incest (*rual*) is like *nueer*. This time, the concept belongs to them; they did not borrow it from the Dinka. If the incest is particularly serious, the guilty parties risk dying from one day to the next. If not, sacrifice provides reparation. In the perspective of the Durkheimian school, prohibition of incest should be particularly 'sacred' because exogamy is the foundation of the social structure. But incest (*rual*) does not pollute any more than the different states of *nueer* do. Affliction strikes only the close family of the guilty parties, and particularly their children (Evans-Pritchard, 1956:184) Incestuous lovers are not despised. On the contrary, the Nuer 'regard incest as a venial offence if the partners are related distantly, and young men certainly often take the slight risk involved' (Evans-Pritchard, 1956;185).

The necessary sacrificial rite under these circumstances consists in halving the animal's carcase; it clearly indicates that the bond of kinship which united the guilty parties is severed. But exactly the same thing is done 'at the closing of an age-set, in mortuary ceremonies, and on other occasions' without any possibility of alleging the notion of sin (Evans-Pritchard, 1956:231).

Where, then, is this state of spiritual impurity which Evans-Pritchard claims is the ultimate rationale of Nuer sacrifice? Shall we find it in the prohibition that forbids a man to have sexual relations with his wife while she nurses a child? Here, the offence belongs to the most general category, *nueer*. There is, however, a specific word, *thiang*, 'to designate the act itself, the consequences which follow from it, and the rite performed to ward off the consequences' (Evans-Pritchard, 1956:187). The function of this rite is to allay the threat of deadly dysentery that weighs on the child. It differs radically from the paradigmatic sacrifice of the ox. In this case, a dog and a goat are part of the ceremony (Evans-Pritchard, 1956:188). Once again we are dealing with a rite borrowed from the Dinka. Evans-Pritchard may partly be regarded as negligent in his analysis in that he overlooks the complexity and diversity of the sacrificial acts. The cild threatened by dysentery is put down by a small termite mound which is surrounded by grass which is set alight: an officiant holds the child above the flames. Then a dog is brought and the child is placed on its back. 'They cut a piece off the dog's ear and it is released and runs off taking the *thiang* with it. Finally a goat is sacrificed and a piece cut from one of its ears is tied with the piece of the dog's ear round the child's neck . . . The rite is performed by old women, though it is a man who sacrifices the goat. The old women eat the sacrificial meat. On the occasion when I witnessed it all the older women of the cattle camp ran, shouting, out of the camp, each carrying a child which she placed on a small termite mound so that, I was told, the *thiang* might go into the mound' (Evans-Pritchard, 1956:188). Why this odd treatment of a dog and a goat? Why is a termite mound chosen for the expulsion of evil? This particular sacrifice, which strongly resembles an exorcism, does not fit in with the usual model in which the sacrifier is seen as paying a debt. Here I shall keep to the interpretation offered by the Nuer. They use the verb *woc* to designate the removal of 'the dangerous influence of this abnormality (*buom*)' that is liable to spread (*dop*) to other families (Evans-Pritchard, 1956:188). What must be got rid of, by quasi-magical means, is an anomaly, which is not otherwise defined. Is it not, once again, to the symbolic order that one must refer?

A man must respect (*thek*) his wife while she nurses a child. He finds himself temporarily separated from her, just as he is permanently separated from cows that are being milked. It is the entire social structure that looms behind these prohibitions. They indicate the general or particular rules that make up life's daily routine; they set up a system of attitudes that is encompassed by a unique set of ethics and etiquette, of *savoir vivre*. Any serious infraction of this code calls for intervention by the divinity or his representatives, creatures of the air. Social order is one with cosmic order. The rules of respect (*thek*) keep men and things that should be separated well apart; in the global system, the celestial divinity and the spirits of the air, or the ancestors, are separated from men. Everyone is in his own place when all goes well, but when an offence has been committed, deliberately or accidentally, this symbolic order is threatened at a precise point. The sacrificial debt must then be paid in order to put the system back in place—God or spirits in the sky; men, defined by their network of prohibitions, on earth.

It should be noted that there is a large variety of sacrifices among the Nuer which differ from the proposed paradigmatic model. They do not all belong to the *kok* category, which establishes, at least provisionally, a communication between the sacrificer and a spirit of the air through the medium of an ox. When an epidemic breaks out, the people go to meet the scourge (*lor*) outside the village in order to put an end to it. When a part of the tribe performs this ritual to conjure away smallpox, they sacrifice goats and sheep, leaving the carcases, with jugs of beer, to set up a boundary (*kegh*) which the epidemic will be unable to cross (Evans-Pritchard, 1956:226). The disjunctive finality which characterises the sacrifices we have already analysed is at this point climactic, and one can find no trace in them of communication with the spiritual world. The nature of the rite is purely magical.

Kok and *lor* designate sacrificial acts of a different kind, whose common denominator is not the idea of expiation or purification, but that of a transaction intended to establish a rupture. The verb *kir* is used for specific sacrifices required when lightning strikes a byre, when a vulture alights on a man's head, or when twins are born to a family (Evans-Pritchard, 1956:227). This word has no equivalent in profane language, and Evans-Pritchard decided to translate it, purely and simply, as 'to expiate'. However, the three cases present an identical pertinent trait which seems to escape him: they manifest an excessive conjunction of sky and earth, since the Nuer liken twins to birds (Evans-Pritchard, 1956:128).

I shall not continue with the analysis of the material gathered by Evans-Pritchard. I shall limit myself to noting here the possibility of an interpretation other than the one he proposes by borrowing a certain number of Hubert and Mauss's concepts on the one hand, and of Catholic theology on the other. The latter provides us with interesting ethnographic material; it testifies to the symbolic system of Western civilisation. But it cannot, in turn, pretend to express a universal anthropological truth on these grounds.

We have not yet finished with Hubert and Mauss's hypothesis. In Chapter 5 of their essay, the authors deal with the problem of the death of God, a central preoccupation of Christianity. Why, in so many religious systems, is the god himself, or his representative, put to death? Frazer's great merit was that he was the first to pose the question clearly. We know his answer in *The Golden Bough*. The sacrifice of God originated in animal sacrifice, and indirectly from the pretended sacrifice of the totemic animal, normally forbidden. The renewal of all nature, and in particular the return of the fertilising rain, depends on the sacrifice and resurrection of the divinity with which the forces of vegetation identify. The gods and kings who are ritually killed would be mere spirits of nature. The sacred king, the divine king, appears everywhere as a privileged sacrificial figure.

Hubert and Mauss take up this thesis partially. They think that the sacrifice of domestic animals in agrarian and pastoral societies is the starting point. They decree that the sacrifice of the god is a 'perfecting' of primitive sacrifice due to 'the imagination of the creators of myths' (Hubert Mauss, 1964:81). We find ourselves in the presence 'of the most perfected forms of the historical evolution of the sacrificial system' (Hubert and Mauss, 1964:77). It is clear that Hubert and Mauss themselves fall into the trap of evolutionism that they rejected in their initial research for a general sacrificial schema. Surreptitiously they reinstate in synchronic analysis a diachronic dimension loaded with moral presuppositions. After having cleared sacrifice of its alleged 'totemic' origins, they assign it a historical destiny, tied to the development of civilisation.

But if one examines the African literature, nothing permits the assertion that the ritual killing of the divine king constitutes an evolved form of animal sacrifice. As we shall see, in Rwanda both rites coexist, on different levels. Marcel Detienne is fully aware that in dealing with the sacrifice of a god, Hubert and Mauss abandoned their initial schema (Detienne, 1979:27). There is no longer any trace of mediation in the sacrificial scene: the most sacred thing, the king or representative of a vegetation spirit, is destroyed in order to assure man's salvation. Therein lies, obviously, a certain theoretical inconsistency influenced by the Christian concept of abnega-tion.

Indeed, no sound information permits us to think that the sacrifice of a god or of the king proceeds, historically or structurally, from animal sacrifice. We shall see that this is part of a very specific problematic (Chapter V). It is no less true that one constant practice pervades the sacrificial field: the possibility of substituting an animal for a man. An ox is sacrificed each year in place of the Swazi king. In Dogon thought, all animal sacrifice re-actualises the primordial immolation of a demiurge whose rebirth is at the very origin of the universe (Chapter VI). What is the meaning of this game of death that produces life in the most varied contexts? A systematic inventory of sacrificial practices is out of the question for it would demand an encyclopaedic, hence superficial, knowledge. Basing our study on a limited number of symbolic systems analysed in their numerous facets, I shall try to outline the ideologies that are set up around the immolation of a human or animal victim. No theological elaboration Christian, Greek, Vedic, Roman or African, could claim a privileged status in this comparative study. One must also reject the opposite position, that of refusing to credit any of these systems of ideas and thus building a universal psychological theory of sacrifice out of thin air. This is what a French essayist, René Girard, recently tried to do in two successive books, *La violence et le sacré* (Violence and the Sacred) (1972) and *Des choses cachées depuis la fondation du monde* (Things Hidden since the Beginning of the World) (1978), in which he somewhat misuses anthropology. The universal truth of sacrifice is this: 'Society seeks to divert toward an uninvolved victim, a "sacrificable" victim, a violence that threatens its own members, whom it intends to protect at all costs' (Girard, 1972:17). Violence is the key word—the key not only to sacrifice, but to all rituals. If sacrifice is murder (but is it really?), it could be but one way of expressing man's fundamental aggression, a means of cheating natural violence by cultural artifice. 'It is the entire community that sacrifice protects from *its own* violence; it is the entire community that it diverts towards victims that are outsiders. Sacrifice focuses on the victim the widespread germs of dissension, and it disperses them by offering a partial satisfaction' (Girard, 1972:22).

This theory is based on a dogmatic bias. Violence never appears as such in the individual ox sacrifice as practised by the Nuer. It is even less apparent in the collective sacrifices, the principal function of which is to 'confirm, to establish or to add strength to, a change in social status—boy to man, maiden to wife, living man to ghost—or a new relationship between social groups—the coming into being of a new age-set, the uniting of kin groups by ties of affinity, the ending of a blood-feud—by making God and the ghosts, who are directly concerned with the change taking place, witnesses of it' (Evans-Pritchard, 1956:199).

Girard abolishes all anthropological differences by virtue of the strange psychological concept he has developed about social life. If sacrifice is the central institution in the history of religions, it is because its function is 'to prevent the outbreak of conflicts' (Girard, 1972:30). Crises that threaten the unity of the community call more especially for the counter-stroke of sacrifice (Girard, 1972:35). Sacrifice would die out where, as in Greece and Rome, judicial systems are set up. As if the vendetta was the common lot of all 'sacrificial societies'! That is to forget a little too quickly that the most civilised Greek cities, during the classic era, did not cease to practise sacrifice, concurrently with the exercise of justice and statecraft, as Detienne and Vernant remind us (Detienne and Vernant, 1979). Decidedly, Girard treats Greek history as lightly as he does anthropology.

On the strength of this encyclopaedic knowledge, Girard thinks he has revealed the foundation of sacrifice by renouncing all the precautions that Hubert and Mauss took. It is very simple: it '*always* aims at calming violence, at preventing it from breaking out' [my emphasis]. Here we have, so to speak, a vulgarised Durkheimian theory, based on the symbolic prevention of crime. Nevertheless, violence is prevalent everywhere—in vengeance, sacrifice and judicial sentences (Girard, 1972:43). No society escapes it, until the teachings of Christ.

Girard then hastily investigates the notion of ritual impurity. Anthropologists will undoubtedly be most astonished to learn of 'this fantastic reality' which they have always denied—impurity is the contact with violence. The latter is contagious. 'The slightest violence can bring on a cataclysmic escalation' (Girard, 1972:51). Does not Girard seem to transfer nuclear panic, the fruit of our military-industrial complexes, into the heart of universal man? Decidedly, ethnocentrism again rears its ugly head. This time we are dealing with a neo-Christian, somewhat heretical, theology. His second book, a sequel to the first, clearly reveals this. In *Des choses cachées depuis la fondation du monde* (Things Hidden since the Beginning of the World), he informs us that Christ, far from being himself a sacrificial victim as official theology teaches us, in reality came down to end the long era of sacrificial violence which had characterised human history, primitive and civilised, since the beginning of time.

These metaphysical excesses do not concern us here. Let it suffice to note that Girard reduces all forms of sacrifice to a theory of the scapegoat, instead of questioning the exact place of that ideology within the field of sacrifice.

In order to examine this, one must begin by listening to what the people say, by understanding what they think of their practices. It is these explicit symbolic systems that the members of a research group (Associated Laboratory 221, CNRS-EPHE, Paris) endeavoured to establish by studying the data from their own fieldwork, during an extensive collective study from 1975 to 1979. First, we tried to situate sacrifice within the general system of 'offerings'. On this particular point, the thesis of Hubert and Mauss seems valid. They maintain, contrary to Tylor, and not without reason, that sacrifice cannot simply be interpreted as a form of gift, as a contractual procedure binding man and the gods.

The ritual immolation of domestic animals is sometimes explicitly included in this category. This is the case, for example, among the Minyanka of Mali (see Chapter VII). But this is merely a superficial explanation masking the fact that the sacrificer manipulates cosmic forces. Sometimes, on the contrary, he affirms—as was the case in ancient Greece—the absolute difference between the gods and men. The sacrifice is, then, a complete ritual cuisine, the expression of social order.

Greek and Mofu ritual cuisine

Marcel Detienne reminds us, following Jean Rudhardt's example, that the schema proposed by Hubert and Mauss is 'inadequate in the Greek case, where neither the sacrificer nor the victim must leave the world at any point, but on the contrary, where it is participation in a social group or a political community that authorises the practice of sacrifice and finds there in return, something to confirm group cohesion and the coherence of the community image *vis-à-vis* the divine powers' (Detienne, 1979:25).

I have borrowed from Vernant the following excellent summary of the position adopted by the French Hellenist school. 'Our analysis should, then, approach sacrifice from two angles, two aspects, that seem different to us, but are in fact one in the eyes of the Greeks. On the one hand, we should see it as a solemn feast where the invited gods are present, where communication is established between the earth and the sky through the smoke and perfumes burned on the altar. On the other hand, we should see it as ritualised cooking, the preparation of a dish according to rules that, in the course of daily life, render the consumption of meat dishes legitimate, even pious. We must focus our analysis on the concrete details of this cooking—the isolation of, first, internal and vital parts, then the long bones with the pelvis and tail and thirdly, the meat divided on an egalitarian basis; the various methods of cooking it—what part is entirely burned for the gods, what part is grilled on the altar fire, what part is boiled in a cauldron. Also, the intended use of these various parts to be eaten or not, to be used for religious purposes or not, to be consumed on the spot or to exercise the right to take some away, or to sell it.

It is through all these details, both ritual and prosaic, that a theology of sacrifice is set up, its schema clearly shown through the founding myths. Greek sacrifice is not like Vedic sacrifice, the proto-type of the creating, founding act that engenders and keeps together the total universe. Being more modest, it recalls the gap which, through Prometheus' fault, occurred between the gods and man; it consecrates, in the very ritual that aims at joining mortals and immortals, the insurmountable distance that will henceforth separate them. By bringing alimentary rules into play, it establishes man in his own status, between beast and gods, at just the right distance from the savagery of the animals, devouring each other raw, and the unchanging bliss of the gods, ignorant of hunger, fatigue and death because they are nourished by nectar and ambrosia' (Vernant, 1975:30–1).

Let us dwell a moment on the code that governs Greek ritual cooking, which is based on a clearcut distinction between the viscera and the meat. 'The viscera are roasted on a spit during the first phase of the sacrifice and eaten on the spot near the altar by a small circle of those who participate fully in the sacrifice, while the quarters of meat, which are boiled in a cauldron, are destined either for a large banquet or for more distant distributions' (Detienne, 1979:20).

At the human ritual table, one thus sees the boiled meat follow the roasted, while the gods content themselves with the smoke of the charred long bones. Why is this so? J.F. Vernant has brilliantly shown that Greek sacrificial rites are inexplicable apart from the Promethean myth that instituted them. In the beginning, men and gods lived together and ate at the same banquets. The wily Prometheus hoped to trick the gods so as to favour mankind. He brought a big ox that he killed and then cut up into two portions. 'Hidden under the savoury dressing of the first portion were the bare bones; under the unappetising skin and stomach of the second were the good edible cuts' (Vernant, 1981, vol. II:409). Zeus chose the attractive portion and left the other to mankind. Of course, the 'good' portion was a trick. 'By eating meat, men behave like "stomachs" (*gasteres oion*, Theogony 26). Their pleasure in partaking of the flesh of a dead animal, their irresistible need for such food, their ever resurgent hunger implies using up their strength, hence weariness, ageing and death. By accepting the smoke of bones and living on odours, the gods prove to be of a different nature. They are immortal and eternally young. Nothing about them ever perishes, and they never come into contact with things that decay' (Vernant, 1981, vol. II:409). The rest of the story is well known. As punishment, Zeus refused to give men celestial fire. Prometheus stole some so that they could cook the meat. Zeus wrought vengeance by offering them a poisoned gift as bait, woman (Pandora). Seduced by Pandora's charms, these prisoners of the cycle of life and death also experienced all kinds of misfortune. Sacrifice must be understood in terms of the stolen fire—and woman-trap, this double trick. 'To make a sacrifice brings one into touch with the divinity and thus commemorates the Titan's [Prometheus'] adventure and accepts its lesson. Namely through the sacrifice and all that it entails (the Promethean fire, cereals and the toil needed to grow them, women and marriage, bad times, and death), Zeus put men in the position they still hold between the animals and gods. By sacrificing, mankind bows before the will of Zeus, who created mortal and immortal beings as two distinct races. Communication with the divinity takes place during the ceremonial meal, a reminder that dining with the gods is over. Men and gods are now separated. No longer do they live together, nor eat at the same table' (Vernant, 1981, vol.II:410). Therefore, the animal's bones were burnt on the altar but the meat was kept for human beings.

Precisely codified culinary practices had an important symbolic function, which another Greek myth brings to light. This time the sacrificial victim was a god-child, Dionysus. Detienne comments on it with insight in an essay entitled 'Orphic Dionysus and the Roasted Stew' (1977). The Titans seize the innocent young god after having seduced him by offering him toys. They cut up his body and start by boiling the pieces in a cauldron; then they roast them on a spit. They devour the meat, except the heart, and then Zeus' lightning destroys them. From their ashes mortal mankind is born.

In this text the origin of man is linked to the subversion of the sacrificial practice, as set up in the preceding myth. Not only is the victim a man-god but, moreover, it is absurd to roast what has already been boiled. Detienne demonstrates convincingly that this singular tale, elaborated in Orphic philosophical milieux, is only comprehensible in opposition to the myth of Prometheus. It constitutes a symbolic protest against the bloody sacrifice practised in the City. The adepts of Orphic thought liken it to a form of cannibalism. These dissident philosophers hoped to rediscover the primordial unity of man and the gods 'by eating only perfectly pure foods such as honey and cereals, by escaping upwards, in the direction of the gods' (Detienne, 1979:16).

This version of the myth of Dionysus should not be connected with the ritual practices of the Dionysian sects at all. The latter express their hostility to the politico-religious order of the City in an opposite way. The ritual that they propose to their followers is 'the tearing to pieces of a living being, hunted like a wild beast and devoured raw' (Detienne, 1979:16). It is in a kind of collective frenzy that the followers of this 'cult of mysteries' refuse to execute the official sacrificial prescriptions of the City. 'By eating the meat raw, the Dionysian faithful want to behave like animals and, strictly speaking, to become wild, in order to escape their politico-religious condition—but this time in a low way, in a bestial way' (Detienne, 1979:16). Nothing about these mystical effusions can be understood if they are not compared with the social function of sacrifice established by Prometheus.

Decidedly, the Greek mythology of sacrifice does not validate the diachronic hypothesis of Hubert and Mauss. First we see Prometheus establish animal sacrifice, which confirms the definitive, tragic split between the gods and man. The opposition between what Hubert and Mauss call 'profane' and 'sacred' appears here as a definitive distance between immortal and mortal creatures. When philosophical sects present a new mythical model, they propose the story of a god (Dionysus), who is cut into pieces and devoured. In this way they mean to stigmatise the sacrifices of the City, which are described as a blow to life. It is not a question of encouraging the spirituality of sacrifice, but of abolishing it.

Loisy has tried, however, to associate the Dionysian model with the Christian model. In connection with these theories, Detienne denounces the astonishing domination that Christianity continues to exercise over the anthropological theory of sacrifice (Detienne, 1979:25–35). Hubert and Mauss, liberal and free-thinking men, do not escape it entirely. In their eyes, theology borrowed its cosmogonies from the sacrificial myths. 'It explained creation by sacrifice, just as popular imagination explained the yearly life of nature ... The recurrent onslaughts of chaos and evil unceasingly required new sacrifices, creative and redemptive. Thus transformed and, so to speak, purified, sacrifice has been preserved by Christian theology' (Hubert and Mauss, 1964:92–3). What seems to me to be particularly questionable in this perspective is that it establishes a unique ritual area in which, from its origins to the present day, differences, far from being symbolic, obey a historical progression, an inescapable moral law inherent in the development of humanity. 'By the same ritual processes our priests seek almost the same effects as our most remote ancestors' (Hubert and Mauss, 1964:93). Whatever scandal such a proposition might have caused in the bourgeois mentality of the early twentieth century, it nonetheless shares in the spirit of the times.

'The function of the Greeks' sacrificial cuisine is curiously reversed in a contemporary African society, that of the Mofu in the North Cameroons' (Vincent, 1976). The Mofu sacrifice, not to distant gods, but to their own ancestors and to possessing spirits. The rite takes place in a different topology from that delimited by far-off Olympus and the City. At the moment of immolation, the ancestors gather 'next to their descendants' (Vincent, 1976:90). But this familiar communicative contact is realised through prosaic culinary contrivances comparable to those which the Ancient Greeks practised in order to maintain a remote communication with the Sky by means of a thin thread of smoke. The Mofu expressly invite their ancestors to come and eat the portion placed on the altar, carved in the same way as the one for the living. Let us consider the meaning of the division between roasted and boiled meat in the two cases. The Greeks insisted that the viscera be roasted without salt. There is much evidence to attest that this initial phase of the ritual was, to them, evocative of a primitive era of human development, intermediary between animal cannibalism and the elaborated art of cooking, symbolised by stew and the use of seasoning (Detienne, 1977:174–182). The consumption of internal organs, roasted without salt and full of vital force concerns only a limited number of guests, those who are most directly involved in the sacrifice. The meal takes place right there, by the altar. The stewed meat, on the other hand, is taken away and distributed more generously. The spit is, then, the centre of a circular social space which encompasses all of the city's free citizens. The sharing of the stewed meat was rigorously democratic.

The Mofu make a different decision, but the priority remains with the roasted parts. The men start by roasting some of the meat near the altar. Then the women proceed with the preparation of the stewed meat in their kitchen (Vincent, 1976:200). They prepare it with a sauce, (but no salt), and add millet flour. The two sexes thus participate directly, yet from different locations, in ritual cooking just as they will be associated in eating the food. The ancestors are invited to this meal as equals, so to speak; unlike the Greek gods, they eat the same good roast, the same delicious stew as the living do; a special portion is even set aside for them. In order to better mark the lack of separation between them and their descendants a predetermined member of the family will then eat the gods' share, which is placed on the altar. The sacrificial democracy of the Mofu encompasses both of the sexes and the gods. This intense participation of the living and the dead is emphasised by the following fact: only the ancestors benefit entirely from the shared meal; as for the possessing spirits, they are merely offered meat, they are not invited to participate in the complete meal (Vincent, 1976:195).

Thus the opposition between roasted and boiled meat is pertinent among the ancient Greeks as well as among the contemporary Mofu, but it relates in each case to different sociological codes. In both, to be sure, the roasting is done first and also as close to the altar as possible. However in the Greek procedure, the two methods of cooking introduce a cleavage between participants who are close and those who are far away; the Mofu practice opposes men and women by underlining their complementary roles. The absence of salt marks the sacrificial meal of the Greeks as well as that of the Mofu.

Similar and different preoccupations thus appear within the same symbolic culinary space. The differences obviously define two strongly dissimilar socio-religious configurations. In one case we are dealing with a democratic City where no meat reaches the altar of the cosmic gods, who are situated at a dizzying distance from men; in the other we are dealing with a restricted familial community or with all the lineage; the ancestors are in close solidarity with their descendants. One cannot find in either case the slightest trace of sacralisation of the victim or the sacrifier. The Mofu require only that the participants' costume be as traditional as possible. The ideal is 'to present oneself to the ancestors stripped to the waist, like them' (Vincent, 1976:189). Thus it is a matter of resembling them as much as possible. The fears entertained by the Mofu are much more prosaic than the supposed terror caused by the mystery of he 'sacred'; if the preparation of the sacrificial meal is meticulous, it is because they are haunted by the ancestors' wrath (Vincent, 1976:196).

From an anthropological standpoint, what is remarkable in the analysis of Greek sacrifice undertaken by Detienne and Vernant is that it reconciles the structuralist approach with the functionalist urge to connect symbolic thought with specific social reality wherever it is found. But it will be noted that the challenge to the City's sacrificial ideology does not in any way convey the tensions of social life, not to mention the class struggle. The circles which protest against the official practice of sacrifice in ancient Greece are on the one hand the intellectual sects, the Pythagoreans and Orphics, and on the other, mystics given to Dionysian possession. Like Girard, the former see in sacrifice a criminal violence, an attack on life; they do not protest against the conditions of slavery, however. These symbolic protesters develop two new alimentary systems that are clearly the antithesis of sacrificial culinary practices. The strict vegetarianism of the Pythagoreans, like the savage devouring of raw meat which the Dionysian sect ritually practises, form one and the same system with the official sacrifice of the City. This kind of symbolic complexity is familiar in traditional societies. When we examine the rites of Rwanda, an African kingdom, we shall see how the initiates of a possession cult of peasant origin built up their own sacrificial system by systematically transforming the rites of the royal court (Chapter V). We shall also see that the Thonga of Mozambique practise sacrifice under different forms depending on whether it is to establish communication with the ancestors or to exorcise a possessed person, who is tormented by a spirit belonging to a neighbouring tribe (Chapter IV). The practice of sacrifice, then, does not necessarily obey a unique schema in any given society.

We agree with Detienne in noting the inadequacy of Herbert and Mauss's theory. We voluntarily admit, along with him, that any attempt to define 'sacrifice' from our own Judeo-Christian religious experience is vain. Must we believe that by approaching this subject from a comparative point of view, we are victims of a 'sacrificial illusion' analogous to that denounced by Lévi-Strauss in dealing with the subject of totemism? Detienne considers that any general discussion of sacrifice could only 'reassemble into an artificial model elements picked up here and there, in the symbolic tissue of societies' (Detienne and Vernant, 1979:34). Is all comparative research then definitively compromised? Is the evident failure of Hubert and Mauss final?

I am not convinced. But it is necessary to tackle the problem from the other end; to renounce defining a formal universal sacrificial schema. One must listen patiently to the ideological speeches of a multitude of sacrificers, in the most diverse societies, before reaching a conclusion. One must ask oneself, in each particular case, what is the symbolic coherence of the set of sacrificial rites which often appear incongruous; one must not fail to connect them with neighbouring rites, with the entirety of the symbolic thought in the society under study. Hubert and Mauss's starting point was decidedly too tenuous. How could they think that they would be able to deduce the universal secret of the sacrificial operation from the Vedic rite, considered as paradigmatic? Unfortunately we can not improve much on the method adopted by these pioneers. We shall take into consideration a limited number of serious monographs on some sharply differing African societies. It is only after having examined their conception of sacrifice that we shall risk asking ourselves if the comparison of symbolic models established around sacrifice is or is not a worthwhile task.

I have now indicated how I intend to proceed. However I must insist on one essential point. If sacrifice belongs to symbolic thought, I must first investigate the status of the domestic animal in classificatory systems. This problem preoccupied my friends and myself during discussions at the Laboratory on Thought Systems in Black Africa. They helped me to clarify a certain number of ideas. Lévi-Strauss elucidated the 'totemic' code and the functioning of mythic thought by basing himself essentially on species of wild animals and plants. A first survey persuaded us that the same approach explains why certain familiar animals are the privileged agents of sacrifice. From this point of view it seems necessary to question the principle of substitution that, according to Lévi-Strauss, threatens to abolish classificatory thought in sacrificial procedures.

Let me refer to the hypothesis he developed in *The Savage Mind:* 'Although distinct things are often destined in a preferential manner for certain deities or certain types of sacrifice, the fundamental principle is that of substitution: in default of the prescribed object, any other can replace it, so long as the intention, the only thing of consequence, persists and although the zeal itself can vary' (Lévi-Strauss, 1966:224). In this important debate, Lévi-Strauss opposes the quantified totemic system based on classification and the rigorous separation of species to the sacrificial system which permits a continuous passage between its terms: 'A cucumber is worth an egg as a sacrificial victim, an egg a chick, a chick a hen, a hen a goat, a goat an ox. And this gradation is oriented: a cucumber is sacrificed if there is no ox but the sacrifice of an ox for want of a cucumber would be an absurdity. In totemism, or so-called totemism, on the other hand, relations are always reversible. In a system of clan appelations in which both figured, the oxen would be genuinely equivalent to the cucumbers, in the sense that it would be impossible to confound them and that they would be equally suitable for manifesting the differentiation between the groups they respectively connote. But they can only play this part in so far as totemism (as distinct from sacrifice) proclaims them to be distinct and not substitutable for each other' (Lévi-Strauss, 1966:224).

However, we shall see that in two Bantu societies the principle of substitution is only played out within strict limits, defined by their particular symbolic thought. Or, as Cartry shows in his study of the Gurmantche (Upper Volta), the problem must be posed differently (Chapter VII). Lévi-Strauss based his opinion largely on Evans-Pritchard's essay on Nuer religion. It suffices to read the latter to realise that its author was not sufficiently attentive to the complexity of the data. Specific rules concerning the choice of animals, the procedures, etc., seem to be mixed up in one paradigmatic model, the fragility of which we have already stressed: the sacrifice of the ox to the spirits of the air to appease their wrath following a breach of the prohibition. Evans-Pritchard makes much of the possibility of replacing this animal with a wild fruit (*cucumis prophetarum*, Crawford) when the sacrifier is in extreme need. Evans-Pritchard unfortunately does not give us any indication as to why this plant is the only representative of the plant world (wild or cultivated) to possess the privilege of 'representing' the ox. We note, however, that it invades all the fields and that it is called either *kwol* or *kwol yang* (cow's cucumber). The privileged symbolic association with cattle is confirmed when one examines the sacrificial rite centred on the cucumber. The fruit is cut in two by a spear. The left half, the bad, is thrown far away while the right half, the good side, is placed in the thatch over the entrance of the byre, after the officiant has rubbed his chest and forehead with the juice. The ritual division of the fruit evokes the lengthwise cutting of the ox carried out in sacrifices exorcising the jeopardy of incest. Actually Evans-Pritchard tells us that the ritual treatment of the *cucumis prophetarum* is currently used when it is a matter of exorcising the 'impurity' resulting from petty incest (Evans-Pritchard, 1956:203). The symbolic satus of the wild cucumber in its relation with cattle assuredly calls for new studies among the Nuer.

The symbolic designation and qualification of species apt for sacrifice deserves greater attention. In order to realise this, it is sufficient to compare the status of the dog among the Nuer and the Minyanka. We have seen how the former turn it into a type of mutilated scapegoat, expelled from man's society because of a very specific offence. This exceptional sacrifice contrasts with the regular immolation of an ox, an animal identified with man's social *raison d'être*.

The Minyanka of Mali, in contrast to the Nuer, have decreed that the dog is the sacrificial victim *par excellence* in the most important collective cult, the one rendered by the villagers to the mysterious Nya power. However, in this case we know the founding myth of the sacrifice, which has been revealed by Philippe Jespers (Jespers, 1976). We shall discuss it in Chapter VII, in order better to situate it in its cosmogonic context.

The comparative study pursued by the members of Associated Laboratory 221 brings to light another remarkable fact. Certain wild animals sometimes turn up mysteriously on the ritual scene. The Mofu use the lizard and the hyrax for certain purificatory rituals (Vincent, 1976:185). Among the Minyanka, the hunters altar is the receptacle for the blood of the hyena, of the aardvark, of the boa and of the antelope, whic are supposed to be captured alive. 'Each hunter possesses also a portable altar on which he slaughters wounded animals', (Jonckers, 1975:96). In other words, the study of sacrifice cannot be dissassociated from the analysis of the ritual hunt. Hubert and Mauss had the great merit of raising this problem as early as 1906 (Hubert and Mauss, 1968:3–11). I shall start there.

II

To each his own

Spirit animals and impure animals (Lele)

One Zairian Bantu society distinguished itself radically from all others, until recently, by an almost total lack of sacrificial practice. This is the society of the Lele of the Kasai. Mary Douglas has made them famous in her brilliant works. They show a complete lack of interest in any type of stock-raising except for raising dogs. Here, we are faced with a paradox. All man's ritual relations with the spirits of nature (*mingehe*) are established through the intermediary of wild animals. The spirits inhabit the depths of the forest, especially the springs. 'They control the fertility of women and make men's hunting prosper. Or they may withhold the game, and turn aside the hunter's arrow' (Douglas, 1954:10). The problem concerning the status of wild animals has been expertly revealed in symbolic terms by Douglas. 'Certain animals and plants', she writes, '*show signs* [my emphasis] that they are associated with the spirits in a particular, close way' (Douglas, 1954:10). The entire network of these relationships reveals to us not only the ritual prohibitions of the Lele, but also their positive rites, the most obvious function of which is to maintain good relations between the village, man's domain, and the forest, the domain of the spirits. Let us try to systematise Mary Douglas's data somewhat, as they are scattered in several essays.

The spirit animals are basically aquatic creatures. Generally women (or only pregnant women) must avoid them (Douglas, 1957:48–9). Fish are always the object of ritual treatment before being brought into the village (Douglas, 1954:10; 1957:52). Terrestrial mammals that show a strong liking for water are also associated with the spirits. One example is the wild pig who spends his time wallowing in streams. The Lele consider him to be the dog of the spirits; he lives and eats with them, he obeys them (Douglas, 1954:10; 1957:49). We can place in the same category the water-chevrotain (*Hyemoschus aquaticus*) 'which hides itself by sinking down into the water until only its nostrils appear above the surface' (Douglas, 1957:49), and the yellow baboon, who loves to wash himself, unlike other monkeys, who avoid water (Douglas, 1975: 301).

Although this is not exactly the point of view adopted by Douglas, one might say that these animals are associated with the water spirits by a metonymical relationship of contiguity. The same type of relationship exists between the spirits of the dead and certain burrowing species (Douglas, 1975:301; 1957:49).

Water spirits come out at night. For this reason, one species is associated with them by virtue of a metaphorical relationship: the antelope (*Cephalophus grimni*). It sleeps during the day with its eyes wide open (Douglas, 1957:49).

Moreover, the Lele's classificatory pattern is by no means limited to metaphor and metonymy. A definitive border theoretically separates the village, man's domain, from the forest, domain of animals and spirits. All species that appear in or near the village are therefore abnormal, suspicious. That is why the Lele did not raise goats or pigs until recently. The only animals tolerated were dogs and chickens even though their presence in the village poses a problem. Theoretically all domestic animals are unfit for consumption; they are impure, disgusting and are defined as *hama*. This reaction is even more intense towards the rats that infect the huts (Douglas, 1957:47).

The *hama* concept has nothing to do with the prohibition of a religious nature that affect the spirit animals. It is rooted in the experience of corporal dirt, it is 'polluting'. It evokes the nausea caused by the sight of corpses, excrement, vermin, etc. (Douglas, 1955:388; 1954:5). Stinking animals like the jackal cause the same sensory reaction. However, the literal meaning of the word *hama* is subject to a remarkable mental extension: certain species are qualified as *hama* impure, and are never eaten because they do not fit into their places in Lele topology and taxonomy. Therefore, these animals present characteristics that are 'unclean' in a figurative sense. This is not only the case for dogs and goats, whose presence among men is out of place, but also for all carnivores. The latter prowl around the village, violating the border between the animal world and man's, just as do the sorcerers, whose familiars they are (Douglas, 1955:391, 395; 1975:301).

One must note immediately that the repulsion felt towards these animals varies. Only the members of the Begetters cult (an association of men who have fathered) can eat the flesh of carnivores with impunity. On the other hand all men willingly eat chicken; only women abstain. The latter also consider as *hama* the flying squirrel, an animal of rather ambiguous status, half-mammal, half-bird (Douglas, 1955:392; 1957:48).

A new aspect of the symbolic topology appears here. The Lele assign specific characteristics to the animals that inhabit respectively the water, earth and air. Earthbound creatures, mammals, walk about on all four legs; birds have wings to fly (Douglas, 1957:48). The flying squirrel is thus anomalous. Its behaviour is unfitting (i.e. 'unclean'); *hama*. Mary Douglas does not explain the reasons why snakes, frogs and toads find themselves in an analogous situation (Douglas, 1955:388, 390). Keeping in mind the preceding remark, one will note that these *hama* creatures do not correspond to the definition of a terrestrial creature (mammals) nor to that of fish, nor to that of birds. One could say they are, so to speak 'monstrous'; they have no place anywhere.

Yet the problem is complicated by the fact that certain species judged aberrant from a taxonomical point of view, far from being qualified as *hama*, enter the category of spirit animals. I discussed this with Mary Douglas a while ago (de Heusch, 1971). I called attention to the need to distinguish carefully the concepts of 'prohibition' and 'pollution', even though there are borderline cases. We have already seen that Evans-Pritchard wrongly combined them (Chapter I). The spirit animals forbidden to women for religious reasons (for they are both related to fertility) are by no means disgusting or unclean; they are laden with a spiritual power; the interdiction concerning their consumption varies according to personal status. Some spirit animals are counted as dangerous food for all except the appropriate group of diviners; others are dangerous to pregnant women or to anyone undergoing treatment for infertility; others are prohibited in other curative rites (Douglas, 1975:301). Women are also more sensitive than men to *hama* animals, but this attitude has nothing to do with the avoidance that keeps them from contact with or consumption of the spirit animals. An ambiguity remains nevertheless. Certain types of bizarre animal behaviour are given value while others (that of carnivores or the flying squirrel for example) are *hama*. The choice is clear when it is the case of terrestrial mammals who show a liking for water, dwelling-place of the spirits (like the wild pig, the chevrotain or the baboon (Douglas, 1975:301). But other unusual types are considered spirit animals for more obscure reasons. For example it is not easy to understand why the tortoise, which women must abstain from eating, is classed among the spirit animals and not among the *hama* animals: 'its shell distinguishes it from other reptiles but, as a four-footed creature, it is anomolous in that it lays eggs' (Douglas, 1957:48).

The Lele themselves seem to draw an uncertain boundary between spirit animals and impure animals. Take, for example, the case of the water lizard (*Varanus niloticus,* Nile monitor). This amphibian has a rather ambiguous status. In a first essay, Douglas presents it as *hama*: the Lele 'feel revolted at the idea of eating anything so like a snake' (Douglas, 1955:390); but elsewhere this same animal is classed among the spirit animals—women cannot even touch the water lizard because it *differs* from the snake as well other related species. 'The Lele describe it as a cousin of the crocodile, but without scales; like a snake with little legs; a lizard but bigger, swifter, and more vicious than any lizard. Like the crocodile, it is a large, potentially dangerous amphibian' (Douglas, 1957:48).

Now if we were to class the spirit animals according to their mystical character, the water lizard holds a privileged position comparable to that of the small pangolin, the most valued animal. Indeed women must avoid all contact with these two species whereas they can touch, but not eat, the tortoise and the baboon and only during the pregnancy do they avoid aquatic species (Douglas, 1957:48–49).

The Pangolin Cult

The small pangolin, as a taxonomic monstrosity, is at the very centre of Lele ritual life. Here there is no hesitation about its status: we are dealing with the spirit animal par excellence and not an impure (*hama*) creature. Why? The small pangolin (*Manis tricuspis*) transcends all categories. 'In our forest [say the Lele] there is an animal with the body and tail of a fish, covered in scales. It has four little legs and it climbs in the trees' (Douglas, 1957:50). Thus like the water lizard the pangolin is associated with water, source of fertility. However, its symbolic power is infinitely greater, for this mammal fish lives in trees, like a bird. Moreover, it has a remarkable human characteristic: it brings forth its young singly, unlike other animal species (Douglas, 1957:50; 1975:302). The small pangolin is a veritable epitome of the universe. It combines the properties of aquatic, celestial and terrestrial creatures. Monoparous, it is also the symbolic representative of moderated human reproduction in a world where fertility is teeming beyond measure. It is the logical or rather dialectical agent of religious communication. It is through its mediation that the village and forest, man and the spirits, enter into privileged relationships.

The greatest gap exists between the leopard (*hama*-animal like all carnivores) and the small pangolin, the most important of the spirit animals (Douglas, 1975:302). The first is a sorcerer, the second man's friend and even his metaphorical representative within the animal world. It is called 'chief' (*kum*) because it fosters female fertility (Douglas, 1957:55). It is the only animal capable of feeling shame (*buhonyi*); it bows its head, like a man who avoids looking at his mother-in-law (Douglas, 1975:302). If it allows itself to be captured by hunters, it is only because it wants to be. The Lele believe that it comes to offer itself of its own free will; it lets itself fall from a tree and instead of fleeing, it rolls itself into a ball and does not move. The hunter merely has to wait until it unrolls itself and lifts its head, in order to kill it (Douglas, 1957:50). It is thus in terms of sacrifice that one must interpret the killing and eating of this animal. A somewhat sacrilegious sacrifice. For it is the actual, quasi-human representative of the spirits that is carved up. The Lele are somewhat ashamed to eat this 'chief'.

The ritual is led by a member of the Pangolin Cult, made up of men who have proved their fertility by fathering a son and a daughter by the same wife and whose high social status complies with specific requirements which we shall examine later on. They alone have the right to eat the animal's meat, which is roasted in secret. The inedible parts, such as the scales and bones, are given to the dogs. The tongue, neck, ribs and stomach are buried under a palm tree whose wine will ultimately be reserved for the members of the Begetters Cult (Douglas, 1975:43).

The capture of the pangolin and its quasi-sacrificial dissection are the centre of the magico-religious life of the Lele, who do not practise any form of ancestor worship. The symbolic rules we have just outlined explain why the Lele do not show any interest in the domestication of animals, either from a ritual or from a socio-economic point of view. The need for meat, or the concern for disposing of a kind of 'money' in order to assure the circulation of women between clans, has never driven the Lele to raise goats or pigs, unlike their southern neighbours (Douglas, 1954:5). All meat comes from the forest. The Lele exploit their own classificatory logic to the maximum. To them, the meat of the domestic goat or pig belongs to the *hama* category; it is nauseating, like excrement or pus 'just because they are bred in the village' (Douglas, 1954:5). The same negativism applies to chickens, but to a lesser degree; as I said men do not deny themselves some chicken while women abstain completely, for they would be more sensitive than their male companions to the uncleanness of this filthy meat. Under no circumstances can the meat of a domestic pig be substituted for that of a wild animal. At the beginning of her stay, Mary Douglas was most surprised to discover that a pig carcase had been carved up and transported a few miles away to be sold to neighbouring tribes despite the fact that several hunts had been unsuccessful and hunger was setting in.

The basic reason for the exclusion of goats and pigs from the diet as well as from the ritual scene, is that the place of animals is not among men. The dog that goes hunting with them is itself *hama*, impure, like the rat that haunts men's houses. This topological division is remarkably rigorous.

The ceremonial attitude of the Tetela-Hamba towards the forest

A few hundred miles east, the Hamba show the same indifference towards the ritual treatment of the domestic animal. But they by no means scorn the raising of goats. On the contrary, the goat is the accounting unit *par excellence* in all socio-economic transactions and more especially in the circulation of women. The goat traditionally figures in bride wealth, as does iron and copper 'money', whereas the Lele confine this role exclusively to raphia cloths. As among the Lele, the goat is likewise absent from the sacrificial scene. The kinship structure (patrilineal and not matrilineal), like their culture, differs considerably from the Lele's. The Hamba of the outskirts of the big forest, like their close relatives, the Tetela of the southern savannah, belong to the Mongo linguistic group that peoples the entire Congo basin. Although they are farmers, the Hamba are more particularly keen on hunting. Contrary to the Lele, however, hunting has not engendered a magico-religious activity. It does not imply any attempt to enter into contact with the mysterious spirits, *edimu.*

The Hamba and Tetela depict these spirits as beings radically different from men, just as the Lele describe the *mingehe* spirits. They haunt both the springs and abandoned villages. In any case, contact with them is dangerous and no positive cult permits conciliation with them. Among the Tetela, the healing rites practised by the *wetshi okunda* (both a diviner and medicine-man) are essentially based on exorcism. The crossroads is the privileged place for this expulsion. One might define it as an anti-altar, at the border between the world of man and that of the spirits. A live chicken is sometimes abandoned there after having been rubbed against the patient's body. Chicken is as a matter of fact, abundantly eaten. It is the perfect welcome gift offered to an important guest. The chicken only appears in one positive rite, of a totally magical nature. Formerly, when warriors left for combat, the *wetshi* prepared a meal (*oselo*) of which the main ingredient was this chicken; the participants ate it with avidity and haste. They were then thought to fly off to combat with the rapidity of the fowl. The same meal is now served, but this time with meat from the squirrel, an animal known for its alertness, in order to fortify the child during the seventh month of pregnancy. The future parents as well as close relatives participate. When I was present at this rite among the Hamba, the officiant refused a lemur that the children had just caught, on the pretext that the child would risk being born with the big sleepy eyes of this animal and would be stupid. Be it a chicken or a squirrel, the judgement that characterises their choice is obviously metaphorical.

The *wetshi-okunda* do not practise any other fertility rite. Nor, when they pick herbs and roots in the forest to make medicines, do they communicate with the dangerous spirits, the *edimu*, or with animals. The effectiveness of the plants depends on God, who is often invoked during the picking. However, the *wetshi okunda* are in contact with a specific spirit of the forest, *Odyenge.* This mysterious entity abruptly possesses a son or daughter of a dead *wetshi* in a kind of violent selection. The chosen one breaks all communication with humans and flees into the forest. There he discovers a bag containing white clay that he will use for purification rituals. During his reintegration into the village, the exceptional sacrifice of a dog takes place. This rite is part of a set of rites that bear the mark of transgression. The candidate approaches his sister (or brother, in the case of a woman) and furtively touches her/his sexual organ, while other members of the brotherhood sing obscene songs. The dog is put to death and the candidate eats its heart in order to acquire, they say, this animal's sense of smell in hunting sorcerers. He will then be initiated into the handling of the divinatory calabash. The acquisition of clairvoyant powers thus lies in an ambiguous zone, one which articulates the realm of the forest and the realm of the village.

Among the Hamba, a new institution, the 'Masters of the Forest' (*nkum'okunda*) have claimed for themselves an important part of the power traditionally held by the lineage chiefs. This closed, strictly male brotherhood practises secret rites in an enclosure forbidden to women and non-initiates, which is built far from the village.

As a group, the *nkum'okunda* claim hunting tributes for themselves, and they impose a certain number of prohibitions on this activity, which vary from one group to another. The taking of three kinds of animals is generally prohibited; they are the leopards, which are authority figures, and the two anteaters, the pangolin, and the aardvark. When a leopard or pangolin is accidentally captured in a trap, it is given ceremonial treatment. The hunter must pay heavy fines for having infringed on the 'hunting prohibition'.

I was present when a dead leopard was brought into a Djumbusanga village. Its legs were attached to a pole which two men carried on their shoulders. They went from house to house, demanding from each family head the traditional welcoming gift (*wema*) to which the lineage chiefs have a right. Then they suspended the animal on a wooden frame. The masters of the forest gathered together; they were welcomed by the chief of the lineage segment to which the hunter belonged. They fined the hunter because when they arrived the animal was still hung on the frame whereas it should have been laid on a bed. The hunter paid for the right to 'pierce' the animal (*otunguna wa nkoy*). The meat was shared among the lineage chief, the masters of the forest, and the hunter and his father. Some days later, the father invited the brotherhood and the lineage chiefs to join in eating the leopard's head. Again he had to pay a substantial fine.

Thus this prohibition on hunting has no bearing on alimentary consumption, but only on the killing of the animal. The ceremonial treatment of the animal and the flow of rare gifts that accompany it are the direct consequence of the accidental death of the leopard, the representative of the elders' power in the animal world. Among the Tetela of the savannah, the lineage chief, eldest of the eldest branch, must provide a great 'potlatch' on the occasion of his investiture, before he can dance the ritual dance. In this, he looms out of the forest like a leopard; his body speckled with white clay, he wears the animal's skin on his back and vigorously flings his arms towards the sky, alternating the left, then the right, thus forcefully expressing his vitality (de Heusch, 1954). The drummers and the crowd joyously escort him to the village. He is accompanied by his wives and close relatives. All their bodies are speckled with white spots, evoking the animal's fur, and some wear necklaces with one or several eye-teeth. The assimilation of the lineage chief to the animal is so strong among the Tetela that he abstains from eating its flesh, for 'the leopard does not eat the leopard'. His closest relatives of the patrilineal line belong, like him, to the segment (literally, 'belly') of the leopard. The flow of wealth I have just described in relation to the leopard dance is again levied at the time of mourning for a lineage chief. Of course one might wonder whether for the Hamba the solemn welcoming of the trapped leopard is not equivalent to a funeral ritual.

What about the pangolin? Its meat is entirely reserved for the Masters of the Forest but an opposite ruling prevails in certain regions—the animal is eaten inside the enclosure, in the forest, if the hunter was himself an initiate. If not, the meat is given to the women and men who do not belong to the brotherhood. The aardvark is the subject of a prohibition because the Hamba say, this animal lives hidden in a deep burrow. Moreover, the aardvark like the pangolin, bears only one child at a time, like man. Thus we find among the Hamba at least one of the metaphorical connotations that the pangolin possesses for the Lele. However, the Hamba do not establish any connection between these forbidden animals and the spirits. Moreover, it was the large pangolin (*Manis gigantea*) and not the tree-dwelling species that I saw the Hamba treat ceremoniously. If, among the Lele, only the small pangolin is the object of a quasi-sacrificial rite, it should nevertheless be noted that the giant species is found, along with the aardvark, on the list of spirit animals. But the position of these two anteaters there is secondary; only pregnant women abstain from eating the *Mani gigantea* and the aardvark is the object of a limited alimentary prohibition (Douglas, 1957:49).

The difference in attitude of the Lele and the Hamba *vis-à-vis* forbidden animals is obvious. The latter merely treat them with the respect due to chiefs, and this ceremonial approach does not influence either women's fertility or the success of the hunt. Hamba thinking has a less complicated classificatory structure than that of Lele taxonomy. By formalising it somewhat, one might say, more precisely, that the chief is the leopard's counterpart in the world of men, just as the pangolin, or indeed the aardvark, is the representative of the human world in the forest. Yet the Hamba do not attempt any magico-religious mediation between nature and culture. The Masters of the Forest limit themselves to joyously imitating the behaviour of wild animals, in entertaining dances.

Contrary to the Lele brotherhood of Pangolin Men, the association of the Masters of the Forest, who appropriate hunting levies and forbidden animals, is of a political, not a religious nature. The objects and traps revealed to the new members in the initiatory enclosure constitute so many secret signs of power. They fill a symbolic void. The Masters of the Forest do not dispense any mythical teachings nor do they engage in any dialogue with the wandering spirits of the forest, whose very nature remains a mystery.

The paucity of strictly ritual activities within the lineage is equally disconcerting. Neither the Tetela nor the Hamba offer prayers or sacrifices to their ancestors. The lineage chiefs maintain their prestige through generosity and not through mystical means. This society, where the competition for women, the desire to procure prestige goods, and rivalry between the elders and juniors are all exacerbated, is obsessed by sorcery. No religious institution has coalesced around the animals of the village or the forest in order to reinforce social cohesion.

Although these results are negative for our comparative study, they do reveal two significant differences in comparison with the Lele. The leopard, a symbol of power and not sorcery, is treated like a pangolin. Among the Manidae the privileged species (*Manis gigantea*) is itself different from that honoured by the Lele (the *Manis tricuspis*). We can learn more on this subject by looking at another society of the equatorial forest, the Lega of Maniema. As among the Hamba, it is strictly forbidden here to hunt the large pangolin, which, in this case, is the object of true sacrificial treatment.

The Small and the Large Pangolin (Lele and Lega)

The Lega reverse the attitude adopted by the Lele—only the large pangolin (*Manis gigantea*) is the object of ritual practices. The Lega set up a hierarchy between the two species. The small pangolin arouses little interest, it is but the younger brother of the large pangolin. On the other hand, the 'elder brother' is respected, protected—hunting it is strictly forbidden. When it is found dead in the forest, it belongs entirely to a closed association, the Custodian of Authority (*bwami*), which is in some respects comparable to the Hamba institution of the Masters of the Forest. Let us take a look at Biebuyck's description.

The large pangolin (*ikaga*) is a cultural hero for the Lega. It taught men the art of building houses. Its overlapping scales evoke the leaf tiles used by the Lega to cover the roofs of their huts (Biebuyck, 1973:224). The higher ranking members (*kindi*) in the *bwami* political group are associated with this beneficial animal because their social function is to 'bring people together', to maintain group cohesion. The dismembering and sharing of the large pangolin involves the participation of several related patrilineal lineages. An impressive number of persons benefit. A uterine nephew of the organising lineage is charged with starting the procedure. He picks off the scales, which will be added to the ritual objects guarded by the high ranking dignitaries. The latter throw a few on to the roof of the house, no doubt in order to confirm their symbolic association with it. Assisted by another uterine nephew, the first officiant then slits the throat of a buck

---

[1] The Lega maintain close social relations with the patrilineal lineages of the parents' and the four grandparents' mother's brothers.

goat, which is grilled whole on the fire. This domestic animal will be shared according to rules somewhat similar to those that operate at the distribution of the pangolin's meat among the initiates of the different, related lineages present (Biebuyck, 1953).

The uterine nephews receive the kidneys as their right. Their participation deserves some attention. Indeed, a proverb likens the large pangolin to a mother's brother. Maternal kinship is a very important aspect of Lega social structure. The society is in fact composed of an extremely extended Omaha network (Biebuyck, 1953b)[1]. Thus one can better understand this proverbial saying 'Pangolin, you are my mother's brother who spreads his burrows far' (Biebuyck, 1953:910). Through the avuncular relationship, it is the entire social structure that is symbolised by this anteater and the deep tunnels it digs in the ground. The role of the male goat that accompanies the pangolin in this ritual is unfortunately not commented on. After the meal, all the participants are obliged to go and bathe in order to purify themselves, for they have just transgressed a very important prohibition (*mweko*) (Biebuyck, 1953:924).

It is as if the group has just dismembered the entire kinship system, in order to better reinforce it. What they are going to carry out is, in truth, no less than the equivalent of a cannibal feast, the sacrifice of the 'civilising hero'. We must compare this with the ashamed demeanour of the Lele when they roast the meat of a small pangolin, their respected 'chief'. From a sociological point of view, the rite of the large pangolin among the Lega parallels the religious function of the small pangolin among the Lele. It is precisely this sliding from one symbolic sphere to another that explains the passage from one species to another.

The Lele do not in any way liken the small pangolin to a relative. The Lele matrilineal clans are dispersed and have no social cohesion, contrary to the Lega patrilineal lineages which constitute residential units. The sociological function of the small pangolin in the first case is of a different nature than that of the large pangolin in the second case. This becomes clear when one examines the Lele rules concerning acceptance into the Cult of the Pangolin Men. Every candidate must be able to display the following qualities: he must have fathered a boy and a girl by the same wife, be a member of a founding clan of the village (thus favouring the reproduction of the matrilineal system); moreover both he and his father must belong to one of the founding clans. Mary Douglas fully realises that these rules encourage intermarriage between these clans in order to combat the exodus of the population to which a village is always prone (Douglas, 1963:209). Thus the small pangolin contributes to the sociological synthesis of two complementary and antagonistic institutions—the village, a permanent political unit, and the matrilineal clan, dispersed and fragmented into local sections which lack their own institutions. This unifying function is centripetal: it affirms the need to maintain within the village a network of endogamous alliances between the same clans. The small pangolin causes men and women who, by virtue of virilocal marriages, were born outside it, to return to the village founded by their ancestors.[2] In Lega patrilineal society, the large pangolin assumes the opposite function in a vast ritual community; it joins together a network of villages, strongly defined by their lineage unity. Still, in both cases, the pangolin is a powerful force for social cohesion.

There is a more important difference. The animal's size is a pertinent element where primogeniture is valued. In Lega thought, the large pangolin is the elder brother of the other. It represents the entire social structure, the hierarchical order within the lineage as well as the extended network of maternal kin. One finds these same fundamental sociological characteristics among the Hamba, who grant special privileges to the large pangolin. Primogeniture determines the hierarchy of the lineages, and the avuncular relationship is one of the complementary cornerstones of patrilineal society. On the other hand, primogeniture is not an organising principle in Lele society; the hierarchy of the two pangolins is reversed for reasons that are no longer sociological but cosmogonic. The *Manis tricuspis* is the only tree-dwelling species of the Manidae family, and as such the small pangolin is situated at the crossroads of the three living orders. As Douglas herself notes, it is 'the only beast that is a fish-like, bird-like quadruped mammal' (Douglas, 1975:46,13). From this point of view, the cosmogonic wealth of the small pangolin is obviously greater than that of its bigger counterpart. This same point of view explains the pre-eminence of the *Manis tricuspis* over the *Manis gigantea* in Kuba royal symbolism, where it figures among 'noble animals belonging to the Sovereign' (Vansina, 1964:109). Is it not the ritual function of sacred royalty to control all natural forces? The sacred king is both at the very heart of human order, and outside it, in the heart of nature, just like the pangolin. When Mary Douglas read my book, *The Drunken King*, in which I started to explore the symbolic foundations of sacred royalty in Central Africa, and particularly among the Kuba, she admitted that she regretted not having ever had access to the esoteric knowledge of the Pangolin Men, and not having analysed a certain number of tales that today seem to her capable of illuminating the cosmogonic symbolism of the small pangolin. Today she is ready to see in it 'the potential sign of the union of the sky and the earth' as realised by the sacred king (Douglas, 1975:x).

The ritual treatment of the pangolin among the Lele and the Lega leads us to pose the question of sacrifice by cutting across classifications that operate within the vast world of wild animals. Lévi-Strauss has taught us to

[2] Here my interpretation varies somewhat from the one proposed by Douglas in *Implicit Meaning* (297–8).

see these as 'good to think with'. The pangolin is first of all the object of a prohibition. The Lele, like the Lega, eat it with a strange mixture of ceremony and repugnance. The latter go to purify themselves in the river after having consumed it, as if they have committed a sacrilegious act. The pangolin is of course not a 'totemic' species, and it is fruitless to try to find in the ritual consumption of this forbidden animal the confirmation of Robertson Smith's thesis, justly criticised by Hubert and Mauss, according to which a pretended communal eating of the forbidden, totemic 'sacred' species is the origin of sacrifice. The pangolin ritual is nevertheless accompanied by an alimentary consumption of mystical virtues. The Lega's social bonds are strengthened during this meal, while among the Lele the Pangolin Men reinforce their special relationship with the very sources of fertility through the medium of the animal. Something in the nature of sacrifice appears on the horizon.

But the comparison is valid only for the final phase, the meal. The initial phase, the ritual killing, is missing. In the Lele schema, on the contrary, pursuing the animal is forbidden and it comes to offer itself of its own free will, to assure communication with the world of the spirits.

It would be wrong to assume that for the Lele the accidental and almost sacrilegious eating of the pangolin replaces the sacrifice of domestic animals which is practised by the majority of Bantu societies, breeders of goats and oxen, and which is not done here. The voluntary victim of this particular sacrifice is the representative of the spirits of nature. On these grounds the small pangolin is, in the Lele symbolic system, the absolute equivalent of the Kuba sacred king, the regulator of the cosmic as well as of the social order. The association of the pangolin with royalty is found throughout Bantu Africa. For example, among the Lovedu of the Transvaal the fat of this animal, captured alive, is an ingredient in the rain medicine used by the Queen Mother (Krige, 1943:274).

The fact that the Lele associate the small pangolin with general fertility by giving it the title 'chief', thus conferring upon it the same power that their neighbours the Kuba attribute only to the sovereign, suggests that this decidedly strange creature is capable of mapping a route for us toward the most singular of sacrificial institutions: the ritual killing of kings. We shall deal with this question in Chapter V.

III

A *calao* for the rainbow,
a black sheep for the python,
oxen for the ancestors (Zulu)

The sacrificial hunt and the value of the black sheep

To state that certain animals participate in one way or another in the spirit world is surely banal. It is more interesting to ask precisely how they do so. Lévi-Strauss approached the subject in *Totemism Today*. The question we face is what is the specific place of the domestic animal within these relationships? We have not yet finished with the ritualisation of wild species, however. Far from it!

Lévi-Strauss briefly establishes that a human group is capable of entering into a relationship with a non-human species, or with a member of that species, just as an individual can enter into a relationship with a species or with one of its members. He brilliantly demonstrates that the so-called totemic system is but one specific aspect of the first case. It is clear that the general behaviour of the Lele toward the pangolin is a non-totemic religious illustration of this. Zulu customs invite us to consider the same type of ritual facts, whose sacrificial nature is undeniable. We base our analysis principally on the excellent data provided by Berglund (Berglund, 1975).

The first species that attracts our interest is the *calao* or hornbill. The Zulu sometimes perceive that the far-off celestial residence of the Supreme Master of the Universe has a slight opening. They can then gaze on the colourful dwelling-place of his virgin daughter, the Rainbow Princess. This benevolent divinity, mediator between the sky and the earth, controls the rain. It is she who sends the glowing arc toward the earth, where it plunges into the waters (Berglund, 1975:178). Two birds are closely associated with the sky—the ground hornbill (*Buceros caffer*) and the eagle (*Terathopius ecaudatus*) (Berglund, 1975:57). The hornbill flies at a great height before the rain is to fall. It is the friend of the Rainbow Princess. Under its black plumage, coloured feathers are hidden. During serious droughts, the Zulu go off to a well watered region to capture a hornbill alive. At early dawn they take it to the edge of a river, where they break its neck or suffocate it, taking care to avoid any spilling of blood. When the body is cold they attach a stone to its feet and throw it into deep water in order to bring on the return of rain. The sky 'will weep' over the death of its favourite animal (Berglund, 1975: 57).

This little drama is by no means mysterious. However, it has considerable interest because it introduces the theme of the sacrificial hunt. The terrestrial representative of a comogonic power is put to death because of a metaphorical correspondence—the colours of the sky are seen under the black feathers (Berglund, 1975:76). But if the metaphor is considered a sufficient reason, it is not the controlling reason for the immolation. There are more substantial affinities between the hornbill and the Rainbow Princess. A bond of kinship links the signifier and the signified. It supersedes the metaphor. The hornbill (always considered female) is the 'daughter' of the Sky Lord, like the Rainbow Princess. The sky 'weeps' over the death of the bird. Does one mourn the death of a metaphor?

Undoubtedly one must, once again, take care not to liken the tragic death of a wild animal to that of a god, nor to see in it a type of 'totemic sacrifice'. That would be completely misleading. Here, all things considered, the bird is but the animal double of an anthropomorphised celestial divinity. The latter has privileged relations with women in general, and more particularly with young virgins like herself. Zulu women affirm, not without some reticence, that the goddess walks about on the earth, in the first mist of the southern spring, sometimes naked, sometimes dressed in a white or multicoloured coat. At that time, she descends on a mountain forbidden to men. Young maidens put on their fiances' war gear and bring her an offering of millet beer (Berglund, 1975:65–66). They leave it on an overhanging rock, where the goddess 'can see it clearly'. They start to sing, inviting the princess, their 'friend', their 'sister', to come and share their food. They have also brought seeds that they take back with them; they will use them to plant the ritual field cultivated in honour of the princess.

It is a rustic and reassuring female scene, in which the young girls laughingly and defiantly take over male prerogatives (on this occasion, the girls even put the men's cattle out to pasture). It contrasts with the dramatic atmosphere that characterises the sacrifice of the hornbill, the goddess's representative. This rough, male procedure, is opposed, from every point of view, to the joyous offering of the beer and the seeds of the future harvest. The sacrifice of the *calao* only takes place as a last resort, when the princess does not play her mediating role, when she no longer sends rain. The cosmogonic function of the sacrifice is, then, even stronger than that of the offering. A part of the goddess herself is menaced by the immolation of the hornbill. The hunters are careful to capture the bird alive, in a distant and well watered region, and not to shed its blood.

There is, however, another exceptional procedure to combat excessive drought. Once again, it is a sacrificial rite. This time, the animal, like the recipient, changes completely. The aquatic python genie is, on earth, the male counterpart of the Rainbow Princess. If this creature is endowed with full sovereign power, it is because it is always 'cool', in both senses of the word. The Zulu say that the python is 'the coolest of all the animals in the whole world' (Berglund, 1975:60). Its temperament is even; its actions, measured. In the presence of a python it is advisable to refrain from speaking 'as when there is thunder, because both come from the sky' (Berglund, 1975:61). This opinion is not shared by all Berglund's informants, however; one of them states that it only involves a respectful attitude towards a great person. These two different opinions clearly indicate that the python is in fact the co-sovereign of the universe, together with the Master of the Sky, who manifests himself through thunder. The former rules over terrestrial waters just as the latter rules over celestial waters. There is some reason to believe that these two representations, which are joined as well as possible in a dualist system in Zulu thought, come from different cultural horizons (de Heusch, 1982). It is most interesting to examine how the Zulu put these two elements together. We find ourselves dealing with a deified animal species, whose members are endowed with fabulous power. The python species, through each individual python, shares universal sovereignty with the Lord of the Sky, a unique anthropomorphised creature, father of the Rainbow Princess, who in turn communicates with men through the hornbill species. This criss-crossing is all the stranger in that the python, like the Rainbow Princess, wields power over rain.

Indeed, the alternative to sacrificing the hornbill, in the case of a severe drought, is the sacrifice of a domestic animal in honour of the python genie. In this case the procedure calls for the participation of a qualified rainmaker (Berglund, 1975:55). The emissaries from the drought-stricken area undertake the sacrifice of an absolutely black sheep (sometimes a goat). It is carried out in absolute silence. If the animal chosen is a goat, they muzzle it to prevent it from bleating. When it has been carved, the rainmaker unaccompanied, carries the skin off to a stream. He settles down on a black rock, in midstream, laying down beside him the horns containing magic medicine, and puts on the animal skin. He remains motionless for a long time. In the dead of the night, a python emerges from the depths of the water and comes to lick off the fat that clings to the goatskin. The python genie then lies down on the magic horns and stays there peacefully, in order to communicate his own coolness to them. He disappears suddenly, silently.

This entire terrifying scene takes place in a dream-like atmosphere, in a mythical place where through the intermediary of a domestic animal, full of symbolic connotations, the greatest physical intimacy is achieved between the magician and python genie. In this vision, one facet is real (the immolation of the animal), the other imaginary (the python's arrival). The nocturnal journey of a brave man to a black rock situated in the twilight Zone between reality and myth may lie somewhere between these two facets. A complex phantasmagorical scenario is substituted for the brutal, but perhaps entirely imaginary, sacrifice of the hornbill, the purpose of which is to force the Rainbow Princess's hand.

How are we to interpret the respective characteristics of these two cosmogonic, homologous sacrifices? The desired purpose is the same, but from beginning to end the ritual procedures are opposed, as is shown in Fig. 1.

Fig. 1

Recipient	Anthropomorphised Rainbow Princess	Python genie
Animal victim	Hornbill, the divinity's double	Black sheep or goat

The ritual topology also varies. The hornbill announces rain by flying high into the sky, towards the dwelling of the Rainbow Princess. When sacrificed, it is, so to speak, dramatically snatched from the sky and thrown into the water. Thus the death of this bird, the sky's messenger, creates a vacuum, which the rain will come to fill. On the other hand, the python brings on rain through an inverse topological pattern. It emerges spontaneously from the depths of the waters and enters into direct contact with the sacrificial animal—in this case a domestic animal. This physical, quasi-carnal contiguity between man and the solicited power (terrestrial, not celestial this time) contrasts with the painful preceding scene in which the sky finds itself separated from a familiar bird. An essential physical property—coolness—circulates from the python to the ritual objects after the intimate conjunction of the rainmaker and the legendary animal.

Metaphor is preeminent in the sacrificial choice of the hornbill. Its plumage signifies a hidden resemblance to the Rainbow Princess. Next, a kinship relationship is formulated between the signifier and the signified. The hornbill, like the rainbow, is the daughter of the Sky Lord. In the sacrifice of the python, the symbolic pattern is quite different. In order to analyse this, let us adopt the perspective proposed by Lévi-Strauss in *Totemism Today*. The religious representation of the python is metonymic; the entire species signifies the aquatic genie and any member *incarnates* it fully. The python is thought to live *in* the water, and in this respect it signifies the entire aquatic realm—terrestrial water as well as rain. This *contiguous* relationship is continued in the ritual: the python approaches the magician and licks the sheep's fatty skin. The sacrificial animal truly constitutes the link between the men who offered it and the god who delights in its fat, without in any way harming the officiant, who is himself, in a way, *identified* with the sheep. In this last case, the metonymic entities take precedence in the symbolic pattern. Step by step, this series of procedures projects the rainmaker into a magic place where he finds himself in the strange position of a 'sheep-man' feeding a python that is also a god. It is clear that the significant gaps between the categories—man, animal, the gods—shrink, just as Lévi-Strauss revealed to be the case with the rite in general (Lévi-Strauss, 1971:600–3). However, in this dangerous situation, classificatory thought does not stop functioning. The choice of a black sheep, from among all the animals close to men, reveals complementary concerns which we shall now explore.

The sheep's fat is also involved in the making of the magic medicines handled by the rainmaker. Two 'female' horns contain ewe fat, for 'the fat of a female sheep is like the fat of women. That is why a female sheep which has given birth is slaughtered to obtain its fat' (Berglund, 1975:54). The informant hints that the fat of a fertile woman would be even better. 'So when there is no woman's fat, then it must be that of this sheep'. The two 'male' horns contain the fat of a ram. A very strong bond thus binds sheep and man.

The black colour of the animal offered to the python genie is part of a symbolic system that is omnipresent in Zulu thought. Two types of complementary magicians handle the celestial dialectic of 'black' and 'white': the rainmakers on one hand, the sky experts (*izinyanga Zezulu*) on the other (Berglund, 1975:46–51). If the first are connected with the python, master of the waters, the latter's function is to keep at a distance the dangerous celestial fire with which the angry Sky Lord sometimes threatens men. These specialists also use the fat of a black sheep in their medicine. Here are their comments on this animal's symbolic powers: the black sheep is like the dark thunder clouds and opposite to the colour of lightning. Further, the sheep are silent, which, again, contrasts with the crack of thunder when lightning strikes the vicinity (Berglund, 1975:50). When a violent storm threatens, the 'sky experts' hasten to cover clear ('white') objects, for they are liable to attract the lightning. They operate with 'black' symbols in the hope of 'driving the lightning to the east, where there is much water (is not water white?), or towards the west, where the great desert is found; that is the place of sand. Sand is white' (Berglund,1975:52). But normally, when there are no storms, the 'sky experts' work with 'white' symbols, *par excellence* the luminous sky's colour and also that of the Sky Lord himself, when he is in a good mood (Berglund, 1975:51–2).

A double code runs through the choice of the animal: a sound code and a colour code. The sheep's silence is a kind of antidote to the clamour of the thunder; its black pelt chases away the white lightning. The logic is that of the law of contrasts.

Yet, the rainmakers sacrifice the same animal to the python genie to achieve a different result. They handle the same celestial dialectic in a different way. The sheep must be absolutely black. If it has any white or brown [spot] it will not bring rain (Berglund, 1975:55). In this case the black colour attracts the clouds. However, it is a 'soft and penetrating rain' (Berglund, 1975:59) that is expected from the sacrifice. The sound code derives from the law of similarity—the animal's silent character is no longer opposed to the thunder's clamour. This sheep fat 'brings soft rain which has no noise' (Berglund, 1975:59). The sheep is a calm animal, unlike the goat. 'So its fat brings about a steady rain' (Berglund, *ibid.*).

The values of this fat are the heart of the matter. Animal fat is 'white' (Berglund, 1975:52), and moreover the rainmaker apparently wears the black sheepskin *inside out* so that the python can lick the fat. The slaughtered animal must be very fat, for 'only fatness will bring rain' (Berglund, 1975:55). This moist and white substance constitutes the perfect offering. The rainmaker, on his rock in the middle of the night, is thus like an Atlas holding up with his shoulders a sky that is now black, now white. In this fearsome confrontation, in which all distance between him and the god is abolished, the magician remains immobile, his head cool. There is something of the determination of shamans in this heroic act, carried out in silence, without useless effusions, at the juncture of the visible and invisible worlds. Nothing could be further from possession or trance than this singular confrontation between the rainmaker and the python genie, brought together after a sacrifice in a quasi-mythical place.

The python god, victim of the sacrificial hunt

The reader may be surprised to discover that the logic used by the rainmakers is not that of the sky experts. The latter carry the reversal of the symbolic categories to such a point that they use the python's fat in their anti-lightning medicine. This animal is theoretically protected by a general prohibition. However, the members of the royal clan can kill it. The circumstances attending this very serious act, which is surrounded by ritual warnings, are unknown to us. The prince, while moving in for the kill, must avoid looking the python in the eye, or shedding its blood. The ritual death of the python has the same psychological effect on the Sky as the death of the hornbill; the Sky Lord experiences it as a cruel loss. The sky experts are the principal beneficiaries of this sacrificial hunt, which again appears as the immolation of a spirit animal. This rite, like that of the hornbill, is bloodless. (Fig. 2.)

Fig. 2

Hornbill	*Python*
Metaphorical and metonymic symbol of the Rainbow Princess	Metonymic symbol of the water genie
Sacrificed for rain	Sacrificed to ward off lightning

The python cult is dominant among the Venda of the Transvaal, who forbid the killing of this animal during the rainy season. When it is killed in the dry season, its skin must be thrown into the water (Stayt, 1968:309–10). To kill a python is to 'cool' the earth. Its fat is an effective medication against burns and also serves as protection against fire (Romeguère-Eberhardt, 1963:16–17). This is the same symbolic system found among the Zulu, where the python, giver of rain, recipient of sacrificed black sheep, itself becomes the sacrificial victim when celestial fire threatens. It is understandable that the ritualists who are engaged in these contrasting procedures are completely distinct from each other. The sky experts are accomplices in the death of a god. We shall see, further on, that the sheep's fat, in which the python delights, is none other than that of a substitute human victim. The sky experts and rainmakers work with the highest values in order to assure an equilibrium between the sky and the earth.

Complementary ritual hunts

The preparation of anti-thunder medicine involves still other animal and vegetable ingredients. It causes, in fact, a sacrificial hunt, of which the python is not the only objective. The sky experts still need varan fat (*Varanus alligolaris*), the skin and fat of a hyrax (*Hyrax capensis*), the skin of an otter (*Lutra capensis*), peacock feathers and tortoise meat. Let us examine the symbolic aspects of these animals. The varan ' . . . is looked upon as the most fearless animal that exists, fleeing from nothing; this animal does not even fear thunder' (Berglund, 1975:50); the hyrax 'is said to drive off the violent rains that accompany thunder because this animal always hides when it rains'; the Zulu assert that the tortoise 'spouts water upwards when it is about to thunder; the peacock is forbidden to common mortals, except the king; it ruffles its feathers when it feels a storm approaching' (Berglund, 1975:51).

All these animals are set apart by their behaviour, real or supposed, when it thunders. They constitute new metonymic signs; they evoke thunder in a relation of negative contiguity. Their blood cannot be shed for 'the sky would be troubled' (Berglund, 1975:50). One must speak to them 'in a nice way', addressing them as 'friend of the Sky', inviting them to do their work and not to 'trouble' the hunter who is preparing to club them. There can be no doubt that this sacrificial hunt is dreamlike in nature. Does not a mythical animal also appear—the *inyoni ezulu*—a kind of celestial hen associated with the flash of lightning? The sky experts dig up the eggs it is thought to lay on earth (Berglund, 1975:39). This creature's fat is supposed to be an ingredient of the anti-thunder medicine; but if it cannot be captured, they will obtain the fat from another celestial animal, the eagle (*Terathopius ecaudatus*) (Berglund, 1975:49).

Let us look at the specific status of this bird. Like the mythical celestial hen, the eagle personifies thunder. The beating of its wings evokes, more precisely, 'male' and 'deep' thunder, whose appearance is not preceded by lightning. This thunder provokes violent rainfall (Berglund, 1975:58). The *inoyni ezulu* bird, on the other hand, represents 'female' thunder, the thunderclap, terrible storms and hail. These manifestations are likely to be followed by a period of intense heat and drought. Female thunder, in this way, is like post-menopausal women. Like them, it makes a lot of noise, releases heat, but does not bring rain, that is, fertility (Berglund, 1975:38). It is understandable that sorcerers are believed to use this mythical bird in their spells (Doke-Vilakazi, 1948:513).

The eagle and the mythical hen, respectively male and female, form a couple. As male thunder, the eagle can replace its female equivalent in anti-lightning medicine. Its symbolic position must be carefully distinguished from that of other (terrestrial) animals mentioned above. The python, master of terrestrial waters, is *par excellence* the anti-fire spirit animal. The varan, the otter, the tortoise, and others demonstrate by their behaviour that they are allergic to violent meteorological phenomena. Together with the python, they set up a symbolic trap, in which the thunder-eagle is in a sense a prisoner.

But this same eagle is also opposed to the hornbill, representative of the Rainbow Princess. The hornbill species is always considered female, and a good omen. The eagle is male, and a bad omen. When the hornbill excrement falls on a person or a house, it is a sign of celestial benediction. The same is not true for eagle excrement, a deadly omen (Berglund, 1975:58). The eagle presages the tornado, while the hornbill brings soft and soaking rain. Do not forget that the latter is sometimes sacrificed to end an excessive drought. Now, in the absence of a hornbill, the rainmakers may capture an eagle and drown it. This substitute sacrifice will provoke violent rain, but the Zulu think this is better than drought. To attenuate the effects of the sacrifice, they will take care to plunge the victim into shallow water, unlike the hornbill.

The eagle is thus situated at the juncture of the two complementary ritual systems that we have just described. It participates at one and the same time in the nature of the hornbill and the celestial hen while also being opposed to them due to certain pertinent traits. Fig. 3 summarises these differing relationships.

The eagle seems more and more marked by the male sovereignty of the Sky Lord, sometimes benevolent, sometimes incensed, whose moods the Rainbow Princess tempers. The eagle's ambiguousness is such that it can presage both excessive rains and drought (Berglund, 1975:57). It can be substituted indifferently, and for opposing objectives, for the two female manifestations of celestial power, the hornbill and the celestial hen. The efficacy of the sacrifice is based on the belief that the eagle is the representative of thunder, and the hornbill of the Rainbow Princess. The

Fig. 3

Hornbill	Celestial Hen	Eagle
Female	Female	Male
Rainbow	Thunder	Thunder
Steady and soft rains	Violent storms followed by drought	Violent rains
Good omen	Sorcery	Bad omen

idea that the latter can be the object of sacrifice is apparently foreign to the
Zulu. The celestial princess is thought to weep at the death of her
companion, the hornbill, captured by men.

From this viewpoint, the sacrifice of birds is different from that of the
python, whose fat is a necessary element in making anti-lightning
medicine. The python really incarnates the water spirit whose terrestrial
sovereignty duplicates that of the Sky Lord and his daughter. The
rainmakers offer him sacrificial victims and only men of royal blood are
authorised to sacrifice him. In this case, the sacrifice is no longer only that
of a messenger or an emanation of an invisible power; rather, the victim 'is'
the power in every respect. A new level has been reached in the intensity of
the rite.

There is reason to think that the python cult is a new element in Zulu
religion, introduced through the influence of the Venda, for whom it is a
dominant figure (de Heusch, 1982, Chapter IX). In trying to reconcile the
cult of the Rainbow Princess and that of the Python, the Zulu sometimes
force themselves to consider both of them dependents of the Sky Lord. The
python's death, as we have seen softens the Sky Lord's mood just as does
the sacrifice of the hornbill, his daughter's messenger. But the Swazi, close
relatives of the Zulu, do not practise the ophidian cult. The hornbill and the
eagle, conversely, are attributes of royalty. The hornbill symbolises 'the
summer of royalty', (Kuper, Hilda, 1947:50–1). It takes revenge on anyone
who dares to kill it. The sacrifice of the hornbill or the eagle, animal
witnesses of celestial sovereignty, is the object of a remarkable displacement in Swazi culture. It is the very person of the king that is symbolically
put to death each year at the summer solstice, to regulate the cosmic order.
We shall examine this new problem in Chapter V.

The Zulu sacrificial hunt is the stuff of dreams. How, indeed, does one
obtain a living eagle? How can it be drowned in shallow water, as
prescribed, without having first been killed? In any case, we cannot
arbitrarily separate this dreamlike aspect from the study of real sacrifices,

the effects of which are equally imaginary. Who can tell where fantasy ends and reality begins?

Let us sum up the situation. Wild animals—real or fictitious—are ritually sacrificed for complementary cosmogonic purposes. In this symbolic game, the hornbill, eagle and python represent the major stakes, because they are singularly close to a divinity. In the third case, the animal truly incarnates it. In this first series of sacrificial victims, the python is also the recipient of a sacrifice, that of the black sheep. We have already examined the selection process that led to the choice of this domestic species. A last question remained—why do the Zulu sometimes allow the presence of a goat on this clearly demarcated ritual scene when they oppose this noisy animal to the silent sheep?

This latitude does not indicate indifference to classificatory thought any more than does the substitution of the eagle for the hornbill in the preceding context. Indeed, the Zulu use a subterfuge. 'If they bring a goat, it must be muzzled while it is killed, so that it does not cry out' (Berglund, 1975:55). By this dodge, the noisy goat is in some sense identified with the tranquil and silent sheep, which is the perfect sacrificial victim. The whole scene takes place in silence. The sacrificers act 'quickly and quietly'; they can only communicate in whispers.

The symbolic position of the black sheep is not exceptional in Bantu Africa. We will soon re-encounter it among the Thonga (Chapter IV). Among the Lovedu, the black sheep enters into conjunction with the pangolin, under the sign of rain (Krige, 1943:274). The pangolin belongs to the queen. It must always be captured alive; its fat is used in making rain medicine, kept the the queen, whose major ritual duty is the regulation of rain. From time to time a black sheep is sacrificed in order to give fresh potency to the magic charm. These two species are again associated with royalty among the Kuba. Here, both the pangolin and the herd of sheep belong exclusively to the king, Master of the Universe (Vansina, 1964:109). Finally, we shall see that the Rwanda attribute a celestial origin to the entire ovine species while contrasting it with the goat as rigorously as do the Zulu (Chapter V).

The ox and sacrifice to the ancestors

It is time to bring on to the ritual scene an animal familiar to the Zulu, the one whose ownership confers the greatest prestige, namely the ox. As the main socio-economic value, cattle serve notably to regulate matrimonial exchanges. A diviner explained to Berglund the Zulu's way of thinking. He began by relating mankind and cattle through a series of metaphors and metonyms. At night, people and cattle share the same family settlement. Women like cows bring forth after nine months of pregnancy (Berglund, 1975:110). For their part, the ancestors (*idlozi*) live in intimacy with their

offspring and are present at special places within the house. Because they
like to dwell within the bodies of people and of cattle, Berglund decided to
call them 'shades'. They are living beings who have lost their human form.
At burial, a dead man goes through a kind of rite of passage. Like a bride
who has left her parents' home and is on her way toward her husband's
(*ibid*:83), he is 'nowhere'. He undergoes metamorphosis into a snake
(*ibid*:94). Various kinds of non-poisonous serpents without forked tongues
embody the ancestor-snakes, which are specially related to water, as we
shall see.

The ancestors also take on another shape, an abnormal human form in
dreams—abnormal in that they are no longer black but 'white' like the
shade they cast. This very property makes the *amathongo*, as they are
called, invisible during the day (Berglund, 1975:89–91). A third name,
abaphansi, refers to the ancestors as beings who live under the ground
(*ibid*:90). The underworld is white. Whether snakes or white shades, the
ancestors remain familiar with mankind. Amazingly ubiquitous, they can
be found particularly in the back of the hut, at a kind of altar (*umsamo*)
where they are presented offerings of meat, beer and tobacco. They like
this cool and damp place (*ibid*:102), but they also like to warm themselves
near the fireplace over which, for this reason, no one may step (*ibid*:103).
Another of their favourite spots is the arch over the entrance where they
hover, particularly at the call of the diviner who interprets their whistling
language (*ibid*:105).

Furthermore, the ancestors have seats in the gall bladder of people and
of animals (*ibid*:111). This organ is at the centre of a network of symbolic
associations. Like a hut, it has only one opening and only one entrance. For
the same reason, it resembles a womb (*ibid*:110). The ancestors are, of
course, responsible for women's fertility. Literally, they are the craftsmen
of conception and of pregnancy. The birth of a child is likened to their own
rebirth as snakes. One of Berglund's informants meticulously described
this process (*ibid*:95–7). A man becomes 'hot' during sexual relations; the
paternal ancestors then leave the water and enter the sperm. As a watery
element ('water is the ancestors'), they are intermingled with the woman's
blood in order to form, in darkness, a child (*ibid*:94). When a man gives his
sperm, he collapses exhausted. He is weakened because the ancestors
have left him and gone into the 'hot' womb (*ibid*:117). Nine months later,
the ancestor-snakes expel the baby in the same manner as they cast off
their old skin every year. The baby sheds its placenta like a slough
(*ibid*:94). The ancestor-snake is reborn at night in water, or rather in grass
wet with dew. Likewise, gestation takes place in the darkness of the humid
womb (*ibid*:95–6).

The making of a baby is also a way of perpetuating the ancestors, of
ensuring their immortality. Death is, however, given with birth. Like a
corpse, the placenta is an impure thing (*izibi*) that must be buried

(Berglund, 1975:95). The ancestor-snake's regularly shed slough is, on the contrary, never handed over to the earth. It is used as a medicine for treating women who suffer from menstrual problems or who give birth prematurely. It re-establishes the periodicity that is indispensable for reproducing life (*ibid*:96).

These watery ancestors who 'heat' the womb cannot resist cooking odours. Among other reasons, sacrifices are made to offer them meat, which they eat in a very strange way.

After the slaughtering, they, supposedly, come and lick some pieces of the raw meat laid out for them on the *umsamo* altar. They thus prove their affection for their offspring (*ibid*:237). Moreover licking produces saliva, and the Zulu associate saliva with fertility (*ibid*:237). The ancestors also lick the victim's bile, a substance that, though bitter to people, is particularly 'sweet' to them (*ibid*:110). As we have seen, the gall bladder, the centre of vitality, is equivalent to the womb. The sacrifier is sprinkled with bile in order to attract the ancestors' attention (Ngubane, 1977:59; Berglund, 1975:238). Depending on the circumstances, the blown up gall bladder is tied to his hair (Berglund, 1975:238; Ngubane, 1977:61), wrist or ankle (Berglund, 1975:239). There are many reasons for a sacrifice, but the ceremony always stands out from ordinary butchery by the way that the gall bladder is handled (Ngubane, 1977:59). Every sacrifice seems to activate the process of reproduction. Let us follow this process to the cooking fire.

The sacrificial sequence

All sacrificial rejoicing invites the ancestors to join their ancestors (Berglund 1975:219). As among the Mofu of Cameroon, the family community increases its closeness in the presence of the immolated animal. The rite takes place in the family compound, for it is there that the ancestors remain closest to the living. The occasions for sacrifice are numerous, but the schema is relatively constant. The principal officiant is always the senior member of the restricted or extended family group. But if the sacrifier offers an animal in order to satisfy a personal wish, then he officiates himself. The sacrificer is merely a skilled butcher. The animal is sometimes selected by a diviner; but the latter is not allowed to shed any blood; he merely indicates the parts that should be reserved to the ancestors (Berglund 1975:225). How do they go about choosing a victim? This question is crucial for our study. The Zulu all agree that although the ox is the most prefered species, the goat will also do, and the latter is increasingly being sacrificed to the ancestors (Berglund 1975:228). The reasons for this substitution are symbolic, the reverse of those by which the sheep is prefered to goat in sacrifices offered to the python genie. In fact, this time the animal must bleat while dying in order to attract the attention of the ancestors, while in the case of the previously mentioned sacrifice, great care is taken to muzzle the animal. In the family sacrifice the goat has another virtue: its gall is enormous and its bile is very bitter (therefore very sweet to the ancestors' taste) (Berglund 1975:111). The animal's colour does not matter in this case, but the diviner (or the sacrifier himself because of a dream) sometimes specifies what features are required (Berglund 1972:228).

The ancestors are invoked in the presence of the animal. They are called by their names; the officiant carefully states the circumstances and reasons for the rite (Berglund 1975:231). The sacrifice clearly expresses the desire for a dialogue; a *bona fide* confession is necessary when an offence has compromised good relations between the living and the dead. The beauty and the perfect physical condition of the animal are praised. The officiant has close physical contact with the victim. Berglund watched a sacrifice performed by a father for celebrating the healing of his son. He saw the father touch the dewlap and throat of the animal as it was dedicated to the ancestors (Berglund, 1975:216). A sacrifice takes place in dignity without any trace of violence. In fact, the animal seems to be 'loaded' with the affection that the living feel for their ancestors. The victim is the meeting place of these two parties. The butcher who kills it approaches 'in a self-conscious and dignified manner' (*ibid*:216).

Before the immolation, the officiant rubs the animal's back with a carbonised magical plant or with beer (*ibid*.:228). *Imphepho (Helichrysum miconiaefolium)* is a plant that is always alive, eternal like the ancestors (Berglund, 1975:113). Ritual precautions are taken to gather it. It must be gathered during the day, preferably early in the morning while the gatherer casts his shadow over it. This act in itself resembles a sacrifice, the taking of a plant's life; the officiant must ask for pardon whenever he breaks the flower's stalk. The diviner who furnished this information to Berglund was convinced that the ancestors are in the ground near the plant (*ibid*.:113). Immortal chtonian beings, the ancestors are united both metaphorically and metonymically to the *imphepho*. This flower must not be pulled up by the roots—as though the sign is consubstantially united with its underground meaning.

Traditionally the ox must be stabbed in the flank with a ritual spear that belongs to the ancestors. This act must be carried out where the ancestors gather in the upper part of the cattle kraal. If the victim is a goat, its throat is cut (*ibid*.:229). The animal must sink down on its right side with its muzzle turned towards the doorway of the principal hut. It is encouraged to bellow or bleat in order to call the ancestors (*ibid*.:216). Not only is this condition necessary for communication but also many people think that a silent death offends the ancestors (*ibid*.:209).

The animal is cut up right away. Although the portion reserved for the ancestors (*isiko*) varies according to the clan, it always includes both meat and fat. When the officiant, along with the sacrifier, carries this portion into the hut, the attendance must be absolutely silent (*ibid*.:232). Berglund has discussed in length the crucial question of the incineration of this portion which, placed on a potsherd or directly on the live charcoal (*ibid*.:273), is burnt in the fireplace within the house. When he asked an informant if simply cooking it would not suffice, Berglund was told that the fire itself 'eats' the offering (*ibid*.:232), that the fire belongs to the ancestors since to make a fire and mold a child is the same work that involves heat. There is no better way to say that the consumption of the meat by the ancestors is a sexual metaphor, a process having to do with fertility.

Let us look closely at the ceremony that Berglund has described. The father is the officiant and the son the sacrifier. They sit around the hearth in the principal hut. The pieces of meat and of fat selected for the ancestors have been placed on a potsherd and sprinkled with blood from the sacrificial wound. When the smoke clears away, the father adds a pinch of *imphepho* grass as he calls upon the ancestors. He grabs the ritual spear and sticks it into the thatch just above the *umsamo* altar, which is dedicated to the ancestors. Letting it stick there, he goes back to his place near the fire. He stays silent (Berglund, 1975:217). The smell of the meat that is being charred invites the ancestors to partake of a meal (*ibid*.:232). Stabbing the roof 'awakens' them. Much more than the consumption of food is at stake. The fire that devours the meat is explicitly associated with the 'heat' of sexuality and of reproduction (ibid:232).

How to interpret the preliminary rite, the stabbing of the roof above the ancestors altar? Located as far as possible inside the hut, the *umsamo* altar is loaded with sexual connotations. It is divided into two parts. The *ufindo* is the framework of the hut comprising saplings whereas the *umbundu* is a mound of earth a few centimetres high, frequently in the form of a semicircular border (*ibid*:102). Together, these two parts form an oval space. *Ufindo* also designates the lower, prominent part of the lumbar vertebrae, in other words, the place in the body where the ancestors cause an erection. The backbone is 'like the arch of the hut' (*ibid*:115).

We can suppose that the household head, who wakes up the ancestors by stabbing the roof in order to invite them to eat the meat on the fire, is asking them to promote fertility. As previously shown, the hut itself is the image of the womb.

The animal's death starts up a process of life, a sexual process. Blood from the spear and from the victim's wound is burnt on the fire along with the ancestor's portion of meat that is reduced to ashes. In another context, one of Berglund's informants used the word *umlotha* (ashes) (Berglund, 1975:221) to designate sperm (*amalotha*) (*ibid*:167). Linguistic research carried out upon my request by Yvonne Bastin and Claire Gregoire (I take this opportunity to thank them) led to the conclusion that these two terms are not related. It is nevertheless interesting to note that a Zulu informant could commit such a lapse, allowed by the symbolic if not by the linguistic system. Sperm is equivalent to saliva. As stated, the ancestors come to lick the offering on the *umsamo* altar and thus help to promote fertility. The ancestor-snakes have acquired this power from the water spirit, Python, the Lord of Shadows, who fertilises women by spitting on them (*ibid.*:143).

The way of cooking the ancestors' portion is, in a way, an anti-cooking. Recall that the aspect and behaviour of the ancestors is opposite that of mankind. Not only is the meat devoured by the fire but also it must not be seasoned. This prohibition perplexed the informant that Berglund was interrogating. Can we see more clearly into this matter?

We need to follow the various phases during which the meat is consumed. When the offering has been reduced to ashes, the officiant puts on the fire two small pieces of meat taken, like the others, from the animal's right flank. As soon as the smoke rises, he cuts each of these barely grilled pieces in two. He gives the first two bits to his son to eat, and he himself swallows the two others while calling upon the ancestors. Each of them then drinks a swig of beer (*ibid.*:218). All the men are sitting around two fires lit outside the hut; one in the byre, the other in the yard (*ibid.*:218). They roast the rest of the meat there. They salt it very little or not at all. Finally, in the house, the women boil the other pieces of meat. They sometimes—but with no obligation to do so—avoid salting these pieces (*ibid.*:239).

The ritual fire of the ancestors is thus located in the centre of a symbolic circle. From the centre to the circumference, the method of cooking is transformed and the prohibition of salt is slackened. Associated with fertility, the anti-cookery of the ancestors gradually loses its mystical meaning. The burning of unsalted meat is followed by roasting (direct contact with the fire). On the perimeter of this masculine ritual space, women boil the meat (indirect contact with fire). The opposition between the roasted and the boiled, which Lévi-Strauss has brought to light in cooking operations (Lévi-Strauss, 1965), is overloaded with religious connotations. The sacrificial cookery institutes a social world that is shut upon itself. Traditionally, neither visitors nor family members from elsewhere could take meat out of the homestead. In the end, the bones too are incinerated; and the ashes are scattered inside the cattle enclosure (Berglund, 1975:240).

Fire, the mystical centre of the socio-religious circle, is the very place where the ancestor-snakes, who belong to the outside world, go to encounter the living. The fire in the principal hut is the juncture of the natural order of biological reproduction and the cultural order defined by cookery.

This culinary space, founded upon the precedence and priority of the roasted over the boiled, has already been discussed in Greek sacrifices. There too, the absence of salt was the mark *par excellence* of ritual consumption. In Greece, the unsalted viscera were roasted and eaten near the altar by members of an intimate circle. But in this case, the immortal gods, kept at a distance, were satisfied with the smoke of the sacrifice; and only people separated from the Olympian gods partook of the banquet. Nevertheless in Zululand and in ancient Greece, the sacrificial cookery has to do with sex and death (See p.19).

Among the Zulu, beer always figures in sacrifices. The ancestors like it as much as meat. Both substances are associated with heat, hence with fertility. The fermentation of beer involves the action of fire. Wanting beer is like desiring a woman (*ibid.*:225–6). The ancestors necessarily participate in any drinking bout (*ibid.*:210). The water used to ferment the millet must be 'alive' and should, ideally, be fetched from a spring or waterfall. Any recently brewed beer must be presented on the ancestors' *umsamo* altar. The religious nature of this drink explains that its consumption can be likened to a sacrifice. The man who wants to bring the ancestors' blessing upon himself is the first to drink (*ibid.*:223). Owing to the difficulty of obtaining animal victims, ritual drinking is more and more often replacing sacrifices. Given the symbolic connections between beer and meat, both under the sign of heat, this substitution is perfectly legitimate.

Water, coolness and the origin of the universe

Heat, the very condition for human reproduction, is, in the eyes of the Zulu, an ambiguous category. It is involved in all states of physical and moral excitation (*e.g.*, hate and anger) that tend to cause conflict. Therefore, the evening before a sacrifice, the officiant sees to it that he is not heated. He must not have sexual relations, must abstain from drinking beer and from eating meat, and must keep away from fire (Berglund, 1975:225). The moral condition for the success of the ceremony is the 'coolness' of participants (*ibid.*:247).

This indispensable condition brings into play the fire–water dialectic that underlies the Zulu's social and cosmological order. Like the Python spirit, the ancestor-snakes are water beings. A diviner told Berglund how he acquired supernatural powers by going down into the depths of water in order to meet these beings. This is the story of an amazing shamanistic trip to the place at the origin of the world. One evening when he was very ill, he was drawn toward a pool by a mysterious white beetle. He went down to the bottom of the pool where he encountered a big python surrounded by a multitude of snakes of all sizes. These snakes were the ancestors, and Python was their ruler (*ibid.*:140–3). The diviner described this pool as being *uhlanga*, the place out of which the first humanity came. According to the Zulu myth, the first people came out of a reedy swamp. The stalks of the reeds sank into the earth and thus impregnated it with water (*ibid.*:144). As a consequence, the first ancestor, Umhlabathi, a chtonian creature, was born. The earth was his mother, the reed, his father (*ibid.*:91).

When a diviner is possessed during a trance, he is in close relation with this ancestor from the beginning (*ibid.*:91). The diviner who recounted his initiatory adventure to Berglund explained that this fantastic trip into the original water was, for him, a death and a rebirth (Berglund, 1975:144). 'A diviner cannot be born of a woman, he must come from the earth' (*ibid.*:167). In this respect, he is like the first people produced through the fertilisation of the earth by a reed soaked with water. This mythical bond involves neither heat nor the action of fire. Born in Ihlunga, the primordial pool covered with reeds, this first humanity with aquatic and chtonian origins was immortal. The chameleon let death come among mankind. Why did the Lord of Heaven choose the chameleon? Because it deceives with its changing colours. Because it tricks its victims by keeping away from them before catching and swallowing them with its tongue. The Zulu describe the chameleon as a monster; its tail resembles a fifth leg, its eyes turn in all directions (*ibid.*:251). Yet this unreliable creature was created by the Sky Lord. It is in the image of the Creator's changing temperament. The creator ordered it to carry the promise of immortality to mankind but then changed his mind and sent the lizard to announce that people are destined to die. The chameleon came too late, after the lizard (*ibid.*:251–2).

This whim of the Lord of Heaven has no other explanation than his unforeseeably changing temperament. In any case, since life has become short, it has been associated with the ambiguous element of fire, the source of excitement and trouble. The fire that the ancestors have given to mankind and that they use in the womb in order to make life out of water, has a dangerous counterpart.

The Zulu make this very clear at the time of sacrifices of thanksgiving for a cure. Let us listen to what the sacrifier who has promised a cow to the ancestors has to say on this occasion. In offering them the animal, he declares that 'the fire which caused the suffering has been put out. Today there is wood for another fire; the fire of food and of sweet smells! The fire of the stomach and of the nostrils! [Yii, you have put out the first fire and the soothsayers have shown us that the other one should be lit!]' (Berglund, 1975:216).

This other fire is the one for sacrifice, for ritual cooking and for gestation. But this fire, by means of which the ancestors aid in the creation of life, itself implies death, the abandonment of the placenta, which is likened to a corpse, or to the skin of the ancestor-snake when he is sloughing it off (Berglund, 1975:95). We are not surprised to learn that a woman who has just given birth is confined to her hut like one who is a chief mourner. 'Indeed if you have given birth, you are like a bereaved person', an informant tells Harriet Ngubane (Ngubane, 1977:164–5).

A serious question then arises. Every sacrifice invites the ancestors to throw themselves into the fire in order to consume their share of meat. This alimentary process is homologous to the fertilising of women by the ancestor's water (sperm) within the 'heat' of the womb. Yet these immortal aquatic beings, unceasingly reborn, create beings whom the Sky Lord has doomed to a short life—because of that detestable creature, the chameleon. Marked by fire, the gift of the ancestors, the birth of a child is already accompanied by death, that of his placenta. Sacrifice, which provides for the ancestors a substitute image for the womb (the gall bladder), is itself an act of fertility which entails the death of a precious animal.

Finally, is not the sacrifice of the ox the price to be paid so that the ancestors will continue to create life by playing with fire—that is, with death?

The anthropological concept which is adumbrated in this sacrificial cooking differs profoundly from that of the Greeks. The tragic emphasis is displaced. Prometheus is no longer present to teach men that in allowing them to eat sacrificial meat he has deceived the gods, has established a definitive distance between the Sky and the Earth, where the altar fire is the very sign of the death which has been foretold to man. The role of Zulu sacrifice is, on the contrary, to reinforce the vital liaison with the ancestors, who circulate freely among them, even in the most intimate areas. Fire, which they love, was not stolen; it was given to man to enable him to eat and to reproduce. If it has a connotation of danger, that is because it is the very antithesis of the primordial water, the source of immortality. That is why the fire that inflames men's hearts must be 'put out'. Every disturbed social state demands a cooling treatment—which we shall briefly consider.

When a family group decides to end a dispute, its members gather around their head. They avoid looking each other in the eye 'because of the heat in their hearts'. The officiant throws ashes into the water and says: 'Here is the water that contains the ashes.' All of the participants then wash their hands (Berglund, 1975:323–4). In this ritual context, fire is indeed the metaphor of conflict, the ashes the agent of the coolness which will allow a united community to sacrifice together once more.

Ashes figure again in a different, non-sacrificial rite. This time an animal is dedicated *alive* to the ancestors.

An unsubdued ritual animal

In any important herd, an animal of exceptional ritual status, the *inkomo yamadlozi*, was formerly to be found. It might be a bull, but never a castrated ox. The Zulu are vehemently opposed to this. 'An ox,' they say, 'is for work. This animal must not work; it is set aside for the ancestors. That is why it cannot be an ox' (Berglund, 1975:200). For this purpose the Zulu usually choose a cow which has proved its fertility, a superb creature, fat and docile, whose long horns are evenly grown. The colour is not important. A nervous or uncontrollable animal would not do. The cow will never be sacrificed or sold. When she dies a natural death, she will be replaced by one of her heifers. The owner presents the animal to the ancestors by rubbing its back with *imphepho* medicine (Berglund, 1975:201). We are familiar with this plant, which is associated with sacrifice because it is a symbol of immortality. In dire circumstances, the owner will approach the *inkomo yamadlozi* and rub its back with ashes in order to appease the ancestors' anger. An informant, questioned by Berglund, himself established the symbolic relationship: ashes are white (beneficial); they come from the hearth, the very place where ancestors like to gather (Berglund, 1975:206).

Another opposition is apparent within the ritual system, that between ordinary sacrificial victims and the privileged animal which is never slaughtered. Through the latter, the Zulu establish another type of communication with the ancestors. The chosen cow, or bull, is soothed with 'refreshing' ashes. The conclusion is unavoidable: the animal dedicated to the ancestors and the sacrificial victim are defined by inverse symbolic relationships.(Fig. 4.)

Fig. 4

Live animal dedicated to the ancestors	Sacrificial victim
Intact bull or fertile cow	Either bovine or caprine
Communication with the ancestors established through ashes	Communication with ancestors established through fire and cooking.

This privileged representative of the ancestors is not isolated from the herd; it walks about freely with its companions, and it sometimes selects them for sacrifice. 'If there is doubt as to which animal is to be slaughtered in a ritual celebration, the animals are all driven into the cattle enclosure; the beast that passes through the gateway nearest the *inkomo yamadlozi* is regarded as the shades' indication of which animal they choose' (Berglund, 1975:204). One should avoid thinking that the *inkomo yamadlozi* is identified with the ancestors. The Zulu firmly reject this idea. What, then, is its status? The chosen cow and some of its female offspring are relieved of all tasks that burden the domestic animal, in order to be used exclusively for religious communication. As a living symbol of the ancestors' presence among men, this animal and its offspring belong entirely to them. They cannot be involved in any sharing out or in any commercial transaction. Thus an animal 'chain of life' is in a way projected into the world of the ancestors by a strange sham. It is linked to man's fire only through the ashes, yet does not really belong to the society of the shades. The *inkomo yamadlozi* cow wanders in a different familiar mythical space that is neither the far off sky of the Master of Thunder, nor the deep water of the python genie, nor yet the realm of the ancestors, the aquatic snakes.

This elect, non-sacrificial animal is in some ways cut off from the cultural pattern in which the domestic species serve man, in order to become the unique representative of the ancestors who easily crisscross the borders of human space. The whole bovine species, on the other hand, is 'sacrifiable', capable of uniting men and ancestors around the hearth. This double purpose contrasts with the ritual use of certain wild species; the hornbill and the eagle represent the cosmic powers, and are sacrificed in order to re-establish a natural balance. Within the man's herds, the black sheep is the only creature to benefit from a similar status.

These diverging strategies are, fundamentally, based on a profound unity. The Zulu associate the python genie and the Rainbow Princess, as well as the ancestors, with water. Each one in its own sphere, from nearby or from far away, shows the same benevolence. Man only needs to know how to manipulate the animal's body in order to control the situation. All in all, it is an optimistic vision that is not even troubled by the fear of death, since the latter is the perpetual rebirth of the immortal snakes.

Death-cries, prayer and silence

Let us compare the sacrificial procedures which relate to domestic animals and try to specify their distinctive characteristics (Fig. 5).

Fig. 5

	Sacrifice to the ancestors	*Sacrifice to the python genie*
Preferred animal	Any ox	Black sheep
Substitute animal	Any goat	Muzzled black goat
Mode of communication	Loud sacrifice	Silent sacrifice
Place of offering	Domestic fire	Midstream

The opposition between the sacrificial animal's loud and silent death deserves more attention. A flow of words accompanies the first sacrificial system, while silence encompasses the entire ritual scene when the python genie is the recipient. Yet in ancestor worship the officiants must themselves keep silent during the most solemn moment, when they place the offering in the fire.

Silence is always essential in the python's presence, and this is also necessary 'when there is thunder, because both come from the sky' (Berglund, 1975:61). This cannot be explained away as a simple show of respect. I will show that silence is necessary in these different contexts to establish a mediatory relationship between two terms which can neither be joined nor disjoined, as Lévi-Strauss clearly demonstrated in connection with other rituals (Levi-Strauss, 1964:300).

Let us begin by noting that the attitude of the rainmaker who is immobile and silent when confronted by the python genie, contrasts with the relaxed attitude of the girls who approach the Rainbow Princess *from a certain distance*. Communication is noisy, free and casual. The girls are full of affectionate words for their heavenly 'sister' and 'friend'. However, in this case the meeting takes place on a mountain, summit between the sky and the earth. There is no sacrificial procedure; the offering of beer and seeds is accompanied by speech. This entirely female rite implies the subversion of the male order since the girls are disguised as men.

In this respect, the sacrifice to the ancestors occupies an intermediary position: the cries of the dying beast and the prayer summon the spirit-snakes. However, silence sets in when the meat meant for them is consumed by the fire. It is as if a linguistic distance must be maintained during this mysterious moment when the dead, the water creatures, return to the hearth in order to sustain life.

The same internal opposition between words and silence is found in Mofu ritual. An aged informant reveals to Vincent, 'The ancestors are there, speaking among themselves; that is why we, the living, should also be numerous, so as to speak to them' (Vincent, 1976:190). The first sequence begins with a long introductory prayer, just as among the Zulu. After the victim's immolation, its blood is poured into a receptacle that is placed briefly on the altar. Part of the coagulated blood is then mixed with millet flour and eaten *in silence* by the oldest participants (Vincent, 1976:193–4). On the other hand, the offering of cooked food to the ancestors is interspersed with many prayers, and Vincent justly notes that 'the freedom to speak which is allowed to each person' contrasts with the strict codification and order of the gestures (Vincent, 1976:197). Vincent wonders about the 'communal' meaning of the silent consumption of blood by the elders. Blood is also rubbed on the ancestors' pottery and the foreheads of participants. The author notes that for the Mofu, this element does not convey any vital force. In this case, the blood belongs to the category of raw food in opposition to the subsequent cooking procedure by which the ancestors are invited to return to the community of the living and to share their meals. The raw blood and the silence mark the lack of communication with the ancestors at the moment when the dying victim is placed on the altar. It is worth noting that only the elders—who have a close relationship with the ancestors—are authorised to consume this raw, coagulated blood.

This type of sacrifice implies the correlation of distinct beings and places. The Zulu observe the same reserved attitude at the beginning of the ritual cooking, during the offering to the fire. No trace of 'sacralisation' of the animal is to be found when this solemn contact takes place. This idea is as foreign to the Zulu as it is to the Mofu. The sudden suspension of verbal communication shows that, despite the artifice of prayer, a radical difference does indeed exist between mortal men and their invisible counterparts, the immortal ancestors. Silence introduces a mediation between both.

From this perspective, the ambiguous notion of 'communion' deserves to be re-examined. In Christian language, it implies a veritable theophagy, the consumption of cooked or fermented vegetable substances (bread and wine) likened to the actual body of a divinity who were sacrificed long ago. This unusual idea is not to be found either in Zulu family sacrifices or in the sacrifice of animals representing the cosmogonic powers. How could they eat an ancestor or the rain genie? Nevertheless, the religious silence of a Christian group when the mystery of transubstantiation takes place also has a topological function: at the moment when the god descends, the suspension of speech confirms in some way that heaven approaches earth. The sacrifice of Christ, man and God, the ritual absorption of his body, introduce a precise mediation between these two terms; they are separated by a dizzying void, which prayer can never overcome.

Bile and chyme

We have not finished with the body of the sacrificial animal. The Zulu specially treat the organ that symbolises the womb, namely the gall bladder. Let us return to Berglund's meticulous account. After meat has been offered to the ancestors inside the hut, the father of the sacrifier sprinkles bile over the body of his son. The gall bladder, emptied of its contents, is tied to the latter's arm. The two men then rub their hands with some of the chyme, some drops of which fall into the fire. The remainder of the liquid is used to spatter the roof. Finally the chyme is scattered inside the cattle enclosure. The blood that has been shed is carefully covered (Berglund, 1975:218).

How to understand the symbolic function of chyme? One of Berglund's informants stated that chyme is, after bile, the most important element in a sacrifice: 'It is for washing. Sometimes it is this thing (the chyme) that is required most of all (for example) at burials' (*ibid.*:129). Washing the hands with chyme is a purifying act; chyme makes the hands white like the ancestors (*ibid.*:129). The latter do not, however, come to lick the chyme or to dwell in it. In this respect, chyme and bile are in total opposition.

The chyme that is spattered on the roof after a sacrifice means that 'everything is clean in that there are no bad thoughts and no ill feelings with anybody' (*ibid.*:234). The purifying power of chyme has to do with the category of coolness, the calming of social tension. Bile, on the contrary, comes from an organ that is the very image of the womb where the ancestors use heat to make life. Sacrifice is like a hot impulse (the cooking of meat, the drinking of beer) betweeen two 'cool' times. Recall that the sacrifier must not be excited in any way the evening before the ceremony (see p. 53). Likewise, the sacrifice ends with a cooling, purifying rite during which the chyme is scattered. This substance is symbolically effective in social affairs. It reaffirms lineage solidarity and the absence of quarrels whereas the bile opens up a personal relationship between the sacrifier and the ancestors. Neither the chyme nor the bile contain magical powers (*ibid.*:239). Sacrifice is not at all a means of therapy; it is entirely symbolic.

But why is this process centred on the digestive system of the animal? Why is it that the contents of the gall bladder and the stomach are necessarily brought into play?

A Zulu author, Harriet Ngubane, tries to answer this question. As we know, the cow has several stomachs. It is the first, the rumen, that contains the chyme, a greenish liquid made up of pre-digested grass that the animal ruminates for a long time. After going through the the reticulum (second stomach) omasum (third stomach) and the abomasum (fourth stomach), the chyme becomes chyle in the intestines. The chyme (*umswami*) is a matter that is 'still intact, with all the life-giving food properties' (Ngubane, 1977:124). The chyme plays an exclusive role in the purification sacrifices which require no ritual cooking. The bladder and bile then disappear from the ritual scene (Ngubane, 1977:125). Ngubane describes a sacrifice where a goat's chyme serves to restore the spiritual well-being of an entire female age set, which was threatened by an offence committed by one member (she lost her virginity) (Ngubane, 1977:130). The man responsible for their fertility gives them a live goat, which they set upon, rubbing themselves with the victim's chyme and leaving it near the river. Later, they go and wash themselves in running water.

This all too brief description requires several comments. What we are actually witnessing is a kind of perversion of family sacrifice. The rite is carried out by women which is an exceptional pattern. The bile is ignored and only the chyme has any symbolic efficacy. Only very old women eat the animal's flesh, which is truly cursed. Ngubane herself invokes the figure of the scapegoat that haunts René Girard's imagination. Yet it is clear that this symbolic figure reverses all the characteristics of family sacrifice in the course of which the Zulu convoke their ancestors for a peaceful meal. There is no excitement at this feast, during which social bonds are reinforced by sharing the animal. On the contrary, all the participants are calm, in the desired state of coolness. When the emotional temperature has to be lowered, when men or the ancestors have to be calmed down, other ritual procedures are used. The purificatory rite carried out with the goat's chyme evidently occupies a marginal place in the Zulu sacrificial system. It is carried out in a strange state of excitement, the young girls throwing themselves on the animal, somewhat like Dionysus' followers on the victim whose raw meat they prepare to eat. The comparison, although excessive, is not without validity. In both cases, the dominant sacrificial system is subverted (see Chapter I).

The opposition between chyme and bile now takes shape. The former substance is used alone in certain purification rites where the sacrifier must regain the state of 'whiteness' after having broken prohibition. On the other hand, the gall bladder is a veritable 'inscription' of the animal upon the sacrifier's body; the sign brings down upon him the ancestors' benediction.

On this subject, Ngubane provides some very interesting speculations as to the symbolism of ruminants' digestive systems, which she tries to relate to colour symbolism (Ngubane, 1977:18–26). The symbolic category 'white', which encompasses all the light colours, connotes life, whereas 'black' connotes death and sorcery. A third category, red, is a mediator between the first two. Green and blue, united under the term *luhlaza*, belong, symbolically to the beneficial category of whiteness (*mhlophe*). Plant life, the sea, water and the sky are *luhlaza*, that is, associated with life. The same is true of bile. If it is so agreeable to the ancestors, it is because its colour *luhlaza* connotes life, just as does the grass that nourishes cattle. The ultimate end of the digestive process is the transformation of this vital substance (belonging to 'whiteness') into black excrement, an impure substance evoking sorcery and death (Ngubane, 1977:120). That is why only old women can eat this part of the intestine, the caecum which is highly developed among ruminants. Inadvertently, Ngubane identifies it with the third stomach. An informant tells her that the caecum is 'saturated by the ancestral presence' and that it 'would interfere with the reproductive powers of younger women' (Ngubane, 1977:123). Thus the ancestors permeate the animal's digestive system and only married women can eat the stomachs and intestines with the exception of the caecum. Digestion can certainly be interpreted as the passage from the natural 'whiteness' of grass to the 'blackness' of excrement. We cannot, however, agree with Ngubane when she introduces the category 'red' into this process. Nothing, in fact, permits us to believe that the chyme, whose green colour obviously belongs to 'whiteness', could 'represent what red symbols stand for', i.e. 'the transformation' of digested grass into disgusting waste' (Ngubane, 1977:125).

Rather, one might seek to comprehend the significance of the ritual opposition between chyme and bile. Clearly, the ancestors are interested only in the latter. One may recall that the bladder is the metaphor for the womb, that torrid place where they work at their own metamorphosis, at the point of articulation between nature and culture. The bile is the very sign of this procreative work. It is as if the ancestors found it tasty because it was cooked. As for chyme, half-digested grass, it belongs to the raw. This substance is the first step in a vital process in which the sacrificial victim's digestion (a metaphor for gestation) is an abridged version of the path from life to death. It is said that a witch caused the death of four children by stealing chyme of a cow sacrificed during their mother's wedding (Ngubane, 1977:35). Chyme is the raw material of life which is built up in the gall bladder. Finally, excrement belongs to the category of the disgusting and unclean (*izibi*), like the cadaver and placenta (Berglund, 1975:95).

The mysteries of the black sheep

Among the Zulu there is a second type of sacrifice which belongs in the scapegoat category. Its purpose is to divert attacks of sorcery from the lineage. A black sheep is used, and the animal is treated like a man. Its blood is not shed (it is suffocated) and it is buried in a grave far from any habitation; there is no consumption of the body. The rite takes place at night (Ngubane, 1977:119). Here again the normal sacrificial schema undergoes a complete reversal. Let us summarise all the sacrificial options involving domestic animals in Fig. 6.

Fig. 6

Recipient	Ancestors	Python genie	Sacrifice without recipient	
Animal	Ox (or goat)	Black sheep	Black sheep	Goat
Procedure	Ritual cooking	Licking of fat	Buried in the earth	Abandoned
Agent	Bile and chyme	—	—	Chyme
Final result	Mediation between lineage and ancestors	Mediation between sky and earth	Getting rid of sorcery	Purification after the breach of a prohibition.

It will be noted that cattle have two remarkable characteristics: only this species, rightfully sacrificed to the ancestors, undergo ritual cooking and complete processing of the organs. For objective reasons (these noisy animals have a highly developed gall bladder) goats can play the same role. Yet goats—used only because of their chyme—can also take over the jeopardy caused by violating a prohibition: the mistreated animal is abandoned without having its gall bladder extracted and without the ancestors having been invited to a ritual feast.

It will also be observed that rites with no recipient have a magical, not a religious, function. They repair a snag in the social fabric; they compensate for the unravelling of its stitches. On the contrary, the sacrifices directed to the ancestors or the python genie assure a positive conjunction on a social or cosmogonic level.

In this set, the status of the sheep is most remarkable. Its sub-species, black in colour, is capable of ending drought and warding off the malefic effects of sorcery. In both cases, as we shall see, the black sheep is treated like a man, not like an animal.

When it is ritually buried (not abandoned or eaten, like the goat or the ox) the black sheep can be considered the substitute for a human victim, the price paid by a family group to sorcerers in order to put an end to their attacks. The study of rain rituals leads us to a similar conclusion. The animal offered to the python genie is not ritually consumed. The magician puts on its skin and exposes it to the god's appetite as if he identified with the animal. Other aspects are even stranger. The rainmakers possess four magic horns. The first two (female) contain ewe fat; the other two (male), a ram's fat (Berglund, 1975:54). Berglund's two informants report that 'sheep are like women' and add that this is a big secret.

All this leads us to emphasise the disturbing nature of the sacrifice in honour of the python. The officiant and the god meet secretly, at midnight. The officiant, identified with the sheep, undergoes a kind of symbolic death. He faces grave danger. It is as if we are dealing with a human sacrifice. It is curious to note that in the Venda myth the python genie's own human wife was compelled to drown herself in the depths of the lake in order to put an end to the drought that had followed its disappearance (Stayt, 1968:333–7). The Lovedu assert that in former times it was a man and not, as now, a black sheep that was occasionally sacrificed in order to prevent the weakening of the royal rain medicine (Krige, 1954:65).

The black sheep is, symbolically, the most potent of all in Zulu rites. It is calm, like man, yet because of its colour it is linked with the disquieting realm of night, with sorcery, as much as with the realm of the rainstorm. Its sacrifice always takes place in dramatic circumstances, when a drought threatens an entire region or when an evil spell decimates a lineage. To be sure, the python genie does not behave in the same way as the ancestors, who eat oxen. Its demands are, in a way, similar to those of the sorcerers. The Zulu are struck by its unusual eating habits: the python kills its victims bloodlessly, then swallows them in one big gulp, unlike men, who must cut up their meat. If the first anomaly guarantees it prestige, the second causes a great deal of concern (Berglund,1975:60–1). When we consider the appearance of the royal figure on the sacrificial scene (Chapter V), we shall better understand the ambivalence of this sovereign genie. Here it is sufficient to emphasise that by licking the sheep's fat, in lieu of a human sacrifice, the python, Master of the Universe, reveals a somewhat anthropophagic solicitude for his people.

Thus, this ritual game obeys a certain number of precise rules. Different paradigms intersect within a topology which encompasses animal, man

and the universe. The ritual killing of certain wild species cannot be
dissociated from the sacrificial sphere. This killing adumbrates the other,
more or less imaginary, side of sacrifice. Theoretically, the hornbill, python,
etc. must be immolated bloodlessly; the same requirement is necessary
when a black sheep is sacrificed in place of a man in order to put an end to
sorcery. In all these cases, the sacrificed animal is truly a 'person',
sometimes representing a man, sometimes a cosmological divinity. This
does not hold true for the ox or the goat in domestic rites. To this initial
splitting of the problem, another kind of dialectic is added: the goat, which
has been expelled and is laden with 'blackness' after the extraction of the
chyme, obviously does not have the same role as the one that is sacrificed
to the ancestors with its special treatment of the entire digestive system.
Zulu sacrifice does not follow a unique schema. Our problem is fragmented
and open to different questions. All of these variants, however, lie within a
coherent semantic sphere, where the differences between species and
organs are clearly set out.

IV

The Thonga's goat

Throughout southern Africa the ox constitutes the index of value *par excellence*; it marks socio economic, political and ritual life with its strong male stamp. The Zulu and Swazi define rank and aristocratic status by the possession of herds. Marriage requires the transfer of many head of cattle to the bride's parents. This transaction, called *lobolo*, allows, the substitution of other valuables in hard times, notably the goat. Among the Mpondo, less wealthy families routinely use the goat (Hunter, 1936:71). There is every indication that the Bantu borrowed the ox from the pastoralist populations of East Africa during their migrations, which began far away near the border of present-day Cameroon and Nigeria. The goat, and to a lesser degree the sheep, is found throughout the Bantu area, and one may assume that the former, at least, was part of initial breeding. We know that the presence of the tse-tse fly in the equatorial forest and in the low altitude savannah region prevented the rearing of large stock in central Africa. The goat competes with other matrimonial currencies, notably copper, in the Mongo societies in the forest of Zaïre (de Heusch, 1955). The goat is not necessarily accepted as a valuable just because larger stock are lacking; indeed, we have seen that the Lele are completely indifferent to any kind of stock raising *for purely symbolic reasons*: they use only raphia cloth in matrimonial transactions (see Chapter II).

One southern African population, the Thonga, neighbours of the Zulu, pose a particularly interesting problem in this respect. During the time that the great ethnographer Junod lived among them (at the beginning of the twentieth century), the sum of the *lobolo* was generally calculated in pounds sterling. However, large stock did represent the dominant valuable during the nineteenth century. Beads and hoes were added after the Zulu raids. From 1840 to 1870 hoes were used concurrently with oxen, when the latter were available. It is remarkable that, contrary to the Mpondo, the Thonga seemed reluctant to introduce the goat into the currency of matrimonial exchanges regulated by *lobolo* (Junod, 1927,I,:275–6).

Here the goat constitutes a veritable sacrificial reserve for the most important ritual acts. All the Thonga own goats, but only young shepherds drink the milk (Junod, 1927, II:49). Boys take care of the goats until they are ten or eleven years old, when they are usually assigned to watch over the oxen (Junod, 1927,I.:62). As among all southeastern Bantu, Thonga women are rigorously kept away from the oxen (Junod, 1927,II:47).

Let us look at a Thonga village as Junod knew it. A circular thorn hedge encloses an extended patrilineal family. To the right of the main entrance, opposite the men's meeting place, is the ancestral altar, a modest cooking pot called *gandjelo*. There, members of the founding lineage normally present offerings of all kinds. If outsiders have placed themselves under the protection of the village chief, each lineage represented will have its own altar nearby. However, in such cases, the chief presents offerings for himself and his family on an altar in the centre of the village, at the foot of the sacred tree (Junod 1927,I:310–4; II:344).

As among the Zulu, ancestor worship dominates religious life, and we must start by examining what is included in the category of offerings (*mhamba*). Junod translates this word sometimes as 'offering', sometimes as 'sacrifice'. As a rule, the officiant is the eldest brother of the family group concerned (Junod, 1927,II:409, 420). He is himself called *mhamba*, as is the powerful talisman made of nails or facial skin taken from the corpse of a prestigious ancestor (Junod, 1927,II:418, 420). Only the elder brother has the right to *hahla*, which means to bring a part of the *mhamba* offering to his lips, to moisten it, and then spit it out saying 'tsu!' (Junod, 1927,II:411). In any case, no one can practise this rite or even present an offering (*gandjela*) before the death of his parents.

Junod begins, somewhat rashly, by translating the verb *hahla* as 'to consecrate'. His analysis of the concept *mhamba*, however, is very subtle. Generally speaking, this word designates 'any object, any act or person which is used to establish a link between the ancestor-gods and their worshippers' (Junod, 1927,II:420). The semantic field is even greater, for all the material signs used in magic are called *mhamba* (Junod, 1927,II:428). This is most troubling; *mhamba* is applied to the entire magico-religious field. It might have passed among old school ethnologists, as a new equivalent of *mana*. In fact, like the old *mana* theorists, the Thonga, say both too much and too little about it. We can no doubt have more confidence in the Thonga, but they, too, may mislead us. *Mhamba* is an overpowering conceptual category which does not acknowledge the implicit internal differences revealed only through ritual practise. This situation is certainly risky for the anthropologist, who in a sense is in the uncomfortable situation of a psychoanalyst faced with a society which has not asked him to explain its behaviour.

When analysing the Thonga's religious offerings, Junod begins by asking himself about their economic value as gifts. He notes that the ancestors' share is always minimal. The offering does not imply any ostentatious expense. It is the act of communication which matters. When the Thonga offer a goat, they eat the meat and reserve a small portion taken from each leg for the ancestors. The principle of substitution of the sign seems to come into full play: when necessary, a fragment of old skin can substitute for the prescribed offering of an ox. (Junod, 1927,II:414).

A certain guile may thus enter into the procedure. An informant volunteered to Junod that the Thonga did indeed 'trick' the ancestral spirits. However, Junod is well aware that this explanation was inadequate. The gods *allow* substitution; for to them, according to another informant— who anticipated Lévi-Strauss's famous precept—a chick is equivalent to an ox (Junod, 1927,I:415).

Before taking a position, let us examine the different contexts in which the *mhamba* offering occurs. Let us begin by analysing the extreme, negative cases. When a village chief is overcome by distress, he 'shows his misery by offering only his saliva' (Junod, 1927,II:391). This 'offering of bitterness', which is always ordered by the divining bones, is sometimes required as a preventive measure. To avert misfortune, the village chief can also present an 'offering of charcoal'. 'He takes a burnt out charcoal, puts it to his lips, utters the "tsu" and adds: "Smoothly! You, so and so. What you want is this ... Gently! This is fire! This is the mouth of the lion. Let that which troubles me come to an end"' (Junod, 1927,II:346).

In Thonga thought, as in that of the Zulu, heat connotes sickness or a dangerous state of excitement. In this general context, the charcoal becomes a metaphorical image. The rite aims at appeasing the lion's burning mouth, likened to the destructive power of angry ancestors. It is in this same perspective that one must consider the 'offering of a thorn': when the village is in danger of extinction and reverting to bush, the chief gathers a thorn in the forest; he sucks it while salivating. He returns to the forest and leaves it in a place indicated by the bones (Junod, 1927,II:392). The thorn, like charcoal, also appears in procedures of magical conjuring in order to stab the enemy or reduce him to helplessness (Junod, 1927,II:418). It is clear that the notion of 'offering' is inadequate. In the cases we have just examined, the *mhamba* object is a metaphorical sign. In the offering of bitterness the object disappears from the ritual scene; only the act of communication itself subsists by means of the saliva and the word.

Let us now examine the vast field of positive offerings. *Mhamba* can designate a chicken, a goat, field produce, tobacco, beer or cloth; even the bracelets dedicated to the ancestors. The very notion of blood sacrifice is not clearly defined in Thonga thought.

The animals or objects presented or handled at the offering place have a a socio-economic significance. They belong to man, they are part of what *he has*. But the *hahla* rite, which puts the offering in contact with his saliva, makes them also take part in *his being*. Far from being a 'consecration,' as Junod thinks, this action clearly show the ancestors that the officiant gives a part of himself. In the perspective adopted by Lévi-Strauss, we would say that the object offered becomes a metonymic sign of the one who offers. The object does not, for all that, share in the 'sacred' nature of the recipient.

Let us examine closely the principle of substitution laid out by Junod's informants. As Junod clearly emphasises, the 'value' of the gift is of little importance. However, one notes that the offering is generally described as an ox when it is, more often than not, a chicken (Junod, 1927, II:381, 396, 415). It so happens that the ox is the highest symbolic form of social wealth. Although Zulu invasions and the epizootic diseases that swept the countryside at the beginning of the twentieth century decimated the herds, the valuables transferred to the bride's father *lobolo* have never ceased to be presented as oxen, even when what are transferred are hoes (Junod, 1927, I:109).

Historical fluctuations in socio-economic values cannot be neglected in a symbolic approach. This makes it even more remarkable that the goat was never considered appropriate for use in matrimonial exchange, even though it is 'certainly the first domesticated animal amongst the Thonga, and, no doubt among all South African Bantu' (Junod, 1927, II:50). On the other hand, the ox is so dominant that it plays the role of the *lobolo par excellence* among the Nkuna, emigrants to the Transvaal (Junod, 1927, I:275). Furthermore, by a sort of verbal inflation, any offering to the ancestors may be described as an ox as if it was important to create the impression of a substantial gift when, as we shall see, this animal was sacrificed only under exceptional circumstances.

To understand these practices one must carefully distinguish three networks of communication. The *lobolo* system allows the convertibility of rare valuables. No such economic calculation enters into the 'system of offerings', for it is evident that neither a chicken nor a piece of skin is worth as much as an ox. In this case, references to oxen are purely rhetorical. Elsewhere, one finds represented among the offerings, objects (cereal, beer, cloth) or animals (chicks, chickens, goats) of no value in matrimonial exchange. The divining bones seem to make every effort to minimise loss, since they often prescribe a semblance of maize beer (*byala bosila*) that no one would ever drink. The officiant may limit his offering to the foam from the brewing or even particles left in the sieve during the beer making (Junod, 1927, II:414). The diviner's prescriptions can, however, be more constraining: he can, for example, indicate that the ancestor would like a handkerchief with a specific design (Junod, 1927, II:413). The offering is not always destroyed. If the diviner recommends a bracelet for the healing of a sick child, it will be placed on his ankle and never exchanged (Junod, 1927, II:397). It also happens that a live chicken or goat may be offered to the ancestors; it is then forbidden to kill the animal which will have to be replaced by another when it dies from natural causes (Junod, 1927, 351).

All these cases show that *mhamba* offerings cannot be assimilated into sacrifice even though animals hold an important place. They constitute so many (metonymic) signs of interest shown by the living for their ancestors or (metaphorical) signs destined to force them to intervene.

Yet within the *mhamba* values, the goat enjoys a privileged status during the great collective rites which we shall now examine. Goats, deliberately kept out of the matrimonial circuit, fulfil an eminent religious function, as Junod duly notes. The Thonga set up their *sacrificial system* around the goat. It is mainly in rites of mourning and marriage that the symbolic value characteristic of this animal appears. In this context, divination no longer intervenes to determine the preferred object required by the ancestors. It is in fact the body of the goat that is used for its symbolic properties, with no substitution permitted. This refers us, as we shall see, to a category different from that of the gift or the offering. The lack of differentiation which governs the system of offerings then ceases to apply, and other concerns are brought into play. A specific sacrificial zone becomes apparent. The terms 'offering' and 'sacrifices' are, then, not interchangeable. A sacrifice may be an offering, but not all offerings are the object of a sacrifice.

The locus of the ancestors

Where do these ancestors, to whom the *mhamba* offerings are addressed, live? They are far from having that familiar status, that closeness and omnipresence, which characterises them in Zulu thought. According to popular belief, they live in underground villages where they lack for nothing. They hand down part of their wealth to their descendants (Junod, 1927, II:375). Sometimes they appear among men in the guise of small, inoffensive blue snakes (*Dendrophis subcarinatus*). When one of them slithers into a house, it is welcomed with joy; killing it is forbidden. They are seen on the thatched roofs and reed walls (Junod, 1927, II:340,384). However, the most prestigious ancestors, those of the chief's lineage, live in sacred woods, which only a priest who is one of their descendants is allowed to enter. There the ancestors take the form of a venomous species, the big grey puff-adder (Junod, 1927, II:384–5). When this fearful animal appeared one day in 1895 to the old priest Nkolele, he recognised it as the ancestor who is Master of the Forest. The snake approached him familiarly and thanked his 'grandson' for the offering he brought. And yet, once again, the officiant tricked the ancestor; he insisted on the beauty of his chicken ('which has just the same value as an ox') and asked in exchange for 'all the trees': the palm trees to build houses, and the trunks to make canoes. This was done to avoid an accident during the felling of the trees. Yet when this same Nkolele was obliged by the Portuguese authorities of Mozambique to remove the main branch of a huge mahogany tree to facilitate the construction of a road through the sacred forest, for which he was responsible, he fell backwards and was taken, unconscious, to his home. His eldest son then went to the forest with a chicken, which he set free. He addressed his ancestors with the following words: 'Here's my ox. Do not slay my father.' Then Nkolele regained consciousness. He consulted the diviner, who recommended that he, too, offer an 'ox-rooster' (Junod, 1927, II:381).

Domestic animals abandoned alive in the ancestors' domain pass into the latter's jurisdiction, as do animals dedicated to them in the village but not killed. A curious story reminds men of this inalienable right to property. Passing near this same Libombo forest on a rainy day, a woman saw an obstinately silent child, perched in a tree, eating berries. She climbed the tree to get him and tied him to her back with the pagne. In the village, the child refused to stand up, to eat or to warm himself at the hearth. He could not be pulled off the woman's back. The diviners, after consultation, revealed that this mysterious creature was none other than an ancestor. The woman returned to the forest and pleaded with the spirits. The guardian ancestor of the forest appeared and hurled these words at her: 'When you find fruit in the forest, do not pick it! If it is maize, leave it alone, or if you pick it, spare at least one ear. If your chicken flies into the wood, do not go after it. If your goat runs away into it, you must not follow. We are worn out, we folk of Libombo, from offering sacrifices to you passers-by.' A priest then sacrificed a white hen, which he presented as an ox, and the child disappeared. But the woman was soon seized by violent tremblings and died (Junod, 1927, II:378–9).

This story is edifying from several points of view. Man's universe and that of the ancestors are rigorously separated. The Thonga's ancestors refuse to come to warm themselves by the hearth, unlike the Zulu's ancestors for whom it is the favourite place. This should be compared to the refusal of commensality, which is the fundamental characteristic of the ancestors in collective, sacrificial rites. (More will be said about this later.) The ancestors also forbid their descendants to encroach on their forest property. To gather fruit or to chase an escaped animal is a serious offence. The reproach addressed to the poor victim in the preceding story is of the greatest significance; it underlines the asymmetrical nature of offerings, even of sacrifice. The ancestors energetically refuse to 'sacrifice' their goods to the living, the latter are required to sacrifice to the ancestors.

The offering is primarily the suspension of a state of tension. The role of the accompanying prayers is often to soften the ancestors' anger, to conjure away misfortune or sickness. When the offering is presented because of a calamity, 'the petition is preceded, or followed, by actual insults hurled at the gods' (Junod, 1927, II:423). Moreover, there are two words to designate prayers to the ancestors: *Khongota*, ('to plead') and *Bula-bulela* ('to reprimand') (Junod, 1927, II:421).

The animal in private offerings

Let us begin by examining the very specific use of the chicken and goat in private offerings. Certain parts of the animal are the objects of symbolic treatment. When an 'offering' of chicken is made for a child, a feather, claw and beak are attached to the child as a kind of talisman (*psirungulu*). These are attached on the right side if the invocation is directed to a paternal ancestor, on the left side if it is to a maternal ancestor (Junod, 1927, II:417). The Thonga kinship system is a variant of the Omaha type, and all men belonging to their mother's lineage have 'a special religious duty towards their nephews,' who are likened to their grandsons (*ntekulu*) (Junod, 1927, II:410). The precise description of an individual, therapeutic sacrifice shows more precisely that the 'uncle' as defined by the Omaha system is the privileged intermediary between paternal and maternal ancestors (Junod, 1927, II:396). When he officiates, he endeavours to reconstitute or strengthen the alliance between the two lines. He starts by abusing his own ancestors. He blames them for being useless, for causing nothing but trouble. He then invokes the solidarity that should unite them, in the other world as in this one, with his nephew's paternal relatives by virtue of these matrimonial ties; he asks his own ancestors to intercede with his nephew's ancestors. He refers to the *lobolo*, the bride wealth publicly transmitted by one group to the other on the occasion of the mother's marriage. Finally, he invites maternal and paternal ancestors to share the hen he offers, represented as an 'ox' for the occasion (Junod, 1927, II:396). This ritual intervention clearly reinforces the fabric of social relations, as if individual healing were possible only through the merging of the two constituent branches of the kinship group. There is also a direct communication with paternal ancestors: the priest may first call his own father and entreat him to go and bring his grandfather, the latter to bring his progenitor, and so on up to the most distant ancestor (Junod, 1927, II:422). But even in this case, 'the ancestors in the main line are then sent to call all the great-uncles, and all the deceased of collateral lines'.

The animal offered has one noteworthy characteristic: if the rite is carried out by a woman, it must be a he-goat or a cock that is offered; if it is by a man, a she-goat or a hen (Junod, 1927, II,:417). The Thonga say the purpose of this rule is that it contributes to 'building up the village'. Their principle of sexual complementarity applies generally; the symbolic conjunction of the sexes is essential to success in any field: 'When a girl is sick, a boy will bring her medicine and vice-versa'.

The chicken and goat are clearly distinguished from other *mhamba* offerings by just this use. They are not only gifts; as living beings, they serve as specific symbolic agents. This is particularly true of the goat. When it is sacrificed, its ankle-bone is carefully preserved as a talisman —*psirungulu* (Junod, 1927, II:427). Now, the goat's ankle-bone is one of the key pieces in the divinatory game staged between men and the ancestors before ritual action is undertaken (Junod, 1927, II:543–7). The bone signifies a man or a woman, depending on the sex of the animal from which it comes. Five ankle-bones from he-goats of decreasing age evoke, respectively: an old man, a mature man, an adult, an adolescent and a little boy. Five such bones from a she-goat signify the corresponding ages of women. These bones connote the 'people of the village' as opposed to the five ankle-bones of the ram and ewe, which 'represent', respectively, the chief and aged members of his family, his widow, sons, daughters and army.

The divinatory system also includes the little bones of wild animals, each designating a particular social status. This system does in no way imply a consubstantiality between man and the billy goat, between woman and the goat. If caprines are used to designate men it is by virtue of a (metonymical) relationship; they both live within the village. As for the ancestors, they are 'represented' (metaphorically) by the small bone of an anteater (apparently the aardvark), for this animal lives under-ground like the dead, and only leaves his burrow at night (Junod, 1927: 376). We know that they are reincarnated as reptiles.

On the sacrificial scene, the goat does not expose the sacrifier to a symbolic death. In private rituals the animal brings forth a fertilising force because of the sexual complementarity between the victim and the sacrifier. As among the Zulu, the gall bladder is attached to the latter's head (Junod, 1927: 443). In the collective rituals which we shall now study, it is the chyme which plays the principal role.

Goat sacrifice and matrimonial alliance

Marriage is the occasion for a battle (Junod, 1927, I:108–113). The girl's brothers confront the fiancé's group in simulated combat. The former guard the village gates, which the suitor's friends take by storm. The fiancé has brought a goat. After the assessing of the bride wealth (*lobolo*), the goat's throat is slit in front of the hut where the bride-to-be is hiding. The women pull her out by force while the future husband's retinue taunts her. The two parties then confront each other in a new verbal duel: they bombard each other with chyme (*psanyi*). When the tension abates, the future married couple squat on a mat laid down where the sacrifice took place. The girl's father, standing behind them, then performs the *hahla* ritual with the same chyme. He takes a part of it between his thumb and index finger, rolls it into a little ball, brings it to his mouth and spits softly, looking straight ahead. He invokes the ancestors. A thin strip is cut along the length of the sacrificed animal's belly, taking care to make a pocket at the level of the jaw, into which he places the ankle-bone from the right foot. The father attaches this protective goatskin belt to his daughter's waist, making sure he does not look her in the face, while she turns her back to him. The next day she leaves her parents to go to her husband's home.

The role of sacrifice now appears in a new light. The chyme marks, simultaneously, the antagonism between the future affines and the brutal separation of the girl from her family. This substance is dispersed in a confrontation. The girl's father uses it to bless his daughter as well as to separate himself from her: 'My fathers, my grandfathers, look! Today my child is leaving me ... accompany her where she will live' (Junod, 1927, I:111). The very attitude of the actors expresses the severance of communication between father and daughter, the breaking of a bond. The latter finds herself, in a sense, abandoned by her retinue, who are forced to surrender her. This temporary solitude of the girl, not yet welcomed into her husband's family, is underscored by the unkind remarks directed towards her by the accompanying women during the prayer. Her only recourse is the ancestors, who never abandon their own people; as maternal relatives, they will never cease to be the tutelary divinities of her children, as we have seen earlier. The ritual belt the girl receives from her father invites this protection.

Let us now examine the specific rite called for in the northern groups when two related people wish to marry (Junod, 1927, I:247–9).

The suitor presents a goat destined to his future father-in-law, who is, by the way, the mother's brother.[1] The victim is destined to 'open the hut'. After the animal is slaughtered, chyme is extracted from its stomach. Then the bridegroom and the bride are called outside and made to sit on the same mat; the man's leg is passed over the girl's leg (this is done to 'kill the shame', *ku dlaya tingana*): they are both anointed with the green liquid of the chyme (*psanyi*); the skin of the goat is then taken, a hole is cut in the middle of it, and it is put over the heads of the two cousins. Through the opening, the animal's raw liver is handed down to them. They must tear it with their teeth—cutting it with a knife is forbidden. They have to bite it, to tug vigorously on both sides, so as to really rip it apart, and then they must eat it. '*Shibindji*', liver, also means patience, determination. 'You have acted with strong determination! Now eat the liver! Eat it in the full light of day, not in the dark! It will be a *mhamba*, an offering to the gods'. The priest will then say: 'You, our gods, so and so, look! We have done it in the

---

[1] Marrying the mother's brother's daughter is, theoretically, forbidden among the Thonga.

daylight. It has not been done by stealth. Bless them, give them children.'
Should this sacrifice not be made, misfortune would indeed come upon
them and the woman would remain childless. When the prayer is ended,
those present take all the solid *psanyi*, put it on the wife's head, and say to
her: 'Go and bear children' (Junod, 1927, I:258).

The predominant role of chyme attracts our attention first. Splattered
with this green substance, the couple find themselves in a situation
comparable to that of the future affines in the normal marriage ritual.
Indeed, the rite transforms the bond of kinship between the incestuous
lovers into one of alliance. Thus the chyme once again demonstrates its
'separating' virtues. However, a new element appears: whereas the
ancestors normally receive part of the cooked animal, the young couple
hidden under the animal skin devour, raw, the victim's liver with their
teeth. The liver is expressly assimilated with the *mhamba* offering
demanded by the ancestors. The incestuous lovers are monstrous creatures outside culture.

In this rite, several topological loci are superimposed. It abolishes the
border between within and without; the positions of the partners are
confused. The two sacrifiers take the places of the victim and of the
ancestors. They are in the goat (under the skin), covered with chyme and
they are also the voracious mouth of the ancestors, recipients of the
sacrifice. By tearing the liver symbolising their obstination, they abolish a
bond of kinship, they devour a part of themselves as if they were cannibals.

In the final episode the chyme shows up once again. Those present
(probably close relatives) place what is left of the chyme on the young girl's
head before sending her away. While the future affines normally battle with
each other with balls of chyme, here all the participants collaborate in an
inverse action which consists of putting all this ritual substance (instead of
dispersing it) on a relative transformed into an affine. The rite combines
two effects of rupture, for it also serves as a substitute for the disjoining
action of the father, who normally spits chyme when his daughter leaves
him. Before taking this analysis any further, let us look at the properties of
chyme in the sacrifices that mark the end of mourning.

Mourning and chyme

Two or three months after a man's death, all his relatives unite to
participate in the rite of 'breaking up the hut' of the deceased (Junod,
1936, I:156–164). The roof is smashed and the debris carefully reduced to
small pieces. A young male goat is brought, which the dead man's uterine
nephews sacrifice, along with two hens and a cock.[2] The kid is the
essential element in the sacrificial rite; the nephews, assisted by the

---

[2] Junod points out that the offering consists of two male and two female animals.

elders, extract its chyme. Then ritual disorder begins. Encouraged by others, several taunting old women begin to dance obscenely. These women, an informant notes, 'have been unleashed by their husband's death; there is no longer any restraint on them' (Junod, 1927, I:160).

While the family provides some chyme, the uterine nephews cut up meat from the sacrificial victims. An old man presses a little pellet of chyme against his mouth and spits. He then addresses a prayer to the deceased. But people start revealing in public the quarrels which ravage the family. Suddenly, one of the uterine nephews interrupts the prayer by making the officiant drink, and immediately the nephews' wives rush at the pieces of kid reserved for the ancestors. They steal the sacrificial meat. At once everyone stands up and chases them, laughing, shouting, and pelting them with the chyme, which they had kept for this purpose. The thieves hide behind a bush and eat the meat (Junod, 1927, I:162).

This ritual agitation is a symbolic disturbance of the social order. It starts with the erotic show that clearly alludes to adultery. It also features one of the most important ritual and social relationships of Thonga society—that between uncle and nephew. In another essay I have examined the permanent debt that the mother's brothers have towards their uterine nephews; in particular, the latter have the right, within some limits, of making off with the possessions of the uncles with whom they have an aggressive joking relationship. Of course one should interpret the ritual theft by the nephews or by their wives within this general framework (de Heusch, 1974).

Let us consider one unusual aspect of this ritual. Whereas normally the uncle does not have the right to protest against his nephew's actions, this time the entire group of maternal relatives rise against the group of aggressive nephews. Good humour does persist, however, in this relationship. It is no less true that the 'thieves' are chased with blows of *psanyi*, exactly as the future affines are repulsed in the marriage ritual, which is played out as a conflict. On the occasion of generalised disorder caused by the death of a member of the group, what is conspicuously underlined is the ambivalence of the avuncular relationship, the keystone of the social structure.

One year after the mourning period ends, another sacrifice takes place during the sharing of the deceased's goods and widows. On this day, 'full of surprises and dangers' (in Junod's own words, Junod, 1927, I:207), the uterine nephews are particularly aggressive. They begin acting up at the beer offering on the tomb. Immediately after the libation, they seize the almost full jug. On their return to the village, they flaunt their matrimonial claim on the deceased's widows ('we go and take our wives with us'). This same claim is asserted even more vigorously towards the end of the afternoon. A goat is sacrificed in front of the deceased's hut and the officiant begins the prayer to the ancestors. One of the nephews insults

him: 'You have no concern for us. Why do you leave us out? You do not give
us our wives! You are killing us!' The whole party of nephews joins in these
recriminations and they finish by seizing the part of the meat reserved for
the ancestors. The crowd pursues them, laughing and bombarding them
with chyme (Junod, 1927, I:208).

All these rites appear to be the strong symbolic expression of a social
tension. One should note, however, that the uterine nephews render an
important liturgical service to their uncles (real or classificatory). The
nephews assume the function of sacrificers. If they take the part of the
sacrifice reserved for their uncles' ancestors, it is as 'representatives' of
these gods, who are for their maternal ancestors (Junod, 1927 I:162).
Everything takes place, then, as if the mourning had interrupted direct
communication between the men and their paternal ancestors. The
mediation of the nephews is required by their privileged relationship with
their mother's kin.

But the mother's brother, for his part, intervenes on his nephew's behalf
in the *private offerings*. He brings paternal and maternal ancestors
together to heal the nephew, reminding them of the legitimacy of the
matrimonial alliance. In this case, the positions of uncle and nephew are
reversed; this time access to the maternal ancestors is through the uncle's
mediation.

Since the uncle and nephew exchange ritual services in a general way,
what we have once more is an asymmetrical exchange defined by Fig. 7.

Fig. 7

Uncle as sacrificer	*Nephew as sacrificer*
Personal service	Collective service
One uncle, one nephew	The lineage of the uncles and all the nephews and their wives
Reinforcement of the alliance	Simulated destruction of the kinship
Animal or object according to the oracle's instructions	Must be a goat (role of chyme)

When the uncle sacrifices on his nephew's behalf, in a private setting, he
reinforces the matrimonial alliance; when the nephews intervene collectively in the public rites at the end of mourning, they pretend to upset it. Or
to be more precise, they can fulfil their duty to their uncles (as messengers
to their uncles' ancestors) only by introducing an element of disturbance.
We are dealing, then, with two distinct ritual modes of expressing the same
social relationship. The category of the uterine nephews in the Thonga's
kinship system comprises a considerable group of people related through

women: sisters' sons and also daughters' sons and paternal aunts' sons.
They are all called *ntukulu*, grandson. Generally speaking, at least two
ntukulu assume the function of sacrificers in all the important family
gatherings—one holds the animal's legs, the other the spear.

This system of kinship terminology has given rise to a controversy. A.A.
Jacques questions whether the uterine nephew has the privileged role
Junod insists he has. Ignoring the Omaha extension of the avuncular
relationship, Jacques believes that the officiant is, apparently, the 'grandson' indeed the son of the paternal aunt (Jacques, 1929,:327–348). In the
Omaha system, however, it is clear that any ego has the same relationship
vis-à-vis the maternal grandfather, his mother's brother, and *vis-à-vis* the
latter's son, his matrilateral cross-cousin (Fig.8).

Fig. 8

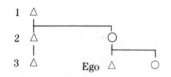

Ego is simultaneously *ntukulu* of 1, 2 and 3.

Nonetheless, Jacques's view has the merit of pointing out a new fact:
the Thonga seem to avoid bringing the real mother's brother (*malume*)
and the uterine nephew into direct opposition in the sacrificial system,
whereas the former is the favoured victim of the latter's ritual acts of
aggression in day-to-day life. However, this reservation leaves untouched
the import of the data reported by Junod: the *batukulu* (uterine nephews
in the Omaha terminology) 'stand before the gods, in their place'; they
'take for themselves the pieces offered to the gods' for they are not afraid
of the maternal uncle's saliva (Junod, 1927, I:270).

On the other hand, the mother's brothers' participation is dominant in
private rites; the mother's kin officiate for their nephews in most cases
(Junod, 1927, I:268). But Junod throws the whole debate into confusion
when he adds that the mother's brother is the 'officiant' in the mourning
ceremonies, whereas the detailed description we have just read clearly
establishes that it is the nephews who play the role of sacrificer-cum-ritual
thieves.

By referring to the text, one can easily verify that Junod confuses two
Thonga subcultures. In the northern groups, the feast of the destruction of
the funeral hut is replaced by a ceremony called 'the beer of mourning'
(Junod, 1927, I:157, 163–4). The latter is characterised by a general
reciprocity of ritual services and not by the asymmetry we have just
described.

'All the relatives, brothers, brothers-in-law, nephews, etc., bring a goat, or half a sovereign, or a sovereign, to the master of the mourning, the heir of the village. That individual must give them back as much as he receives from them, a goat for a goat, a sovereign for a sovereign, and all the animals are killed according to rule. There were fourteen of them at a certain gathering held in the Nkuna capital to mourn one of the chief Shiluvane's wives in 1905. A sacrifice is offered; the men sit on one side, the women on the other; the *kokwane*, viz. the maternal uncle of the deceased, takes the *psanyi* and squeezes it on them all while praying, or rather insulting the gods who have afflicted them with such a bereavement. All rub their chests with this green liquid and add their insults to those of the priest ... The *batukulu* then come to take that portion of the victim which has been put aside for the gods. It does not appear that they steal it, as is the case amongst the Ba-Ronga.' (Junod, 1927, I:164).

The differences are obvious: the roles are reversed. In the northern groups, it is the maternal uncle and not the uterine nephew who is actually the principal officiant; it is he who makes use of the chyme while insulting the deceased's ancestors in a ritual act where, once more, the disjunctive role is clear. In this region, and only here, the *psanyi* is used in mourning rites with the same emphasis as in the rites that break up an incestuous relationship. It seems to emphasise the break established by mourning between an entire social group and its ancestors. The latter are subjected to insults. However, as in the mourning rites practised by the southern groups, the deceased's uterine nephews intervene as representatives of the ancestors.

Among the southern groups, the mother's brothers who make up the deceased's lineage pursue all the uterine nephews while pelting them with balls of *psanyi*; among the northern groups, a mother's brother smears all his relatives, in-laws and nephews with *psanyi*. The ritual tension is shifted. In the first case, the chyme sets the lineage of the deceased against the uterine nephews; in the second, it sets all the kin of the deceased (including the uterine nephews) against the ancestors. Yet the chyme's symbolic role does not change; it establishes a dividing line, either within the social community or between the world of the living and that of the dead. Basically, the northern groups are just extending to collective rites the mediating role that all the Thonga entrust to the mother's brother within the framework of private offerings. We have seen that the uncle will even abuse *his own paternal ancestors* in order to remind them of their duty to protect his uterine nephew. It is the same role he assumes, but with anger and without hope, when he reproaches them for being responsible for his nephew's death. Like the sacrifice of separation performed for incest, the sacrifice of mourning, involving insults to the ancestors and the smearing of chyme, is a strongly dramatised rite of passage among the northern groups.

It is in this sociological context that the meaning of chyme takes on more clear-cut significance. Junod's analysis is ambiguous. He asserts that the *psanyi* mixed with the blood of the victim is spat out by the officiant in order to 'consecrate' the offering, or to dispatch it (one might say) to the ancestors (Junod, 1927, II:410). But elsewhere he interprets the chyme (more correctly) as a purificatory element; he recalls that 'to remove the danger of death', pellets of *psanyi* are thrown on the roof of the deceased's hut when it is ritually shut; in the same way, the role of the chyme placed on the girl's head during the marriage rites for an incestuous couple would be to 'dispel the dangers of a consanguineous marriage and assist procreation,' (Junod, 1927, II:416).

Let us reexamine the specific examples available to us. In the marriage ritual the father spits out the chyme (which comes from the sacrificial goat), the instant his daugher leaves him. At this moment, he certainly invokes the protection of the ancestors, but he begins by drawing attention to the fact that the young girl is leaving his group: 'my child is leaving us'. (Junod, 1927, I:111). Now this is exactly the same formula used to open the prayer in the ritual for the end of mourning, after the officiant has spat out a little of the *psanyi*: 'You, Manyibane, you have left us' (Junod, 1927, I:160). All in all, Junod's evidence suggests that chyme functions, here and elsewhere, as the symbolic agent of separation or transformation of status.

What seems to me particularly illuminating is the fact that 'in certain cases of special misfortune, the officiant squeezes the green liquid contained in the first stomach over his hearers, who rub their bodies with it' (Junod, 1927, II:410). The specific virtues of chyme are also exploited in therapeutic magic in the course of the ceremony of purification, *hondlola*, which marks the end of any major medical treatment. The medicine man offers a piece of the sacrificial victim to the ancestors, asking them for the power to cure his patient. He then mixes chyme with various drugs; the patient smears his body with this mixture and the practitioner carefully gathers the particles that have fallen on the mat. The divining bones will indicate the place where these scraps, carrying misfortune with them, will be burned (Junod, 1927, II:470–1). The magic effectiveness of chyme acts here in a way thoroughly opposite to the religious offering of meat.

Thus there is reason to believe that chyme assumes an original symbolic role which has escaped Junod's attention. To better understand this role, chyme must be defined in relation to the other parts of the sacrificial victim. The sacrifice of a goat is in fact accompanied by a rigorously coded cooking ritual. The villagers *boil* their portion; it is eaten without peanuts. On the other hand, relatives invited from outside the village *roast* their share, without salt, on the road home. In both cases, it is a curtailed cooking, deprived of condiments. Lévi-Strauss's hypothesis, which holds that roasting is associated with exo-cooking and boiling with endo-cooking, is borne out among the Thonga (Lévi-Strauss, 1965). The shared meal that follows sacrifice brings into opposition the villagers (in theory, members of the same extended family) and the other relatives, particularly the uterine nephews.

How does chyme, which intervenes specifically to separate members of the lineage from uterine nephews, figure in this system? If we accept the suggestions of Lévi-Strauss, we would concede that on the spectrum ranging from the raw at one extreme to the cooked at the other, roasted food would be near the raw, boiled near the cooked. Now chyme is a raw, inedible substance. From a sociological point of view, chyme emphasises both the opposition and the complementarity between the people of the extended family (who will eat the victim in boiled form) and the uterine nephews, who are both stealers of meat and eaters of roasted meat. The nephews are thus in two ways outside the villager's system of sharing and eating the goat: both the method of cooking required of them (roasting), and the chyme, with which their wives were spattered, belong, in a sense, to the same symbolic category, though in differing degrees. The superficial cooking of a roast is comparable to raw chyme, which is specifically used to chase the uterine nephews out of the village, where they can freely roast (and only roast) the sacrificial meat they have stolen. (Fig.9).

Fig. 9

Chyme	Roasted	Boiled
Raw food, half-digested by the sacrificial victim	Half-raw meat	Completely cooked meat
Signalises the opposition between the patrilineal family and the uterine nephews	Signalises the guests from outside the village	Signalises those belonging to the village

Thus the sacrifice at the end of mourning follows a precise topology. On the occasion of a crisis, it underlines differences in social status and residence. It is based on the separation of men and the ancestors; the latter's messengers, the uterine nephews, are sent outside the village area. There is no alimentary communion between the ancestors and their descendants. As outsiders, the uterine nephews are necessary intermediaries.

One must return here to Junod's interpretation of chyme as a means of purification. Indeed, everything happens as if the uterine nephews, chased by pellets of chyme, become the bearers of misfortune (*khombo*), even of the pollution of death. However, this explanation is too summary: it cannot be applied to the marriage ritual, where the two parties pelt each other with chyme, before cementing their tie. The factor common to all these uses of chyme is a more general one. Chyme has a disjunctive function; it foreshadows a transformation of status. All this is merely a variant of Zulu symbolism in which the dispersed chyme protects the sacrificial locus from harmful forces: heat, hate and witchcraft. The chyme is in fact the first stage of the very vital substance which nourishes the ox and goat, sacrificial victims.

The sacrifice associated with marriage or death expresses a secret violence, a certain social tension; it underlines the difficulty of the alliance between men on the one hand, and between men and the gods themselves on the other. If the prayer that is part of every offering succeeds in establishing direct communication with the ancestors, the ritual cooking short-circuits it. Junod notes without explanation, 'the sudden end' of the invocation: 'one of the uterine nephews puts a portion of the victim into the officiant's mouth, thus "cutting off his oration" (*tjema*)' (Junod, 1927, II:423). 'When the victim is a hen', he specifies, 'it is the gizzard, which has been half-roasted during the long prayer, that is used for this purpose. The priest eats it, and so is the first to partake of the flesh of the offering'. From this perspective, the ritual cooking assaults the word; literally cuts it off. It is significant that here again the mother's brother/nephew opposition is expressed by the eating of barely cooked meat provided by the nephew, the roaster *par excellence*. The prayer is similarly interrupted during the marriage ceremony: when the elders have had enough, they send a young man[3] to cut a piece of meat and to put it into the old man's mouth. Thus they 'cut' his prayer and he keeps still (Junod, 1927, I:111).

Within the general category of offerings (*mhamba*), then, there is a purely sacrificial zone. It is delimited, however, only by ritual practice. Junod leads us astray when he writes that the Thonga have recourse to sacrifices involving bloodshed 'when some notion of guilt may be implied' (Junod, 1927, II:416). It seems more accurate to say that blood sacrifice accompanies a dramatic situation that involves a temporary rupture of fundamental social bonds, between groups or between men and the ancestors. This explains the rigorous coding of the goat sacrifice during the important collective rites of passage. Blood sacrifice simultaneously affirms and conjures away a danger inherent in the articulations of the social body.

The sociological import of goat sacrifice among the Thonga is decided not the same as that of ox sacrifice among the Zulu. The latter reinforces the cohesion of the patrilineal lineage. The sacrificer is a qualified butcher, acting on behalf of the family chief; no writer has noted any participation by the uterine nephew. The Zulu and the Thonga express two different social structures through the contrasting ritual uses of the sacrificial animal. But these rituals bring into play the same vocabulary based on the animal's digestive system. The Thonga attach the gall bladder to the sacrifier's hair; it brings him 'happiness and luck' (Junod, 1927, II:443). That is all Junod says of it. It is clear, however, that the gall-bladder is opposed to

[3] His status is not specified, but he is probably a uterine nephew.

the rumen (the first stomach containing the chyme) in the Thonga ritual system as well as in the Zulu's explicit symbolic thought.

The Thonga, however, have considerably elaborated the symbolic function of the chyme. Whereas the Zulu use the cud only as a means of purification, the Thonga use it as an active operator for separating or disjoining two partners or even for transforming a person's social status. The gall bladder has apparently lost its special function. There is no evidence that this organ is associated with the ancestors' fertilising power. This transformation can be related to a new phenomenon—keeping the ancestors at a distance. Unlike the Zulu, the Thonga do not maintain familiarity with the ancestors. These beings do not directly intervene in conception and pregnancy. Instead, they are dreaded, and offerings are usually intended to appease them. Among the Thonga, the dead are separated through the immolation of a goat after the rite during whic the hut of the deceased is torn down. In contrast, the Zulu perform a sacrificial ceremony (*ukubuyisa*) in order to bring the shade of the deceased back into the house after burial (Berglund, 1975:220). Sacrifices during marriages are just as radically different between these two peoples. An ox, led by the Zulu bridegroom, is immolated along with the one provided by the bride's father; this double sacrifice is the sign that the ancestors of both spouses accept to work together in procreation (ibid.:118). The bride herself stabs each of the victims in the stomach. The most important rite is the pouring of bile on her feet and the fixing of the two gall bladders in her hair. In the Thonga marriage ceremony, the emphasis is laid upon the chyme as a sign of the antagonism between the two families. There is no evidence that the bride receives the gall bladder of a single slayed animal that was provided by the bridegroom. In fact, chyme is sometimes placed upon her head in order to accentuate the rite of separation (See p.74). These two sacrificial rituals are related through transformation in yet another respect—cooking. Ousted from the village, the Thonga ancestors—through the intermediary of 'sisters' sons'—eat unsalted, roasted meat whereas, inside the principal hut, the Zulu ancestors are offered—in the fire—an unsalted portion of meat. The zone of boiling is on the periphery of this ritual space among the Zulu but in the middle among the Thonga.

Goat sacrifice and exorcism

Man's body can itself become the theatre of violent conflict with the spirits. The strongest religious form of blood sacrifice is associated with the ritual of exorcism of the possessed. Sacrifice is in this case, the act that itself assures the expulsion of a pathogenic spirit, a spirit from outside the maternal or paternal lineage. We have seen that the ancestors are capable of venting anger on their descendants, thereby setting in motion a therapeutic ritual founded on offering and prayer. Mental illness (*the madness of the gods*, in Thonga terms) has a completely different origin. It appears to be exogenous, while illnesses originating with the ancestors are endogenous. Mental disorder is always attributed to aggression on the part of a spirit belonging to another tribe (Junod, 1927, II,:482–495). The Thonga affirm that the first possession that occurred among them was caused by the spirits of the Nguni. Divining bones diagnose the nature of the illness; they also determine the specialised therapy to be sought and where it will be carried out. All those formerly possessed assist the officiant in the dramatic struggle with the pathogenic spirit. Amidst a great din, the musicians and the chorus of those formerly possessed endeavour to induce a trance in the prostrate body of the patient, during which the spirit will be forced to reveal itself, and its name. When the crisis comes the patient abandons himself to a violent dance. This first phase of treatment can last several days. The second phase consists of 'opening the eyes' of the patient by plunging his head into a basin (the *gobo* rite). We shall dwell a little longer on the third phase. Junod calls it, 'appeasement by blood'. Essentially, it consists of a bloody and violent sacrifice that ensures the expulsion of the pathogenic spirit from the patient's body and its transfer to an altar:

'In most schools a she-goat is taken, if the patient is a man, or a he-goat in the case of a woman. The exorcist who has been in charge of the cure orders the by-standers to repeat the song which had induced the first crisis. The possessed once again shows excitement and exhibits the same and the symptoms of raving madness that I have previously described. Then the animal is pierced beneath the foreleg . . . and the patient throws himself on the wound greedily sucking the flowing blood, and, in frenzy, filling his stomach with it. When he had drunk his fill, he has to be dragged away from the animal by main force; certain medicines (one of which is called *ntshatshu*, apparently an emetic) are administered; his throat is tickled with a feather and he retires behind the hut to vomit all the blood he has absorbed. By this means the spirit, or spirits, have been duly appeased and expelled. The sufferer, who is now recovering, is next washed again and smeared with ochre.' (Junod, 1927, II:491).

Junod takes a careful look at what happens to the remains of the sacrificed animal. The gall bladder is attached to the exorcised patient's hair; his body is covered with strips cut from the animal's skin; these strips are attached to each other by strings made from the roots of a tree, which has a pleasant odour and 'brings joy to the nose' of the spirits. An act of ritual cooking follows the sacrifice:

'From each limb a small piece is cut and these pieces are cooked in a separate saucepan, with a powdered drug prepared for this special purpose. The head exorcist breaks off the branch of an acacia bearing enormous shiny white thorns, on each of which is spitted a piece of meat between his teeth in passing. While eating it, he rushes towards the east. He comes back, seizes another piece in the same manner

and runs towards the west, and so on towards all the four cardinal points In this way
he propitaties the gods, the spirits of every country, in whatever direction they may
lie. The young *mathwaza*, viz. those who have lately passed through this initiation,
must also seize the piece of meat with their teeth ... The remainder of the goat is then
cooked and eaten.' (Junod, 1927, II:492).

Let us attempt an initial interpretation. During the sacrifice, the
possessed person, who is beside himself and completely identified with the
spirit, hurls himself on the animal's blood as if he would devour the victim
completely raw. To expel the spirit, he must be forced to vomit. Yet even
having done this, the patient has not returned to a human state. It is as if the
mental patient's reintegration into cultural order passes through a phase of
identification with the victim. The ritual act of running away, performed by
the patient wearing the animal's skin, assures positive communication with
all the spirits, while the consumption and vomiting of blood, assure the
expulsion of the pathogenic spirit. The ingestion of food during all this
running around indicates that the patient is now his own messenger
vis-à-vis the gods. If the manner in which he grabs the food places him
outside the human world, the passage from raw blood to cooked meat
suggests a real dialectical process of rehumanisation. The mechanism
seems to be the following: the possessed person who is alienated in the
strict sense of the word (a stranger to himself) finds himself brutally
projected into the universe of a violent, bloodthirsty god. The sacrificial
victim is the agent of metamorphosis: thanks to the animal victim, the
possessed person rediscovers a marginal identity. He also reorients
himself in space by running towards the four cardinal points. Achieving
normality will require prolonged convalescence; formerly the patient wore
the strips of skin for a year before undergoing final purification. One can
synthesise these initial conclusions by contrasting, item by item, the two
phases of sacrifice (Fig. 10).

Fig. 10

Exorcism	*Alliance with the spirits*
Raw blood spurting from one leg	Cooked meat coming from the four legs
Vomiting	Digesting
End of identification with the pathogenic spirit	Return to the human state through the mediation of the animal

Figure 10 shows that passage from an abusive 'divinisation' (evil
possession) to the normal human state implies a temporary 'animalisation'.
The sacrificial victim is first of all the object of violent aggression, which
demonstrates alienation in its extreme form (the patient is a cannibalistic

monster); the animal then becomes the means of constructing a new personality. This therapy merits attention from psychoanalysts. As far as the trance, it develops the fantasy of identification with one god. Transference is carried out on the sacrificed animal, which serves a dual function: it permits both exorcism (under the sign of raw blood) and the restructuring of the social persona (under the sign of cooked meat, untouched by hands).

These two complementary elements have not been differentiated by Junod, who says 'the flesh of the sacrificed goat also supplies the means of finally exorcising these mysterious spiri powers' (Junod, 1927, II:492), whereas, on the contrary, it marks a new alliance with pathogenic powers, which will be worshipped by the patient.

This is an enriching experience for the Thonga, for the cured patient who was possessed and who 'saw the spirits' during the *gobo* rite of the basin in which he 'crosses the sea' enters a community of iniiates. Junod notes that 'by the drinking of blood he has become a superior being, a man who does not fear things which make others tremble. He has *thwaza*. This word is the same as that employed for the renewal of the moon' (Junod, 1927, II:495).

The exorcism of a possessed person is an individual rite of passage. It is surprising that the animal victim's chyme is not used to mark the break with the pathogenic spirit. Do the collective sacrifices follow a distinct code, or does exorcism rather constitute a mere transformation? That is the problem we shall presently try to resolve.

A general symbolic code

Let us begin by stating that the rites of marriage and of mourning can be interpreted as tension in the social order and recourse to the ancestors whereas possession is a psychic rupture, implying recourse to the spirits of all countries'. In the first two cases (collective rites), the symbolic element that stands for separation is the *chyme*; in the third's it is *vomited blood*. A fourth rite should be included in this series. It will be recalled that the sacrifice that ends an incestuous bond utilises the animal's *liver*, which the couple, hidden under the hide, must devour raw, tearing it with their teeth. The blood in one case, the liver in the other are the shares demanded by a violent god who eats raw food. What makes the two rites comparable is the fact that they both effect a change in personal status: they always imply, in some way, an *identification* of the officiant or officiants (the possessed, the incestuous lovers) *with the god and with the animal*. The incestuous couple concealed under the goat's skin are no more than a voracious, divine mouth; the possessed person personifies the spirit when, during his trance, he throws himself on the spurting blood of the animal, whose remains he then wears. This brutal projection of the sacrifier into the divine world eliminates the mediation of the uterine nephew, who normally assumes the role of messenger in the collective rites, under the sign of roasted meat.

We can try to reconstruct the general scheme which regulates the sharing of the sacrifice and the ritual cooking (Fig.11). Within the goat's digestive system, the strong opposition is between chyme and bile; the roasted/boiled opposition defines ritual cooking. The second reproduces the first, in a way.

Fig. 11

Goat's digestive system		*Ritual cooking*	
chyme	*bladder*	*roasted meat*	*boiled meat*
a change of status (sickness, death, marriage)	luck, prosperity	outside the village	inside the village
opposition between in-laws and relatives, maternal uncles and nephews, men and ancestors	familial harmony	ancestors' and outsiders' share	alimentary communion of the relatives

Indeed, chyme, like roasted food, is found on the side of the nephews, ritual thieves, messengers of the gods—these same people who were chased from the village with pellets of chyme assume during the mourning rites the role of divine roasters, outside the local community (who boil their food). Harmony, luck and prosperity, connoted by the gall bladder, correspond to internal social cohesion, connoted by boiled food. It all happens as if the goat's digestive system was the image of the human community. The interior of the village is to its exterior as the gall bladder is to the stomach (the first repository of raw food). But from then on, an ever-clearer relation shows up: roasted, i.e. superficially cooked meat, is to chyme, half-digested vegetable substance, what boiled, i.e. totally cooked meat, is to bile.

We discovered the same type of relationship in Zulu thought, where the position of terms is no longer the same. There, the roasted and bile connote a positive rapport with the ancestors within a masculine socio-religious space protected by the chyme, while the boiled, entrusted to women, is cast off to the periphery.

But let us return to the Thonga. In the mourning rituals, the ancestors, through the intermediary of the uterine nephews, normally eat their share of meat roasted; among northern groups, during the wedding of an incestuous couple, they devour the liver raw via the bride and groom. Only foreign spirits, responsible for possession, drink blood. These three modes of consumption in their turn, make up a system. The ancestors are nearly always on the side of cooked food; the particularly aggressive spirits from outside the lineage are shunted to the side of the raw, and become a kind of vampire. The ancestors are only 'raw eaters' devouring the liver in one exceptional case—when a bond of kinship between a future couple must be broken. Among the groups who, like the Ronga, do not practise such an extreme form of this ritual, the couple simply refrain from eating the flesh of the goat sacrificed for them (Junod, 1936, I:249). From this a new division emerges (Fig.12).

Fig. 12

Ancestors		Foreign spirits
Normal situation	*Abnormal situation*	
Roast meat	Raw liver	Raw blood

One might observe that blood plays only a weak symbolic role in private, family offereings. A little blood is mixed with the officiants's saliva during the 'presentation' of the victim (Junod, 1927, II:416). Blood has no real symbolic content outside the rite of exorcism. The slaughter of the animal stresses this strange contrast; while in all the family rites, the goat's heart is pierced, exorcism requires that the victim be wounded in the foot.

The prominence of blood as a central element in an exceptional process can only be interpreted within a lexical set, that includes parts of the sacrificial animal we have not yet mentioned.

The rite of exorcism rests on the poles of the culinary axis: the bones of the goat are *burnt* to ashes in the shade of a tree, in order to 'refresh' the spirits, that is, to appease them, to keep them from getting too wild (Junod, 1927, II:493). Thus two forms of offering occupy similar roles at the beginning of the sacrifice and at the end: blood is placed *before* cooking and the burnt bones (from which the marrow may not be extracted) are placed *beyond* cooking. Meat cooked ritually (and eaten by the possessed during the ritual flight) occupies a central position on this axis. Unfortunately Junod did not specify the cooking method used: he simply says that the meat is placed in a pot 'with a powder prepared for the occasion'. The basic lexicon of the rite can be found in Fig.13. The division of blood, meat and bone cannot be studied more thoroughly with the information now in hand. The way the bones are treated introduces the category of ashes, the cooling function of which is clearly attested.

Fig. 13

Raw	Cooked	Burnt to ashes
Blood	Ritually cooked meat	Bone

Whatever its peculiarities may be, the exorcism rite is part of the general system of Thonga sacrifice, from which it borrows two traditional protective elements: the sacrifier wears the animal's gall-bladder on his head and the ankle-bone over his sternum.

The animal's horns and hooves are kept on the roof of the patient's hut, above the entrance, to protect his home. The reintegration of the mentally ill patient into a collective universe is thus sealed by establishing a protective screen between the formerly possessed person and 'malign influences' (Junod, 1927, II:493). Thus in every way the sacrificed animal comes between the sacrifier and the wrath of alien gods.

The patient is surrounded with a large number of ritual precautions because 'he is susceptible to severe attacks of nerves, especailly in the first weeks following the exorcism' (Junod, 1936, II:498). From then on, he maintains a new relationship with the exorcised spirit: he deposits offerings (especially tobacco) on a particular altar—a forked branch erected inside his hut. A personal bond, stronger than the one between a man and his ancestors, is established after the cure; thus, 'a real communion' is established with the pathogenic spirit, who becomes a benefactor (Junod, 1927, II:499). Moreover, the situation of the possessed person who once healed and initiated, becomes an exorcist himself, differs from the ordinary man's. The sacrificial rite radically transforms his personality, which is enriched by these new powers.

Illness, death and insanity are three critical situations, which each in its own way breaches social cohesion. To these threats, the Thonga oppose three social and ritual displays of progressive intensity. *Illness* calls for the union of uncle and nephew, the consolidation of the alliance of maternal and paternal ancestors; sacrifice is merely a modality of the offering. *Death* tears a rent in the social fabric. Uncles and nephews oppose each other in a symbolic space marked by the opposition of roasted meat (outside) and boiled meat (inside); sacrifice and the use of chyme are at the heart of the rite. Finally, *insanity* is the destruction of psychic space. It is violently reconstructed in paroxysmic tension marked by extreme opposition between raw blood and the incinerated bones, which both operate to transform madness into union with the spirits.

Thus, among the Thonga it is in blood sacrifice that a successive and dialectic 'destructuring' and restructuring' is expressed. During mourning, society plays out its own contradictions, mocking itself with blows of chyme. When a man loses his reason and excludes himself from society, foreign spirits are blamed, and the reintegrating of the possessed into the social order brings into play sacrifice in its strongest form. Played out at times lightheartedly, at times dramatically, the sacrifice as a ritual elaboration becomes a specific act. It is introduced to emphasise a rupture and to offer a solution to it to reconstitute psyhic or social unity.

The symbolic elements brought into play are similar in nature. As the most extreme threat, madness calls for extreme measures. These are the affirmation of the greatest distance between the raw and the cooked, between nature and culture, between spirits and men.

A black ram for the sky

The Thonga sacrificial system is not a mere variation of the Zulu rites. The underlying spirit is completely different. Far from establishing a permanent and affectionate communion between patrilineal lineages and ancestors, the Thonga put a distance between them. They call for mediation by uterine nephews, sacrificers *par excellence* and messengers of the patrilineal ancestors. They prefer the goat to the cow, giving the *former* a specifically religious value. Among the Zulu, the cow serves to unite the living and the dead, who share the same 'having' (the herd) and the same 'being' (the child is the reincarnation of an ancestor). Among the Thonga, the goat kept outside the economic system, serves to separate out antagonistic parts of the society in a problematic communication with the ancestors. The story of the ancestor-baby whom the woman tried to bring from the forest to the hearth exemplifies the separation of respective spheres in which the living and dead move about. The Thonga do not share the sacrificial meat cooked outside the village with their ancestors, whereas the Zulu invite theirs to join them in their hut, near the hearth.

One animal however, retains the same characteristic in both systems—the sheep. On the occasion of a severe dry spell, the Thonga sacrifice a ram chosen for the blackness of its wool (Junod, 1927, II:405). A pot is buried in a thicket of thorny bushes. Around it, four furrows are dug in the shape of a cross, it ends oriented towards the four cardinal points. The black ram is offered to the chief's ancestors by his uterine niece (Junod, 1927, I:269). She takes part in the sacrifice of the animal whose belly is pressed just over the pot so that the chyme will flow into it. Little prepubescent girls fill the pot with water, letting it overflow into the furrows.

This cosmological rite inverts all the characteristics of the paradigmatic goat sacrifice. The goat and the sheep are opposing figures in the divining bones. The first represents the villagers, the second symbolises the chief, his family, and army, that is power. Goat sacrifice is always carried out by men, that of the ram by women, in particular prepubescent girls grouped around the chief's uterine niece. One should realise that mothers have a negative relationship with sheep; they are forbidden to carry their babies in a sack (*ntehe*) made of sheepskin (Junod, 1927, I:46). The sheep is used only when a mother has previously lost several children and finds herself destitute (*buwumba*). Yet we note that symbolic implementation of the inversion: a newborn carried in a sheepskin *ntehe* will wear girl's clothing if it is a boy and vice-versa (Junod, 1927, I:194).

The sacrifice of the black ram is directed to the chief's ancestors. It brings into full play the symbolic properties of chyme; ritual cooking disappears. In this new context, what is the magical efficacy of chyme in association with water? To answer this question, we must look to the Lovedu, who seem to have the same sacrificial system as the Thonga. The Lovedu sacrifice goats in honour of their ancestors; although oxen are unquestionably the animal of highest socio-economic value, they are never sacrificed for religious purposes (Krige, 1943, :43–4). Like the Thonga, the Lovedu resort to sheep for important cosmological sacrifices (Krige, 1943, :278–9). The Lovedu entrust the control of rainfall to the queen, who has the appropriate medicines. The latter must be kept in a permanent state of 'coolness'. In the case of an exceptional drought, the queen sacrifices a black sheep on the grave of a maternal ancestor. She beseeches him to prevent his people from being 'burned by the sun'. The contents of the sheep's stomach are divided into two parts: the liquid chyme is poured into a hole dug in the grave, while the solid elements are placed on its surface, beside the cooked meat.

The Thonga sacrifice of a black ram can easily be interpreted as a transformation of the royal Lovedu ritual. The Thonga chief's uterine niece takes the place of the Lovedu queen. In both cases the cooling action of the liquid chyme is a primary consideration; it puts an end to the excessive, burning conjunction of the sky and earth. Chyme's disjunctive function, which we have already noted in the family goat sacrifices, is transposed onto a cosmological level. The prinicpal role shifts from the uterine nephew to the uterine niece.

Let us take this comparison a step further. Thonga divinatory symbolism associates sheep with the chief and his army, that is, with violence. The warriors, after killing an enemy at war, are in a dangerous state of 'heat' and 'blackness' (Junod, 1927, I:479–80). I have shown elsewhere that in Thonga thought, any release of heat endangers the social order as well as cosmological order (de Heusch, 1982, chapter IX). This is where the exclusive use of chyme and water takes on its full significance. The Lovedu require the personal attendance of the Rain Queen during the black sheep sacrifice. This sovereign, responsible for the 'coolness' of the world, is herself a woman condemned to death. Her life span is shortened. Normally she is supposed to kill herself when the fourth age set of young men initiated during her reign are promoted (Krige, 1943 :114). Moreover, the original tradition of the Monomotapa dynasty, to whom the Lovedu queens claim kinship, required the sacred king to take poison when a disaster arose (Krige, 1943 :166). The cooling of the earth by means of the black sheep's chyme is, then, a way of delaying the ritual regicide. We shall return later to this theme of Frazer's. In any case, the black sheep sacrifice, among both the Lovedu and the Thonga, belongs to a different register than the sacrifice of a goat in honour of the ancestors. The exceptional killing of the black sheep is all the more readily interpreted as the equivalent of a human sacrifice because the latter, among the Thonga, is an alternative solution. Long ago, in instances of severe drought, a young man was abandoned, alive, in a sacred wood (Junod, 1936, II:383, 405). As for the Lovedu, they used to sacrifice a man in order to revitalise the rain medicine (Krige, 1954, :65).

These practices are very widespread in southern Africa. They are still found among the Tswana where the chief's main ritual function is to make the rain fall (Schapera, 1971:70–72). Among the Kgatla, during the annual ceremonies preceding the planting, a black sheep (never a goat) was sacrificed. The chyme was spread out over the receptacles containing rain medicine. It was also sprinkled on a horn full of bile and urine. Old men and little girls ate the animal's meat. The victim's sex was determined through divination; if the bones demanded a female, the rain would be soft and steady; a male, on the other hand, called down a heavy rain. The Tswana justify the colour of the hide in the same terms as the Zulu—the clouds are dark. In an emergency, a black sheep with a little white spot could be chosen, but then lightning must be expected along with rain. The Tswana used to sacrifice a young man (Shapera, 1971:104).

The hypothesis that the black sheep sacrificed by the Zulu to the python is a human surrogate is thus confirmed in the comparative context. Among the Thonga, as among the Zulu, the same break within the sacrificial sphere can be detected (Fig.14).

Fig. 14

	Thonga	*Zulu*
Sacrifice to the ancestors:	Goat	Ox or goat
Sacrifice for rainfall:	Black ram	Black sheep

Among the Zulu, the sex of the black sheep sacrificed in honour of the rain genie is not specified. But unlike the Thonga, they emphasise the peaceful character of sheep, which they contrast to the turbulence of the goat. The Zulu tend to associate the former species more especially with women (see p.63) We find ourselves faced with a new transformation: the male Zulu rite uses a surrogate female victim sacrificed in silence by men, whereas in Thonga rite women sacrifice a male victim (a ram) associated with warlike violence and authority.

Cooked chyme

We have just mentioned the 'heat' of war. Let us see how the Thonga warriors regain their normal status. When they have killed an enemy, they cannot re-enter the village until they have undergone a purification rite. Their hands are 'hot'. They cannot have sexual relations with their wives until they have rid themselves of *nuru*, their victims's spirit, who yearns for revenge (Junod, 1927, I:478–80). One of the procedures used is itself part sacrificial; it involves goat's chyme. All kinds of seeds, along with the contents of the goat's stomach and various medicines, are roasted in a potsherd. The warriors breathe in the smoke. Then they rub their hands with this mixture and rub it on their joints. I have elsewhere discussed this rite, which belongs to a paradigmatic series, the role of which is to 'cool down' or 'heat up' the object of the treatment (de Heusch, 1982, Chapter IX). The presence of cooked chyme is what interests us here. One will remember that this substance is always used *raw* in the sacrificial rites. This time the chyme is roasted and, in a sense, 'consumed' through the nostrils.

After undergoing the rite, the warrior is authorised to participate once again in village life, to share his wife's bed and to eat the food she prepares, without taking all kinds of ritual precautions. It is the union of husband and wife, interrupted by war, that is played out in the roasting of the seeds and chyme.

This rite of passage is comparable to the one carried out by the adolescent just after his first nocturnal emission. To gain the strength to approach women, he roasts pieces of wild animal skins mixed with goat chyme in a potsherd. He eats a bit of this strange mixture, then vigorously rubs it on his joints (Junod, 1927, I:95). The young man's union with women is thus facilitated.

The puberty rite, like that of the warrior, does not evoke the ancestors. Their efficacy is magical. Moreover, these rites bring into play an 'anti-cooking', based on the roasting of substances unfit for consumption using a potsherd or broken pot. Sacrifice, on the other hand, is meant for the ancestors and involves the cooking of an animal and rejection of its chyme. Thus, in these rites, the sacrificial system undergoes a genuine perversion (Fig.15).

Fig. 15

Collective sacrificial cooking	*Individual rites of passage* (Anti-cooking)
Chyme rejected raw	Chyme cooked and eaten

The symbolic system, as well as its role, is inverted. The cooked chyme serves to introduce (or reintroduce) a man into women's society; raw chyme eliminates the heat of illness (*hondlola* rite) or drought (the 'black ram' rite); it also separates prospective affines before the marriage is concluded, just as it marks the antagonism between the lineage and the uterine nephews in mourning rites. Raw chyme is disjunctive, while cooked chyme is an essential element in the rites that aim to conjoin the sexes.

Chyme, quarrel and beer

The sacrifice of an ox is an exceptional event among the Thonga.

Theoretically, it is required when a family group meets for the 'big millet' offering, which celebrates a happy event, such as the cure of a serious illness (Junod, 1927, II:401–2). Junod writes: 'It is one of the rare offerings not dictated by fear or misfortune'. One of the rite's manifest roles is to reinforce marriage bonds. Daughters must take part with their husbands even if they live a long way from the paternal home. This offering, interpreted by Junod as a *thanksgiving act*, presents a new, unusual characteristic. *The chyme of the sacrificed animal is poured on the altar along with the millet beer.*

The important ceremony that took place in 1924 near the Shiluvane mission, in which almost two hundred people took part, seems to belong to this ritual category. First, libations of beer were offered at the graveside, then a cow was sacrificed. From our point of view, what is particularly remarkable here is that the portion reserved for the gods included meat and 'all the grass contained in the first stomach' (Junod, 1927, II:402). While addressing the ancestors by name and calling for their protection, the officiant deposited the offering bit by bit, on the ground, in the centre of the family circle. What is even more curious is that the whole group ate *roast meat*. We know little about the circumstances of this ceremony, except that it was performed by the Kabaloyi group living among the Nkuna, in Transvaal. Be that as it may, the use of chyme as a positive offering unquestionably poses a new problem.

Let us compare the rites of 'big millet', of marriage, and of mourning. The first brings together affines and relatives of all kinds in a communal meal, an extraordinary occasion in all respects; the second stresses the division between future affines, and the third expresses a tension between the patrilineal lineage and all its uterine nephews. The 'big millet' rite eliminates these distinctions. Not only do the relatives and affines gather to share equally in the ritual but, what is more, raw chyme is part of the offering along with beer and cooked meat. Moreover, the opposition between roasted and boiled, between interior spaces and exterior spaces, disappears. The sacrifice of an ox or a cow brings together the complementary components of kinship; the sacrifice of a goat emphasises their underlying antagonism.

The non-ritual slaughter of an ox by the village headman seems to present the same characteristics. In another passage, Junod tells how the meat is divided. The maternal uncles receive part of the loins, the parents-in-law and brothers-in-law the tail, etc. (Junod, 1927, I:329). Junod adds that none of these rules apply to the sharing of a goat (Junod, 1927, I:340). Thus we are faced with two different symbolic systems. Both sacrifice of the ox and its non-ritual slaughter underlines the unity of kinship and alliance of the maternal and paternal sides, while the ritual treatment of the goat exposes a crisis in which the constituent parts of society confront one another. The introduction of beer along with chyme in the symbolic code dictates an enlargement of our field of investigation. By a happy intuition, Junod sets us on the right track by bringing under the same heading ('special family sacrifices') the offering of the 'big millet' and the 'offering or reconciliation' (Junod, 1927, II:398–9). When two brothers have quarrelled, the younger one must initiate the reconciliation, for the elder alone is entitled to present offerings and sacrifices to the ancestors. In the northern Thonga group, the solemn ceremony of reconciliation is called *byalwa bya huwa* ('the beer of noise') because of the din a quarrel makes (Junod, 1927, II:399). The offering to the ancestors consists of several types of grains from the granaries of those involved in the dispute. 'Two handfuls of the grains are brought to the altar and thrown onto it and the brothers who wish to be reconciled recount their grievances' (Junod, 1927, II:399–400). The cereals offered are 'neither ground nor cooked'. And yet they expressly 'represent' beer. The Thonga observes Junod, 'do not think they have said anything contradictory in expressing themselves in this way', but he leaves this problem of symbolism unsolved. Let us try to clear it up.

In the capital, the first millet harvested is solemnly offered to the chief's ancestors (Junod, 1927, I:396). Agriculture is not central to Thonga ritual preoccupations. Field produce is, however, 'the most common kind of offering' in private rites (Junod, 1927, II:413). The ancestors appreciate beer. Beer is poured on the grave before the goat is sacrificed in honour of the deceased, and the uterine nephews steal the jug just as later they will steal the meat reserved for the ancestors. The big millet offering is exceptional in that this antagonism disappears. The symbolic function of the 'offering of reconciliation' and the 'big millet' offering are comparable: in both cases, it is a matter of bringing together parts of the social body separated by tension (structural or accidental). The symbolic elements are of the same order. The offering of reconciliation transforms raw grain into brewed beer: the symbolic passage from the raw to the cooked consecrates the reintegration into the same community of two brothers separated by a quarrel. The 'big millet' offering brings together a large family community; it links beer (cooked grain) and roasted meat with chyme, which normally belongs in the raw category. Male pastoralism and female agriculture are rigorously separated. The simultaneous presence of the beer (prepared by women) and the ox in a sacrificial rite that refers explicitly to agriculture (that of the 'big millet') obviously reinforces group cohesion; it proclaims the union of man and woman, of paternal and maternal relatives, through the complementarity of seed and ox, of the raw and the cooked.

Chicken's blood, bran and weaning

To complete the picture we must examine one last aspect of the Thonga sacrificial system.

In the *mhamba* system of offerings, though the chicken may often 'represent' the ox, demanded by divination, the chicken is not central to the problematics of sacrifice. It does, however, have a particular role in the weaning rite (Junod, 1927, I:58–9). The mother prepares a light maize beer, being careful to keep part of the bran left over from the sifted seeds. The medicine man kills a chicken and sprinkles its blood on the bran. He mixes his saliva with this offering while invoking his ancestor and the child's. He then rubs this mixture on the child's body, which had been previously smeared with oil. The mother carefully picks up the bits which fall on the mat. She makes a little ball of them, which she hides in an anthill at sundown. She is forbidden to look back when she returns to the village lest she bring illness to her child.

It is indeed to the *hondlola* category (expulsion of illnesses) that this rite belongs. The sacrifice of a chicken introduces a variant in the paradigm. In this case the victim's blood fulfils the purifying function usually assumed by the goat's chyme with which the body of the victims is drenched (see p.79). Yet the blood, like the bran with which it is mixed, belongs to the raw, in opposition to the light beer, which introduces the child to the world of the cooked. The mother has also prepared a pot of millet into which she pours a medicine to help it forget her milk. In this context the chicken blood plays the same disjunctive role as goat blood in the exorcism of the possessed. This convergence is not the product of mere chance: like the possessed person before the cure, the nursing child is, to a different degree, in a state of heat and weakness. During the therapeutic rite, the possessed person goes from a raw diet (he drinks the victim's blood) to the consumption of cooked meat. The weaned child, covered with the chicken's blood, abandons raw milk to accept boiled millet.

Let us draw some conclusions. Both chicken and the ox with which it is so often assimilated in the rhetoric of offerings occupy only marginal positions in the Thonga sacrificial system, to which goats are central. Goats have a role in individual therapeutic rites as well as in the rites marking the major collective crises (marriage, death and insanity). The purpose of family sacrifice is not exactly the same as among the Zulu, where the goat and the ox assume a more positive ritual function; they unite the living and the dead around the domestic hearth. No more than the Zulu do the Thonga develop a unique sacrificial paradigm. Yet each rite is built around a particular species, or at least it assigns a specific use to parts of the same animal. To cut up a living being, to cook the meat according to certain rules, to remove the chyme, the bile, or both are interdependent preoccupations aimed at restoring or maintaining group unity or individual integrity. Sacrifice is a symbolic labour on living matter.

Commenting on the assertion of Hubert and Mauss that destruction of the victim is the essence of sacrifice, Herrenschmidt states that this operation is 'the only way of making it pass from the visible to the invisible' (Herrenschmidt, 1978, :12). This does not, however, account for the importance of the treatment of the internal organs. It would also be overlooking the fact that the offering of a living animal dedicated to the ancestors suffices to establish communication with the invisible. The Thonga sometimes dedicate to the ancestors a chicken or a goat without sacrificing it. A perpetual debt thus begins; indeed when this animal dies, another representative (from the same species) takes its place (Junod, 1927:351). We have seen that chickens and goats can also be delivered alive to their ancestors, in the forest (see p.70). In each Zulu herd, a consecrated (but not destroyed) animal is the living sign of an invisible presence. Neither the 'consecrated' nor the immolated animals are projected into another world: on the contrary, Zulu sacrifice calls upon the ancestors to join their descendants around the hearth, to participate in a party. The killing in this case allows for the marking of boundaries between men and the ancestors, while arranging for passage points. We have seen that this topological disposition varies among the Thonga. In any case, the manipulation of an animal brings into play symbolic categories for the benefit of an individual or a collectivity.

To kill an ox or to isolate it from the mass of sacrifiable animals in order to dedicate it to the ancestors, are different ritual acts. This dialectic is universal. It exists among the Mongols (Hamayon, 1978).

The Buriates 'consecrate' a bull, which will never be killed, sold or mistreated: it becomes the 'bearer' of the Bull Lord, the mythical ancestor of the tribe. Yet the Buriates sacrifice horses and sheep (warm-muzzled animals) to the clan ancestors, masters of the mountains. The meat will be eaten by the participants. However, they painstakingly scrape the bones, taking care not to break or scratch them. Then these are burned and thus the animal is transferred *intact* to the ancestors' ghostly herd, for the skeleton is the animal's framework. The remains, the organic support of the vital breath, are one piece, comprising the head, respiratory apparatus, lungs and heart; it is speared on a stake and left to the predators. Obviously these preoccupations diverge from those of the Bantu of southern Africa. The Buriates separate the flesh and bones and are careful to recompose the victim's body so that it may pass on to the other world, while the Zulu call on their ancestors to settle themselves in a special organ attached to the sacrificer's body: the gall-bladder. For the Zulu, the 'consecrated' animal as well as the immolated animal constitute two complementary means of attracting, if not trapping the ancestors. Among the Buriates, the two approaches are however, in a relationship of opposition defined by Hamayon in these words: 'Whereas the sacrificed animals ascend from men towards the spirits, the consecrated animals represent the descent of the spirits to men. Through a pattern of sacrifice and consecration the circuit between men and the spirits, or rather between the living and the dead members of the clan, is closed' (Hamayon, 1963:174–5),

Animal life and human life are not comparable. It would be monstrous to dissect a man's body; cannibalism to eat it. This is why animal sacrifice is not murder. Yet the evidence is irrefutable: among the Zulu, a specific species, the black sheep, representing man, is substituted for him in rain rituals. This marginal and unsettling sacrificial zone is often the area where religions base the founding myth of their ritual practice; the death of a man-god assures the creation of the world or the salvation of men. In Christian iconography, the man-god is sometimes depicted as the lamb of God. The famous Van Eyck painting reflects a familiar anthropological image; that of a peaceful animal transformed into a celestial agent. The lamb represents the crucified Christ. Changing the ancient image of water, universal source of life, to a mystical plane, the Van Eyck brothers paint a fountain in front of the altar where the animal-victim, metaphor for the human god, awaits sacrifice. We shall investigate this new problem more thoroughly in Chapter VI. To understand the sacrifice of a god, one must begin by developing the reasons for the King to be the preferred object of the sacrificial process when it has a cosmological purpose.

V

The king on the sacrificial
stage (Swazi-Rwanda)

Let us return to our starting point. As we saw in Chapter II, a small, strange animal called 'chief', offers itself to the Lele from time to time—an animal they have refused to kill outright. The pangolin, symbol of the universe, voluntarily 'sacrifices' itself for man. We have not yet explored all the aspects of this sacrificial capture.

The Kuba, who are the Lele's close neighbours, point the way for us. Their king monopolises this animal, which is laden with cosmological significance. He also takes on the mystical roles assigned by the Lele to the Pangolin Man ritual group. The *Nyim* (king) like the pangolin, belongs to nature while, at the same time, being master of cultural order. He is. invested with dangerous power, indispensable to the orderly functioning of the universe and of society (Vansina, 1964:98–116). He derives this unique mystical power from the enthronement rites, which sever his ties to his clan. He has sexual relations with a sister and marries a grand-niece from his own matrilineal family group. From this time on, he is regarded as a formidable sorcerer who is considered, strangely, to be both filth and the representative of God on earth. When he dies he will become a spirit of nature.

The king is surrounded by a network of prohibitions. He is hot, like the leopard and the sun, and may scorch the earth should he venture across a field. He is able to transform himself into a leopard, the sorcerer's familiar, to take revenge on his enemies. We should keep in mind that the Lele classify the leopard and all carnivores as *hama*, impure animals that arouse disgust. The Kuba king has attributes both of the pangolin—a benevolent animal spirit, guarantor of fertility—and of the deadly leopard. He is ambivalent.

In an earlier book (de Heusch, 1982) I discussed the general nature of this politico-symbolic entity in Africa. Along with Alfred Adler (1978) and Jean-Claude Muller (1975), I have resolutely joined Frazer's camp. It cannot be doubted that the sacred king, the formidable master of natural forces, is, after a reign of varying length, condemned to die prematurely, to become a sacrificial victim. The ritual killing of the king is part of his fate; it is the ultimate expression of the prohibitions that hedge in his excessive power, his monstrous counter-cultural nature.

And among the Kuba? Tradition confirms that formally, the king's throat was cut when his physical strength declined (Vansina, 1964:100). It has been many years, however, since this custom was last observed. The Kuba king is an essential cog in a flourishing economic system, and the master of a strong army. There can be no doubt that these facts weigh heavily on the historical evolution of sacred royalty.

It is primarily in small societies, such as the Rukuba (Nigeria) that the symbolic structure of this political institution is most evident. Each Rukuba village constitutes an autonomous political unit. However, Muller convincingly shows that its chief (*utu*) has all the characterisitics 'of the sovereigns referred to in the literature as divine kings' (Muller, 1980:151). If his mystical power proves ineffectual in coping with any kind of catastrophe, he is deposed. Though he is not put to death, as the classical Frazerian schema would have it, Muller demonstrates that the theme of regicide haunts Rukuba ritual thought and practice. The nominating procedures for a new village chief vary, but they are always shrouded in mystery. The ideal candidate should cut a fine figure and speak with ease and authority, and also respect the customs. Moreover, he should possess a mystical power the Rukuba call the Eye; as should the Blacksmith, the clan chief and the diviner. However, the village chief differs from the other possessors of the Eye because of the remarkable characteristics conferred upon him by the installation rites. The candidate elected from the clan in power, is truly 'bound' to the chieftainship (Muller, 1980:156). He hides in the home of his mother's brother and his head is shaved as if he were 'in mourning for himself', for his agnates have symbolically killed him (Muller, 1980:157). In the end, the uncle gives back his nephew, who is 'resuscitated' like a child emerging from initiation. He then prepares to bear the 'burden of chieftainship' by drinking beer from the skull of one of the previous chiefs (Muller, 1980:158). In three leading villages, the chief is symbolically put to death during his enthronement through a substitute human victim: the ritual organisers seize and smother a sickly newborn baby belonging to the chief's clan. Then a ram is immolated. A bit of the infant's flesh is secretly added to a few pieces of the ram which are cooked and then eaten by the chief. He is now anthropophagous, without realising it. He becomes dangerous; his mystical power can infect those who eat or drink from the same receptacle as he.

Muller subtly observes that the substitute sacrifice of the new-born must be interpreted as the transformation of the ritual regicide carried out by some neighbouring groups, notably the Jukun. Unlike the latter, the Rukuba do not kill their chief after the seventh year. On the contrary, his reign is theoretically unlimited; however, the 'first seven years of the reign are considered a probationary period, a sort of competence test' (Muller, 1980:161). 'Instead of killing the chief at the first sign of ageing or on a prearranged occasion, Rukuba ideology chooses to accomplish this at birth—or shortly afterwards; the eating of the baby's cadaver assures an effectively long reign' (Muller, 1980:172). Moreover, the chief is sacrificed by proxy during the great periodic ritual, *kugo* which theoretically, but not in actual practice, takes place every fourteen years. Before the opening of the ceremonies an old man is seized: unlike the newborn baby immolated during the enthronement, he does not belong to the chief's clan. The victim is rendered repulsive and terrifying. With utmost secrecy the officiants kill a ram and the old man eats its flesh. The latter then becomes 'so impure that he could never again live in the village nor be in contact with his fellow citizens' (Muller, 1980:173). According to the Rukuba, the rite serves to 'repair the world' or to 'put it back in place' (Muller, 1980:175). Muller shows most convincingly that the rite is based on a double displacement. The ram, which the Rukuba never eat, 'represents' the chief; the old man who broke this alimentary prohibition 're-enacts the chief's transgression during his enthronement. He also ate the chief, in the form of the ram, and he will suffer the consequences' (Muller 1980:175). He is doomed to live in exile, in a hut situated outside the village's social space, begging for his food at a distance. He is supposed to die suddenly during the seventh year. The old man is eliminated in place of the chief himself, who finds his position strengthened.

Muller undertakes to apply here the hypothesis proposed by Girard in *La violence et le sacré*, 1972 (*Violence and the Sacred* 1977). The king is supposed to be a potential sacrificial victim, an ambivalent figure, both a guarantor of order and a troublemaker, created for the sole purpose of serving as a scapegoat. I shall attempt to prove that this interpretation results from an error of perspective. The precise problem posed by both Rukuba chieftainship and Kuba sacred royalty is to understand why the investiture rites make the holder of power a 'being at fault', guilty of the crime of anthropophagy or incest. During my early research on this theme, I indicated that, upon enthronement, many African sovereigns were called upon to break the law of exogamy by practising, like the Kuba king, an incestuous hierogamy (de Heusch, 1958). He is thus projected outside the social order and the Kuba do not hesitate to identify their sovereign with both a spirit of nature and a sorcerer (Vansina, 1964:102). The ritual anthropophagy imposed on the new Rukuba chief belongs to the same category. Muller discovered a very apt phrase to define it: 'alimentary incest' (Muller, 1980:171). The very choice of the candidate defines him at once as a marginal being, outside the group for which he is now responsible (de Heusch, 1981). One must question this topology which fixes the sacred chief in a contradictory or ambivalent position. Within the human sphere he is the guarantor of prosperity and the fertility of crops, yet it is as if he could not act upon natural forces unless he presented himself as a desocialised, even monstrous creature, belonging entirely to the mysterious realm which encompasses culture and upon which the latter's survival depends. Indeed it is in order to protect themselves from the excesses of this uncanny force that the very person of the sacred chief or king is surrounded by a network of prohibitions.

In a penetrating article dealing with the Mundang of Tchad, Alfred Adler pays particular attention to this aspect (Adler, 1978). The king of Léré's strength lies in a substance (*ke*) which gives him the power to control rainfall. His palace is 'likened to a microcosm and the king is like the sun of this universe' (Adler, 1978:34). The numerou prohibitions he has to obey 'both in his physical life and in his social relations' impose constraints 'whose function is', to paraphrase Frazer, 'as much to protect the king as to protect the people from him' (Adler, 1978:34). Adler proposes interpreting ritual regicide as royalty's 'supreme prohibition'. The king's life will be shortened. Yet this premature end is delayed by various tactics. Each year a double takes upon himself the tragic fate to which the Léré king is doomed. A man, a 'sort of scapegoat for the king' sacrifices an ox and, during the night, flees from the palace with the hide . 'The burden he carries condemns him to die soon in place of his glorious double' (Adler, 1978:36). During the feast honouring the soul of the millet, which takes place at the end of harvest, a servant replaces the king: he places a large sheaf of millet in the palace's central granary: 'naked, his body covered with ashes and wearing a penial sheath, the young man is indeed dressed like an initiate emerging from initiatory death'. The king 'throws pebbles in his direction three times hurries to a room to avoid seeing him' (Adler, 1978:36). Finally, the annual cycle is brought to a close with the feast of the guinea fowl. This time the sovereign himself, naked, takes part in a collective hunt to bring on the rain. He is subjected to bullying and ridicule. From all this data Adler concludes that 'each ritual year is, for the sovereign, equal to one unit in a countdown ending with the regicide' (Adler, 1978:37–8). Indeed his conception of sacred royalty is like mine: 'the many specific prohibitions and the ritual death of the king make him a unique being, at the very edge of society, somewhat like Archimedes' locus which allows, if not the raising of the earth, at least—which is almost the same thing—the comprehension of society's union with nature' (Adler, 1978:38).

All these characteristics, more or less developed in each particular case (royal incest, anthropophagy, the assimilation of a king with a sorcerer, the prohibitions surrounding him, and finally regicide), must be brought together within the same symbolic structure. They all define the formidable magic force which abolishes the border between culture—from which the chief is separated when he is sacralised—and nature, of which he becomes the sovereign master. In the end, the king is, in the Latin etymological sense, a sacred monster.

Therefore the Rukuba chieftainship does indeed deserve to be described as 'sacred'. However, Muller prefers to qualify it as 'divine' reserving the first term for kingdoms that do not require a violent death of their king (Muller, 1980:163). This differentiation seems to me somewhat arbitrary. Though the Kuba sovereigns' military power allowed them to end regicide long ago, the symbolic complex defining their ritual role is indeed that of the minuscule chieftainships described by Muller. It is more likely that the 'divinisation' of sovereigns is a historical pattern, originating in sacralisation as we have just defined it. It accompanies the politico-economic development of the machinery of state.

Sacred royalty is a symbolic structure which has broken from domestic family and lineage order. It is a topological machination which must be interpreted as a meshing of the human space and the realm of the bush or forest where the mysterious forces of fertility live; it could also be the locus where the sky meets the earth. The king's body, identified with inhabited and cultivated territory, and with its wealth, is also symbolically outside its laws. It is this paradox, this phantasmagorical project that must be elucidated if we are to understand why the sacred king is a multiplicative mechanism of productive and reproductive forces on the one hand, and a dangerous being surrounded by ritual interdictions, condemned to a premature death, on the other. In some cases the royal body is not used for this purpose as long as it is perfect, intact. In others, this essential cog must be replaced after an arbitrarily fixed term, unless a substitute sacrifice can bring about the indispensable regeneration.

Among the Rukuba, the substitute animal figure is a sheep. It is noteworthy that the Kuba, for their part, make the sheep the property of the sovereign: 'only the king owns two or three herds. The rams are most especially the symbol of the king' (Vansina, 1964:109). A Kuba myth tells us that the niece of the cultural hero Woot gave birth to a lamb at the very moment when the dynasty's founder voluntarily exiled himself after being blamed by his people for the incest he committed secretly with his sister (de Heusch, 1972:121).

We have already noted the special symbolic character of the ram in Africa. We should also note that among the Thonga sheep symbolise chiefdom. It is again the sheep, and not the ox or the goat, that we find representing the human race among the Zulu on the occasion of the sacrifice in which the rain maker, far from calling on the ancestors, bravely sets out for the aquatic home of the python genie (see Chapter III). There are not traces of ritual cooking, of 'alimentary communion', here. There is no other sacrifice like this in the Zulu scheme of things. It is played out as if the rainmaker is risking his life, alone at midnight on a black rock in midstream. In this role the magician is really the king's surrogate. It would normally fall to the sovereign to assure control of cosmic forces; and the Zulu resign themselves to calling on a specialised rainmaker because the kings no longer accomplish their ritual duties. The Zulu say, 'the trouble is that our kings do nothing today. They simply sit in an office, dressed nicely, and write letters' (Berglund, 1975:53).

Thus the Zulu rainmaker takes on a dangerous royal function. Furthermore, it is the chiefs themselves (*induma*) who call on the rainmakers directly; there is no more royal mediation. The chiefs send emissaries asking them 'to plead with the sky'; it is the chiefs who furnish the black sheep for the cosmological sacrifice (Berglund, 1975:55).

However, among the Swazi, who are related to the Zulu, the sacred king has never stopped assuming his ritual function each year during the southern summer solstice. Hilda Kuper has written a masterly description of this great ritual of regeneration which starts with a quest for the 'waters of the world' (Kuper, H., 1947:201). Elsewhere I have proposed a complementary analysis (de Heusch, 1982, Chapter VII). Here we shall consider only the central sacrificial episode. The second part of the ritual, the great *ncwala*, is launched at full moon following the solstice. That night, young people go out to gather acacia leaves, a fertility symbol. It is a good omen if it rains as they return to the capital where the sovereign comes out to meet them. The next day, old men cover the sanctuary of the royal palace with this green vegetation. A black ox stolen from a commoner is brought to the young people. They pummel it with their fists while driving it into the santuary. There the priests kill it and from the animal's corpse extract a number of parts which are used in making a magic, revitalising medicine given to the sovereign. The blows inflicted on the ox by the young people also have magical power; they enhance the effectiveness of the 'waters of the world'. The young officiants bring a second black ox into the byre. This time it is the principal ox of the royal herd, the *incwambo*. The animal is thrown to the ground and the completely naked king is seated on it, to be washed with ritual waters made foamy by plants. The sovereign thus becomes the 'bull of the nation'. This event introduces a brief period of mourning. The next day (the 'Great Day'), the still-naked king walks through the crowd, wearing only an ivory penial sheath, and heads for the royal enclosure where he spits out beer ('stabs') before ritually eating ('biting') the first shoots of a certain number of green plants mixed with sea water. Women cry; mournful songs deplore the hate and neglect to which the sovereign is subjected.

Later, when the excitement has become paroxysmic, the king, accompanied by members of his clan, surrounded by the tightly packed crowd, enters the ritual hut in the byre while the princesses cry. Suddenly he emerges, disguised as a nature spirit. A head-dress of black feathers falls about his shoulders, hiding his face; he wears a lionskin headband. His body is covered with green grass. Brandishing a shield in his left hand he performs a mad dance, facing the young warriors who hail him as 'Thunder'. After going back inside the hut several times, the king comes out one last time brandishing a bright green gourd, which he finally throws at the warriors after tantalising them with it. One of them catches the gourd on his shield, held horizontally. Then a new period of mourning and 'darkness' follows, during which all sexual relations are forbidden to people until the final purification. During the final rite, the king's fabulous costume is burned along with the gourd. No one doubts that this ritual fire will be extinguished by rain.

We shall not repeat here the detailed analysis we undertook elsewhere, in the wake of many other writers. Suffice it to say that the Swazi sovereign is the principal participant in the great cosmological game. As a lion, a master of nature, the Swazi king is situated outside cultural order; like the Kuba king he is literally a 'sacred' monster; he sleeps freely with the 'sisters' of his lineage. The ritual acts he accomplishes are characterised by violence. When he eats the first fruits he is supposed to 'bite'; when he couples with his ritual wife, while all his people are sworn to continence, he affirms his virile strength by 'stabbing'. By walking about naked among his people, he shows off as a creature of nature; he carries the burden of royalty in shame and the women pity him. When he emerges disguised as a violent nature spirit, he gives himself over to a true ritual combat with his army, while the princes try in vain to take him elsewhere. Naked or dressed, the king is 'other', at once monstrous and indispensable for the wellbeing of the universe.

It is in this general symbolic perspective that the sacrifice of a black ox must be interpreted. Ordinarily the Swazi, like the Zulu, sacrifice cattle and goats to honour their ancestors (Kuper, H., 1947:192). But unlike the Zulu, the Swazi are not on comfortable terms with the ancestors. They do not worship the ancestral spirits, they scold them. They get angry when they feel that they are persecuted by them (Kuper, H., 1947:192–3). Hilda Kuper does not go into much detail about the rites which are dedicated to them. Describing the annual sacrifices carried out on the royal graves, she states that each animal is 'identified' with the particular royal ancestor to whom it is dedicated. This assertion is very doubtful if one recalls Berglund's excellent description of the complexity of Zulu ritual communication between ancestors and descendants. Surely the fact that only widows and descendents of King Bunu are authorized to eat the flesh of an ox sacrificed in his honour is not sufficient evidence that the animal 'is' King Bunu (Kuper, H., 1947:193–5).

Moreover, as among the Zulu, each Swazi family singles out from the herd an animal that will never be killed. Designated by the term *licabi*, the chosen beast is dedicated to the ancestors, and animals that are to be sacrificed are always led up to this one before being slaughtered (Kuper, H., 1947:192). Hilda Kuper specifies neither the sex nor the exact role of the *licabi*. We do know, however, that the Zulu adamantly refuse to have a castrated ox represent the fertilising power of the ancestors. It is always an intact bull or a very fine cow. Now the animal which fulfils this same role within the Swazi royal herd, the *incwambo*, is expressly described as an ox. Strangely enough, *incwambo* 'is a physiological term applied to a muscle near the testicles' (Kuper, H., 1947:214). This is the first paradox. There is a second. This animal, which 'holds a unique place in the royal herd', is never slaughtered. It is replaced by a younger animal when its strength declines, but is still allowed to die a natural death (Kuper, H., 1947:214). It can never be 'beaten, maltreated or used for any menial task', but it is 'forced to the ground' during the *ncwala* rite, when the kings sits naked on it to be proclaimed 'bull of the nation'.

To understand the symbolism brought into play, one must of course recall that shortly before, another black ox stolen from a commoner was indeed sacrificed in order to regenerate the king's magical power, which affects all of nature. There exists an obvious link between the sacrificed animal, *incwambo*, and the king. When the king carries out the *ncwala* while he is still a mere child, the two ritual animals are 'measured against the king himself, so if the heir is very young it is a small animal, and if he is already nearly full grown the animal is large' (Kuper, H., 1947:222). There is in this case no room to doubt the double identification of the king with the sacrificed ox and with the principal ox of the royal herd. It is obvious that the first is a substitute for the second, and that it is itself the bovine double of the king, proclaimed 'bull of the nation'.

To shed light on this mystery, one must first realise that the naked king, seated on the *incwambo* ox, is wholly a creature of nature; he is completely 'deculturalised'. This symbolic figure of royalty, linked to a domestic animal, withdrawn from the socioeconomic circuit, is the symmetrically inverted image of the 'lion-king', master of savage nature. Yet in the very instant that the naked king confirms his bovine affinities, he appears as a *castrated bull*. Beidelman was the first to ask why the sacrificial animal was deprived of his reproductive power. He tries to explain it by the animal's marginal position ('betwixt and between'). It is taken from the herd and used to establish a link between the nation, the king, and his ancestors (Beidelman, 1966:396). I think the explanation lies elsewhere. Within Nguni culture, there is a striking contrast between the castrated black ox representing the Swazi king and the intact animal—bull or cow—representing the ancestors within the Zulu herds.

To appreciate the importance of this opposition, we must include the neighbouring Venda in the discussion. Ancestors of each Venda lineage are always represented by a black bull, in whom important religious roles are invested (Stayt, 1968:242–3). The Venda, however, .symbolically castrate their king. Indeed, after his enthronement, the sacred chief drinks a depressant that renders him impotent (Stayt, 1968:242–3). In Central Africa, in certain parts of Penda country (Zaire), the same dignitary is forced to wear a penial sheath, which dooms him to sustained continence (de Sousberghe, 1963:66). These prohibitions can only be explained within the general symbolic context of sacred royalty; the master of nature wields an excessive, menacing power over men, close to sorcery (de Heusch, 1982). It happens that the Swazi king, the lion-king, does walk about naked with an ivory penial sheath when he walks through the crowd to couple with the ritual queen whom he is supposed to stab the day after having been proclaimed 'bull of the nation'. This pulse of violent life which is the bull's has been acquired after having been symbolically put to death through the intermediary of a substitute ox. Thus he renews the living forces of nature at a particularly critical moment; during the summer solstice the sun indeed retires to its 'hut in the south'. All these data are summarised in Fig. 16.

Fig. 16

Black ox sacrificed	*Black ox Incwambo*	*King*
Stolen from a commoner	Principal animal of the royal herd	'Bull of the nation'
Hammered by fists	Never mistreated or slaughtered but forced to the ground during *ncwala*	Symbolically put to death during *ncwala*

What is played out each year on the *ncwala* sacrificial scene is the precise equivalent of the slaughtering of the ram, substitute for the sacred chief during the Kugo ritual in Rukuba country. Only the choice of animal and the periodicity of the rite differ. The status of the Rukuba 'kinglet', however, is more unstable than that of the Swazi king, a sovereign firmly established in the political order. When the former is unable to assume his permanent mystical duties, when the harvest is not plentiful, 'the villagers use the grain reaped on the chief's farm for themselves, and the chief receives nothing and may even be deposed' (Muller, 1977:3).

The cult of the ox *incwambo* is perverted in this sacrificial context: representative of royal power, this animal is itself thrown to the ground after a substitute ox has been hammered with blows and slain. The sacrilegious character of this act is somewhat lessened by a deliberately created gap between the two animals: the implicated victim, (the *incwambo*) is the most respected member of the royal herd; the actual victim was stolen from a commoner.

The transference is obvious. But what does it mean? Is Girard right in saying that the sacred king is a scapegoat on whom the whole Swazi nation projects its own violence? If so, does it follow that the royal figure was fabricated wholly for this purpose? It is true that the king is, in a way, a 'potential sacrificial victim, a condemned convict awaiting his execution' (Girard, 1972:154). Yet to assert that his 'true function' is to 'convert sterile and contagious violence into positive cultural values' is based on a misunderstanding (Girard, 1972:155). One must start by defining the positive aspects of sacred royalty itself. As I have already stated, the symbolic intrigue is not the one imagined by Girard. He quite simply mistakes the consequence of a particular ontological status for its cause. By arbitrarily isolating one of the pertinent features of the structure defining kingship as a symbolic institution, he obscures its very function. He fails to specify that the substitute sacrifice of the king is but one episode among many within the vast, grandiose ritual in which the Swazi king figures as master of the sun and the cosmic rhythms. To assert that the sovereign is divinised because he is a scapegoat who rids the nation of its violent impulses is to reverse the data. Elsewhere I have shown that the *ncwala* can no longer be interpreted, as it was by Gluckman, as the symbolic expression of rivalry among the constituent groups (de Heusch, 1982, Chapter VII). The violence expressed by the young men when they attack the sacrificial ox is entirely directed at the one person who, because of his position within the symbolic space, is likely to accumulate 'filth'. I shall try to explain this complex notion.

The ox sacrificed by the Swazi indeed stands out because of its black colour, which links it to death and sorcery. We have already spelled out the fundamental opposition between 'white' and 'black' among the Zulu (see Chapter III). These conceptual categories are also used to organise ritual activities among the Swazi. As the principle of life, the king is associated with the light of the sun and the full moon. Any contact with death throws him into a state of 'blackness' that weakens the entire nation (Kuper, H., 1947:86). However, the royal compound (*lusasa*) built during the young monarch's minority comprises two parts: the 'white' part is where he receives his mother and visitors; only the dignitaries who initiate him into kingship, a few companions, and later his young mistresses, may enter the 'black' part of the house. Faced with such a clear line between the luminous and the obscure aspects of royalty, it is hard to agree with Beidelman, who considers the black category as ambivalent (Beidelman, 1966:381). Though a song of praise glorifies King Sobhuza as being born 'amidst the black shields', it is directly followed by the assertion that he is 'fearful' (Kuper, H., 1947, Chapter IX).

Surely the slaughtering of the black ox sacrificed during *ncwala* is part of the same symbolism. If not, why must the pre-pubescent youths who eat its flesh purify themselves in the river (Kuper, H., 1947:214), as must those who are in contact with the *incwambo*, the 'sacred' ox of the same colour, the king's double (Ziervogel, 1957:67)? In truth, it is the dangerous character of the king that is expressed in the choice of a black ox which is then brutally slain. One will also note that at the end of the *ncwala*, the victim's remains are burned on a purifying pyre along with the costume worn by the king

when he was disguised as a violent nature spirit. All these objects are
polluted. The Swazi say: 'the filth of the king and all the people lies here on
the fire' (Kuper, 1947:220). Even the great King Sobhuza was polluted. His
song confirms this by insisting on the purifying virtue of water:

> Waters cleanse Sobhuza, wash his feet,
> Cleanse him of pollution.

It is again a black animal—this time a goat—identified with the young
sovereign that is slain when the prince reaches puberty and undergoes
symbolic circumcision. The warriors dig up a big stone from a humid place
and the prince sits on it. 'A pitch black goat is killed, the head is cut off and
the contents are removed. Into the empty space in the goat's head, the
specialist puts the king's hair, then he places the goat's head in the hole
from which the stone has been dug and rolls the stone back into its place'
(Kuper, H., 1947:77).

In these two sacrificial rites an accursed black animal represents the
king and is used to drive out the 'blackness' in him. We have already
encountered this violent system, quite distinct from the one developed in
ancestor worship, among the Nguni. A goat is mistreated by Zulu maidens
to rid themselves of the danger caused by some transgression. Harriet
Ngubane compares this sacrifice to the slaying of a black bull that used to
be carried out during the ritual of first fruits, which was similar in many
ways to the Swazi *ncwala* (Ngubane, 1977:130).

The reader may be tempted to compare these practices and the
sacrificial customs of the Nuer (Chapter I). As a matter of fact, the different
registers in which these rites are inscribed cannot be confused. By slaying
the ox, the Nuer do not expel a pollution. On this subject, we have argued
against Evans-Pritchard's interpretation: by transgressing, the Nuer
threaten the equilibrium of a cultural code controlled by the spirit world;
they perform a sacrifice in order to repay a debt. On the other hand, the ox
sacrificed instead of the Swazi king is indeed the bearer of a curse, as is the
goat on to which the Zulu maidens transfer their pollution. The Zulu have a
specific word for this concept, *umnyama*, which literally means 'darkness'. It is associated with heat, sexuality and birth, as well as with death.
This pollution is concentrated, as we have seen, in the royal person, the
focal point of energy. The *ncwala*, which the monarch must carry out each
year can be interpreted as a huge purification ritual, the restoration of
'whiteness'. We shall find this royal conceptualisation again, but transformed, in Rwanda.

The 'saviour' king and animal sacrifice in Rwanda

The actual body of the Rwanda sovereign was identified with the physical
territory of the kingdom, which was held to belong to him completely (men,

women and cattle). The king was forbidden to bend his knee lest the country shrink like a piece of leather (D'Hertefelt and Coupez, 1964:5–8). As among the Swazi, the royal herd, called 'the respectables', had a chosen animal, here an intact bull and not an ox. Called *rusanga*, it was killed when the king died and its skin was used to shroud his body (Pagès, 1933:356–7; D'Hertefelt and Coupez, 1964:207, 486, 489). The *rusanga* bull was associated with a ram that bore the same name; the latter underwent the same fate as its bovine counterpart during royal funerals. Its hide covered the legs of the royal corpse (D'Hertefelt and Coupez, 1964:207,362). Unlike the Swazi, the Rwanda never castrate male animals. The *rusanga* bull differs in another from the *incwambo* ox; his hide is *white*. This is what can be deduced from Bourgeois's information: the royal cadaver is rolled in the skin of a white 'ox' (Bourgeois, 1956:46). This contrast is even more surprising because the symbolic connotations of white and black are similar in Swaziland and Rwanda. The former 'connotes the idea of good omen, joy, victory and plenty', while black evokes the idea of bad fortune and infertility (D'Hertefelt and Coupez, 1964:247).

The beneficent white royal bull does not have a sacrificial substitute that is put to death annually, as is the case with the black ox *incwambo* when it appears in the *ncwala* rite in Swaziland. Yet the Rwanda king shares many characteristics with the Swazi sovereign. He reigns with his mother; he practices incest within his lineage. Moreover, far from being the principal actor in a unique annual national rite, he is ready to intervene at any moment to assure fertility and to regulate world order, while observing a very precise ritual code. The 'damned' (*sacer*) aspect of royalty seems to disappear. It is, in fact, transformed.

Dynastic history teaches us that a certain number of kings, known as 'saviours' (*umutabazi*), willingly sacrificed their lives in the manner of the first so called 'historical' king, Ruganzu Bwimba. However, this important 'sacrificial function' was in fact ensured by a substitute human victim in cases of national crisis. 'In the case of major battles ... a 'liberator' designated by diviners and representing the king had to go out and meet the enemy alone and sacrifice himself voluntarily as Ruganzu Bwimba had done. The shedding of his blood was in fact thought to buy or rebuy the earth mystically. It was then invaded or reconquered by the warriors' (Smith, 1970:18). Now this august sacrifice had its evil side. 'Monstrous human creatures' automatically suffered the special death reserved to the king or his representatives: pubescent girls whose breasts had not developed, single mothers—even twins of different sexes and disturbed people. They were led to the border and slain on foreign soil so as to transmit the curse to foreigners (Pages, 1933:404; Bourgeois, 1953:159; Sandrart, 1939 I:30).

It is as if the 'sacred' character of kingship had been divided into two antithetical and complementary figures in Rwanda. On the other hand the king, associated with the intact white bull, is the perfect pure and beneficent being. On the other hand, the monstrous creatures (monstrous either biologically or, like single mothers, morally) are expelled from the kingdom to strike a blow at the integrity of an enemy country. In this division something that resembles a scapegoat is evident. A threat is avoided, transferred elsewhere.

In the case of 'floods', an accursed animal accompanies the monstrous human victim in the sacrifices carried out to regulate rainfall. The secret ritual code then prescribed the slaying of a woman without breasts from the inferior Twa caste, and of a black goat, symbol of barrenness (D'Hertefelt and Coupez, 1964:27). The ritual procedure brought into play on this occasion has two complementary aspects which should be carefully distinguished from each other. A bull and a sterile cow are placed inside the shelter built in honour of the ancestor designated as 'favourable' by the diviners; the Twa woman and the black goat are *outside*. The first are sacrificed in honour of the protecting ancestor, to whom sorghum beer and hydromel are also offered, while the officiant copulates. On the other hand the Twa woman and the black goat are visible bearers of the curse carried by the ancestor designated as 'unfavourable'; they are led to a deserted place where they are put to death. A black bull is sacrificed along with them. The absolute externality of this second type of victim is easy to explain. The woman without breasts is not only stigmatised by her monstrous nature; culturally she also belongs to the peripheral Twa, who do not pay tribute to the king. (D'Hertefelt and Coupez, 1964:27). It is sterility, as a principal alien to Rwanda society, which is expelled; a Twa woman 'beyond childbearing age' would also do.

The role of the black bull merits discussion. He is chosen from the herd of cows called 'ashen' (i.e., white) which is controlled by a high dignitary known as 'King Kono'; he represents the three clans of celestial origin from which the queen mothers must be chosen. A black bull in a herd reputed to be 'white' (i.e. beneficent) is obviously abnormal, monstrous. The animal suffers a significant reversal: it is killed *head down*. The officiants damn Rwanda's three principal enemy countries, wishing their people would sleep with their 'heads down' (D'Hertefelt and Coupez, 1964:31). However, the principal purpose of the rite is to ward off excessive rainfall. To turn the black bull upside down is of course also to invert the relationship of sky and earth. The animal is prevented from grazing on the way 'for they do not want him to touch the ground'; this is why it is hand-fed with grass (D'Hertefelt and Coupez, 1964:29), and its dung picked up in a basket (D'Hertefelt and Coupez, 1964:31).

All sacrifices of expulsion are carried out by specialised officiants, the *rembo*, organized like an army corps. They are in charge of ridding Rwanda of those nefarious signs that are 'the black goats, unfavourable divinatory material, unwed mothers, girls without breasts or not menstruating'. In the event of war, the *rembo* accompany the armies to hurl their incantations in the face of the enemy (D'Hertefelt and Coupez, 1964:485–6).

These ritual acts cannot be dissociated from those of the king's emissaries who sow disorder in the enemy ranks while exposing themselves to their blows. The formidable and dangerous character of the royal person is used against the country's adversaries. The sacrificial role is inverted by being militarised; instead of purifying the country's pollution, the substitute royal victim takes a curse away to the outside. Royal sacrifice, however, has not altogether lost its Frazerian character. The death from smallpox of Mibambwe III at the end of the eighteenth century was considered a 'redeeming' act, for it put an end to the epidemic that had been ravaging the country. A historical chronicle tells us that a son of King Ndahiro Cyamatare agreed to give his own life, along with those of his wife, children, and herds, on the top of a hill, to put an end to a severe drought (Pages, 1933:237). We have just seen that, conversely, the sacrifice of sacred monsters in a deserted place conjure up floods.

There are even stranger examples. If one can credit the 'trustworthy' accounts reported by de Lacger, periodically the king himself became an expiatory victim, charged with all the crimes of the nation (de Lacger, 1939:208–17). King Musinga, who reigned at the turn of this century when the Belgian Colonisers arrived, displayed himself in the role of an expiatory victim on several occasions. De Lacger correctly interprets this dramatic ritual as 'simulated capital punishment'.

The officiant is a court diviner, designated by the readers of signs. The king and queen mother spend the night preceding their symbolic execution tied up like prisoners near a pen containing a bull and a cow. The next day the sovereigns, freed of their shackles and preceded by the sacrificial animals, are led to the capital's public place. The bull is stabbed in the neck (in everyday life, a butcher would slit the animal's throat) and his blood gathered in a bucket. It is then bludgeoned to death. The king climbs onto the victim's side and is covered in blood while the officiant charges him with all the crimes committed in the kingdom. When he leaves the animal's body, his feet are carefully washed with the juice of the *gisavura* plant (*Acanthaceae Thunbergia alata*) the name of which is derived from the verb meaning 'help out of a difficulty' (D'Hertefelt and Coupez, 1964:431). This plant is also used during the enthronement (D'Hertefelt and Coupez, 1964:229).

Thus delivered, the king is acclaimed by the crowd. The officiant covers his forehead and chest with purifying white clay. The cow is sacrificed and the queen mother climbs on its side where she undergoes the same treatment as the king. The second act in the ritual drama is played out underground. The king, followed by the queen mother carried on a litter, starts out on foot into a tunnel specially built for this ceremony. Soon a bull calf and a ram are seen leaving from the other end, with the king attached to the calf and the queen mother to the ram, by a cord tied to one of the legs. The redeeming bull calf and ram are designated as *Imana*: they are thought to have pulled the sovereigns from the grave, in the name of the Supreme Being.

De Lacger presents this death-rebirth ritual as an expiatory action, destined to appease the spirits of members of the royal family who died in palace intrigues. Musinga's ascendance at the end of the nineteenth century was indeed marked by bloody events, worthy of a Shakespearean tragedy. This substitute sacrifice does not seem to be of a cosmological nature. The king and queen mother offer themselves to the ghosts of their close kin, victims of political crimes. However, the scenario should be compared to the central episode of the annual rite of regeneration, during which the naked Swazi king is identified with a substitute victim. This comparison is even more valid in that according to Bourgeois the Rwanda rite was supposed to have been acted out each year (Bourgeois, 1956:17).

Perhaps this is a recent phenomenon, for the secret ritual code, which describes in detail all the king's ritual acts in the most varied circumstances, does not refer to it. Whatever, it is congruent to the logic of the sacred royalty. The affinities between the king and the bull, strongly emphasised in the dynastic poetry, are not a mere rhetorical game. They can be explained by an original consubstantiality. Indeed the most venerated Rwanda myth relates the bovine and celestial origin of the dynasty. The wife of Thunderbolt, king of the heavens, had become sterile. She stole the heart of a cow that had been used in a divinatory sacrifice adjudged 'favourable'. She placed it in a jug of milk, and after nine months a perfect child (*Kigwa*) was born. However, Thunderbolt refused to acknowledge paternity of this mysterious infant, even though he had given his saliva to the divinatory bull-calf. Kigwa went into exile with his elder brother and sister. He brought with him a bull and a cow, a ram and a ewe, a cock and a hen (D'Hertefelt and Coupez, 1964:221; Lestrade, 1972:105). These animals are precisely those that the signreaders use in divinatory consultation, as we shall see later.

Black and white

Let us look more closely at the similarities and differences in royal sacrifice in Rwanda and Swaziland.

Are we dealing with the same symbolic system, the same fundamental conception of sacred kingship? I think we are. The Swazi and Tutsi pastoralist civilisations have too many cultural features in common for us to doubt that 'whiteness' and 'darkness' have the same connotations for both (Smith, 1979; de Heusch, 1982, Chapter VII).

The institutions we have described are involved in a transformation relationship. In both cases the king and his mother rule together. However, the sociological meaning of sovereignty differs in the two cases. In Swaziland, royalty belongs to the nation. It is the Swazi people who, through their chiefs, furnish the cattle legalising the marriage of the future queen mother. From then on, she is considered 'the mother of the people of the country' (Kuper, H., 1947:54) and the future king 'the child of the nation'. Furthermore, on several occasions during the *ncwala* the king is kept from members of his lineage to make clear that he now belongs to the nation (Kuper, H., 1947, Chapter XIII). Son of the terrestrial clans through his mother, the Swazi king is capable of assuming the 'blackness' of the past year in a ritual that assures the regeneration of both society and the universe. The king is naturally destined to accumulate 'pollution'. The Swazi call him the 'black hero' (Kuper, H., 1947:xii).

In Rwanda, however, the queen mother is always chosen from one of the three aristocratic clans that, like the royal clan itself, is of celestial origin. Rwanda's mythical history is at pains to show how once settled, the royal ancestors renounced marriage with native women so they could be endowed with a celestial umbilical cord (de Heusch, 1982, Chapter II). Affirmation of the transcendent 'purity' of royalty dominates this legendary chronicle, as it does the symbolic concerns of Rwanda rituals. This divergence is manifest in the respective sacrificial systems of the Rwanda and the Swazi. The *incwambo*, the animal double of the Swazi king, like the substitute that is slain during the annual rite of regeneration, is a black ox, bearer of his formidable magic power. In Rwanda, by contrast, a white bull represents the king's fertilising power. The cursed aspect of royalty is split. It is assumed on the one hand by black animals and human beings marked by monstrosity and 'barrenness', and on the other by the representatives of the king, who substitute for him as victims on the battlefield. However, the expiatory sacrifice of the king and queen mother brings together these contradictory aspects in one signal dramatic sequence.

Rwanda royalty implies distinct sacrificial practices. It was born of a divinatory sacrifice, constantly replayed at court. In consulting the viscera of the bull-calf to which he gave his saliva, the king evokes the origin myth of his celestial ancestor, the birth in the sky of a bull-man.

The sacrifice of their own lives by the king's representatives, known as 'liberators' (*umutabazi*) refers to a different mythic paradigm; it re-enacts the heroic deed of King Ruganza Bwimba, with whom the series of 'historical' kings begins; I have discussed this point at length elsewhere (de Heusch, 1982, Chapter II). Here it is a matter of saving a terrestrial enterprise—the State. The sacrifice of a 'liberator' is merely a mystic means of waging war, of routing the enemy, just as the sacrifice of women without breasts brings down a curse upon him. In this role the king in a sense duplicates the symbolic power of the monsters. But the secret ritual code also states that, in certain circumstances, the sovereign must sacrifice a couple of bovines—a bull with a sterile cow—to appease the wrath of an ancestor designated by the diviners. Unfortunately, we do not know the details of this ongoing ritual practice. At any rate, it is not based on any specific myth, and we have no reason to believe that the animals represent the king and queen mother. The people usually content themselves with minimal offerings to the ancestors: in the miniature hut in each family compound that is set aside for ancestor worship, they leave a little beer or milk, seeds and some beans or peas (Maquet, 1954:107; D'Hertefelt and Coupez, 1964:284).

Terrestrial Men and Animals

The sky/earth opposition divides men and domestic animals into two categories. Of celestial origin are the royal clan and the aristocracy, as well as the ox, the sheep, and the chicken (all special instruments of 'noble' divination). The sacrifice of bull-calves for this purpose was a royal privilege (Coupez and Kamanzi, 1962:32–2). The royal sacrifice of the calf is accompanied by a communal meal that symbolically unites the three castes: whereas ordinarily the Tutsi herdsmen, the Hutu farmers and the Twa hunter-potters never eat or drink together, the meat is roasted and eaten in 'common by the king and those subjects who are present, whatever their social standing' (Coupez and Kamanzi, 1962:32). The blood of the bull calf judged 'favourable' is sprinkled on the royal drums, symbols of dynastic perpetuity (Lestrade, 1972:105). An eminent religious dignity was conferred upon the sheep. Indeed they symbolised 'purity, silence and peace' and thus the Supreme Being himself (Smith, 1975:36–7). This is why the Tutsi herdsmen were always careful to see that a few sheep accompanied the herds of cows. During the new king's enthronement a ram called Rusanga (like the head bull of the royal herd) was slain and his hide placed on the throne where the new queen mother silently took place to end the mourning for the former king (D'Hertefelt and Coupez, 1964:261). The peculiar affinities between the queen mother and the ram explain why this animal was charged with assuring her 'resurrection' in the expiatory sacrifice described above (see p. 111). In popular beliefs the ram represents the thunderbolt (de Lacger, 1939:229; Lestrade, 1972:51). Now, Thunderbolt, the King of Above, is in the myth the husband of Gasani, the original mother, who is represented on earth by the queen mother (de Heusch, 1982:133–4). It is in the sheepskin called 'placenta' that the Rwandan mothers carry their babies (Smith, 1975:238). The skin of the sheep is attached to the throne during the annual rite celebrating the first fruits (D'Hertefelt and Coupez, 1964:81).

Upon falling to earth, the ancestors of the king and aristocracy, accompanied by the domestic animals of celestial origin, found the natives Hutu, with their dogs and goats.

The sheep is rigorously opposed to the goat, an animal loaded with 'negative and interconnected connotations of dirtiness, immodesty, noise, boisterousness, indiscretion' (Smith, 1975:36–7). Only the Hutu, terrestrial creatures, sometimes sacrificed a goat to an ancestor (Lestrade, 1973:134). We have seen that a black goat represents the exact opposite of royalty, incarnated in a white bull and a ram. Now this same black goat is, among the Swazi, a prop for the royal figure when the adolescent future king is symbolically sacrificed a first time before taking power.

The Rwanda diet is greatly influenced by the classification of domestic animals in terms of their celestial or terrestrial origins. The sheep, a celestial animal, is never eaten except by the Twa, considered to be gluttons and always famished. The Tutsi, but not the Hutu, abstain from eating the goat, a dirty and boisterous terrestrial animal. The cow has a dual mythic status. Although the ancestor Kigwa brought the first pair of cattle from the sky, King Gihanga, who married a native princess to become the veritable founder of the dynasty, domesticated a large herd of wild cattle who one day mysteriously rose from the depths of a lake. The scale of religious values is translated on an alimentary level (Fig. 17).

Fig. 17

	Meat diet	*Hierarchy of religious values*
Tutsi	Cows	Sheep (celestial)
Hutu	Cows and goats	Cow (celestial and aquatic)
Twa	Cows, goats and sheep	Goat (terrestrial)

Paradoxically the diet richest in protein is theoretically that of the despised lowest caste. The aristocrats' attitudes toward food defy any interpretation of history in dietary terms. The Tutsi in fact rarely slaughter cattle, the instrument of their socioeconomic domination. They pretend to live essentially on milk and display the greatest disdain for cooking.

Here we are at the opposite pole of the Greeks' conception of sacrifice, unique source of meat in the city.

Human sacrifice and the Mysterious Death of Kings

Enthronement ends with a ritual war against a distant province, the Bukunzi, the purpose being to capture alive a man destined for sacrifice. The unfortunate victim's fate is particularly horrible. Gagged and lying on his left side, he is stabbed through the right armpit with the royal spear. (D'Hertefelt and Coupez, 1964:277–9). This ritual act is interpreted as the new king's vengeance against the poisoners and sorcerers responsible for his father's death (D'Hertefelt and Coupez, 1964:365, 392). The text describing this in the secret ritual code ends with these enigmatic words: 'The corpse's head goes to *Myambazo*. The way of enthronement is then ended.'. D'Hertefelt and Coupez could not identify the mysterious *Myambazo* (D'Hertefelt and Coupez, 1964: 277–9). However, Pages sheds some light on the essence of the rite. Until recently, he says, the Bukunzi had to deliver a young man who was sacrificed by means of a dagger; his blood was caught in a wooden jar which was left on enemy territory (Pages, 1933:297).

The status of this expiatory victim is ambiguous. His death avenges the sovereign's but it also presents some features of the sacrifice of the liberator king, whose blood can never be shed on native soil. It is as if the foreigner, captured in a peripheral region and brought to the court to be slain, is but a new substitute for the royal person. Indeed, one of the king's duties is precisely that of carrying malediction beyond the kingdom's border through his own bloodshed. In a way, the victim announces the sacrificial role the new king is supposed to fill, should the occasion arise, to save the kingdom, just like his remote ancestor Bwimba. However, this glorious death is in turn but an alternative to ritual suicide carried out in secret. Folklore consistently maintains that kings had to swallow poison before becoming physically decrepit.

The 'way of impropriety', as the king's funeral is described, starts with an enigmatic formula. 'When the situation has returned to normal, that is when the king is dead . . . ' (D'Hertefelt and Coupez, 1964:205). Coupez and Kamanzi propose the following explanation: ' . . . if the king ages, Rwanda weakens along with him; the situation becomes normal with the introduction of a young and vigorous successor' (Coupez and Kamanzi, 1970:26). Yet this 'normalisation' seems to follow a ritual plan that regulates the lifespan granted kings according to their position in the dynastic cycle, itself subject to the idea of a progressive loss of vitality in royalty itself. In an earlier book (de Heusch, 1982, Chapter IV), I put forward the following argument. The succession of Rwandan kings was cyclical. One of four dynastic names is given to every king of Rwanda, depending on his position in the cycle. They are Yuhi, Mutara, Kigeri and Mibambwe. The secret ritual code promised the king who began the cycle, as well as his immediate successor, that they would reach a ripe old age. They have specific mystical functions related to the fertility of man and cattle. On the other hand, the Kigeri and Mibambwe kings had a military vocation. Dynastic history teaches that all the sovereigns who ruled under the name Mibambwe either met with a dramatic death or, for various reasons, were graced with the title of 'liberator', like King Ruganzu Bwimba, who voluntarily exposed himself to the enemy to prevent the annexation of Rwanda by a foreign power. This sovereign died in his prime, shortly after recognising the legitimacy of his successor who had just been born. King Mibambwe III died as a 'liberator' from smallpox, after a reign of barely five years; his son of a few months succeeded him.

Taken together, these facts allow us to reconstruct the following 'weltanschauung'. The dynastic cycle has to end with the sacrificial death of the Mibambwe king before the Yuhi King, who is promised a ripe old age, regenerates the life forces of the universe by extinguishing and then relighting the sacred fire for four generations. However, no king can die a natural death. This drama is obscured. The monarch's death is attributed to sorcery. That is why the enthronement rites include a ritual war against the Bukunzi and the sacrifice of an outsider, who suffers the same fate as the sacred monster inside the country. Brought by force to Rwanda, the victim is treated like a damned person, yet his blood is poured on foreign soil, following the very scenario for which the saviour or liberator (*umutabazi*) kings or their representatives volunteer, following the example of Ruganzu Bwimba. The ritual murder that ends the enthronement is, in a way, that of an anti-king.

The Sacrificial Death of a god-king

Besides ancestor worship, many Rwanda practise a cult of possession: the *kubandwa*. Within this mystical kingdom, caste differences between adherents were theoretically abolished (de Heusch, 1982, Chapter V). The cult recognises the sovereign power of a hero totally ignored by dynastic tradition, King Ryangombe, surrounded by his companions, the *imandwa* spirits.

This divine figure is clearly forged from symbolic elements compounding the portrait of two historical sovereigns:[2] on the one hand Gihanga, the cultural hero who brought fertility and prosperity, and on the other Ruganzu Bwimba, the king of sacrifice (de Heusch, 1982:180–94). Like Ruganzu Bwimba the god-king Ryangombe is doomed to a tragic end, which is likened to a voluntary sacrifice. Like Gihanga, the founder of the kingdom, Ryangombe is a great hunter. Let us briefly review their similarities and differences. Gihanga races madly across Rwanda, searching for a distant bride. This matrimonial quest is also a quest to attain terrestrial kingship, the absolute life giving principle. Gihanga, a wandering hunter, finally establishes himself. From the earth he extracts materials for pottery making, and the forge, for which he invented the techniques. Although Ryangombe is also a hunter, he is certainly not a craftsman. The prosperity he promises his followers is not the fruit of a creative labour. The myth at the basis of his cult develops, to an exaggerated degree, the theme of the life giving powers of hunting. A close intimacy with nature is the exclusive source of all the benefits he bestows (much in the manner of a sacred king) upon his faithful. The matrimonial quest characterising Gihanga's wandering becomes *hubris*, lubricity; Ryangombe never settles down.

Among other things, the myth of Ryangombe tells us that hunting, a pursuit he practices excessively, is a threat to cultural order. It is as if the sacred king was completely and dangerously involved with nature, ignoring matrimonial bonds as well as the respect due to women. Ryangombe is particularly impudent with his mother; yet her position within the dynastic order is that of queen, a full co-sovereign. 'King' Ryangombe, disregarding social rules, and known as 'a lover of vaginas', has only three interests: gaming, hunting and sex. This insurgent anarchist does, however, bear a royal title: he is the king of the *imandwa*, the chief of a small band of uncouth and bullying types, who have themselves become helpful spirits: after his tragic end, they follow him to the Afterworld. If we are to believe one version of the myth, Ryangombe was killed by a disturbing female creature, who was doubly monstrous: an unwed mother without breasts who suddenly transformed herself into a raging buffalo. With his dying breath Ryangombe established his own cult, calling upon the Tutsi, Hutu and even the Twa to pay him homage in order to benefit from a prosperity which was often obstructed by the ancestors and which the rites performed by the king were insufficient to materialise.

I have elsewhere analysed at length this strange myth and I only wish to mention here its sacrificial aspect (de Heusch, 1982:196–224). The tragic end of this god, who was a chimerical king, is indeed but a carbon copy of the voluntary 'sacrifice' the historical king Ruganzu Bwimba is supposed to have made of himself in order to save the country (see p. 109). Like him, Ryangombe is hailed as 'liberator' (*umutabazi*).

We are confronted with a spectacular reversal of the sacrificial schema previously presented. We saw how unwed mothers and breastless women were executed at the border as a curse on the enemy. In the myth of Ryangombe, a sacred monster belonging to both these categories becomes an agent of royal sacrifice. By wildly throwing herself upon 'King' Ryangombe, the monstrous woman banishes him from his earthly kingdom thus investing him with sovereignty over the Afterworld. He henceforth rules over a kingdom of shadows from the top of a volcano. However, from this vantage point between sky and earth he is constantly reincarnated by possessing the body of one of his followers who presides over the liturgical ceremonies organised in his honour. Ryangombe's 'sacrifice' inaugurates a new kingdom, while the ritual death of kings or their representatives saves the country from dire peril. In this transformation, an accursed victim (the breastless unwed mother) attacks the very person of the king, the august sacrificial victim. This half-woman-half-animal is in turn cut to pieces by Ryangombe's son, who after his father's death takes on the title of king of the *imandwa*.

Thus the emergence of a god-king in the realm of the imaginery is based on the telescoping of two human sacrifices which present some strange affinities: that of the royal person assuming the role of *umutabazi* and that

[2]I have examined their mythical make-up in another work (1982).

of his monstrous counterpart. The dangerous woman, playing the role of sacrificer before becoming herself the sacrificial victim, lies beyond the cultural sphere and biological normality; she belongs completely to nature, due to her ability to turn into a buffalo. Ryangombe, the hunter-king, is thus the victim of his own excess. Yet it is precisely this exceptional status which permits him to achieve the Frazerian standing of gods who die in order to be reborn. More precisely, Ryangombe is a king who becomes a god through sacrificial death.

This shifting of the sacrificial function assumed by Ruganzu Bwimba leads us to the discovery of a new magico-religious phenomenon. Indeed, Rwanda's 'historical' kings, the magician-kings controlling natural forces with the help of Lightning, 'the king of the sky', are not 'deified'. After their death they are merely powerful ancestors. Ryangombe is not in this category. This ephemeral 'king' of unknown lineage and origin is a helpful god; he communicates directly with his followers by possessing them. The initiates assert that Ryangombe's death freed them from a 'profane' condition. They are sure to join his kingdom, that pagan paradise he set up on top of a volcano.

This doomed god does, however, partake of earthy kingship. He draws upon most of the functions progressively established by the exploits of various sovereigns recorded in the official historical mythology (see the first part of *Rois nés d'un coeur de vache; Kings born of a cow's heart*). Like Gihanga, Ryangombe is responsible for fertility and economic prosperity; like Ruganzu Bwimba he sacrifices himself and through his magical power over nature he surpasses Ruganzu Ndori, the warrior king. Yet unlike the latter, neither Ryangombe nor his companions can boast of the slightest military exploit. This lack also characterises Ruganzu Bwimba, the king of sacrifice, who during a hunt submits to the blows of an adversary. A human victim finds himself treated like a wild animal. All this happens as if this type of sacrifice constituted a third pole, between the hunt (the source of fertility) and war in the symbolic space of Rwanda. These oppositions can be summarized in triangular form (Fig. 18).

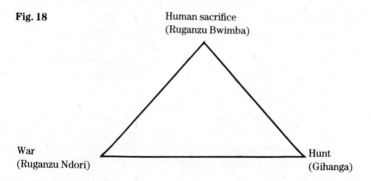

Fig. 18

Human sacrifice
(Ruganzu Bwimba)

War
(Ruganzu Ndori)

Hunt
(Gihanga)

The sacrificial practices of Ryangombe's cult are exceptional. They immolate, according to very particular procedures, the bull-calf, an animal normally reserved for divinatory sacrifices carried out for and in the presence of the king. This pre-emption of the royal animal on behalf of the initiates takes place at night during a strange secret ceremony (d'Hertefelt and Coupez, 1964:295–6; Coupez, 1956:137–151; Arnoux, 1913:123–9). It is accompanied by a change of meaning: the sacrifice of the bull-calf takes on a regenerating function; it is strictly homologous to the sacrificial death of the god himself; as if the animal victim, dead and resurrected, had become his double.

It begins with the presentation of the bull calf to the devotee master of ceremonies, personifying 'king' Ryangombe. Nine times the beast is sprinkled with water whitened with kaolin. It is hacked to death and cut up. D'Hertefelt and Coupez recapitulate the sharing procedure: 'the participants put the head, liver and first stomach aside for the rites of the following night. The front legs, ribs, heart, intestines, tail and genitals are given to specific members of the cult group while a sufficient quantity of meat is cooked for a communal meal' (d'Hertefelt and Coupez, 1964:295). The hide is placed over the skull, back, and hind legs. 'Thus', one of Coupez's informants states, 'it becomes like a living cow' (Coupez, 1956:139). Ryangombe attaches two pieces of meat to his elbows and two to his little fingers (Coupez, 1956:147). His arms outstretched, he then begins a strange march: nine times he tramples over the animal's remains while crossing the enclosure. His first assistant and then the animal's donor, imitate him. A sheep is dragged in and covered with the bull-calf's skin; when the animal frees itself it demonstrates 'the resurrection of things' (Coupez, 1956:143). According to Arnoux, Ryangombe himself topples the sheep and wraps it in the skin; when it stops moving a jug of cold water is poured on it. When it stands up, the audience proclaims 'it is reborn, we have restored its life' (Arnoux, 1913:126). Ryangombe neutralises the evil spirits by throwing the victim's chyme to the cardinal points (d'Hertefelt and Coupez, 1964:295).

The initiates meet again the following night. Ryangombe begins by burying the bull-calf's bones with the remains of the chyme. He is seated on a throne and receives the homage and prayers of his devotees, who hail him as 'the living principle of fertility and prosperity (*imana nzima*) (d'Hertefelt and Coupez, 1964:295). Ryangombe and his followers consume the meat set aside the previous evening: minced liver and first stomach, mixed with the meat from the head. At dawn the horns are buried in a trench full of bull dung (d'Hertefelt and Coupez, 1964:295–6).

Now, the analysis. The central episode of the rite, the solemn march of the officiant, decked in the strips of meat taken from a victim considered to be 'alive' (and soon to be reborn through the intermediary of a sheep) could be compared with Ryangombe's death-rebirth. The rite conforms with the myth, expressing it in sacrificial terms. The initiates constantly re-enact the 'saving' sacrifice by which the hunter-king, always on the move, took over the kingdom of shadows from which he dispensed an abundance of benefits. The sheep, agent for the bull-calf's 'rebirth', fulfils the same function as the ram, charged with pulling the queen mother out from under the ground after the expiatory sacrifice during which she and her son were symbolically put to death. We have already examined the important place of this animal within the symbolic system (see p. 114). It is worth noting here that Ryangombe's myth tells us that his mother, as well as all her companions, committed suicide to join him in the Afterworld. Though the myth is modelled on the edifying sacrifice carried out by king Ruganzu Bwimba, the paradigm of 'liberator' or 'saviour' kings (*umutabazi*), the *kubandwa* ritual evokes the periodic purifying sacrifice performed in public by the sovereigns.

Now Ryangombe does invite devoted subjects to subvert the royal sacrificial code. When possessed they are projected into an imaginary kingdom free of prohibition. The democratic communal meal held by the *kubandwa* sect is itself a radical transformation of the one held at court, in the presence of the king, during divinatory sacrifice.

Let us consider this aspect more thoroughly. Remember that despite the rigorous barrier separating castes, men of all conditions take part in the royal divinatory rite (see p. 114). The cult of 'king' Ryangombe symbolically abolishes the sociopolitical differences. On a strictly equal footing, the initiates take part in the sacrifice of the bull-calf. Even women are allowed to participate in the *kubandwa* ceremonies. Let us compare the sacrificial procedures in these two 'royal' contexts. In the cult of Ryangombe, the calf's hind legs and back are covered with a hide after the carving. The adept incarnating the mystical king tramples this with his feet. In the royal divinatory sacrifice the victim's hide is put back on the viscera after the seance and the king touches the remains (Coupez and Kamanzi, 1962:32). A moving king opposes an immobile king. By attaching the strips of meat to his arms, the first is, in a way, identifying with the animal who is to be reborn; he accomplishes the passage from death to life by his march. The sovereign, for his part, identifies with the bull-calf before immolation by giving it his saliva (Coupez and Kamanzi, 1962:32). The treatment of the internal organs is also reversed. 'King' Ryangombe eats the carefully minced liver and first stomach. In the other rite, after the royal diviners have examined the abdomen and entrails, 'certain pieces' are placed (intact) in a carefully plugged churn; this receptacle is incorporated with the royal treasure. This pre-emption is designated by the expression *jiishuur* meaning 'to untie' (Coupez and Kamanzi, 1962:32). We cannot avoid comparing this intention (however obscure) with the profound meaning of the sacrifice executed by Ryangombe who has tied strips of meat to his arm. His march contributes to the animal's rebirth.

Let us consider another transformation. The followers of *kubandwa* take great care in carving the bull-calf. Not only the liver and first stomach are minced but also each participant must eat a small piece of every part of the animal, including the tongue (Coupez, 1956:139). It is as if the ritual carving contributes to the rebirth—as a whole, intact creature—of the animal decked out in a sheep's skin. This process entails an overall regeneration, 'the resurrection of things'. Concurrently, at the royal court, the burying of the most precious organs in a churn which will be kept with the royal treasure re-enacts, in a certain way, the artificial gestation of Kigwa. The latter was made in the sky from a cow's heart immersed in a jug of milk. It was just after a divinatory seance that this organ was stolen from the officiants by the sterile wife of Lightning, the king of the Heavens (de Heusch, 1982:32). The divinatory rite evoking the celestial birth of the dynasty's ancestor corresponds, in *kubandwa*, to the rite celebrating a king's rebirth as an immortal god, a king who went to meet death because he unwisely left his earthly mother (de Heusch, 1982:200–6). In this connection it is worth noting that the paradigmatic sacrifices of Ruganzu Bwimba and Ryangombe follow the same schema: in both cases the hero breaks the maternal bond by jumping over the belt she placed before the entrance of the house to prevent her son from leaving (de Heusch 1982:204). Ruganzu Bwimba's sacrifice replays in reverse the astonishing birth of the ancestor Kigwa. This fabricated child is born without an umbilical cord; he leaves his unnatural celestial mother and goes into exile on earth. Ruganzu Bwimba, on the other hand, symbolically breaks his terrestrial umbilical cord in order to sacrifice himself in a neighbouring kingdom. I have shown in *Rois nés d'un coeur de vache* (*Kings born of a cow's heart*) that he thus renews ties with the sky, with the celestial womb of the dynasty (de Heusch, 1982:43).

We may conclude that the sacrifice practised by the *kubandwa* sect celebrating the death and rebirth of its king draws it inspiration directly from royal myths and from the royal divinatory sacrifice. Not only is the same victim chosen (a bull-calf) but moreover the procedures followed are related by a process of transformation.

The 'resurrection of things', the actual aim of the sacrifice honouring Ryangombe and in which he is intensely involved, must be understood in a totally pagan sense. Coupez's informant states: 'if it [the thing] is sick, it heals; if it dies it is reborn' (Coupez, 1956:143). We must not forget, however, that by dying Ryangombe established for his followers—and for them alone—a pleasant sojourn in the Afterworld, situated between sky and earth, and in this respect *kubandwa* is a religion of salvation.

Finally, the sacrifice of a bull-calf commemorating the death and rebirth of 'king' Ryangombe has a dénouement comparable to that of the divinatory sacrifice: a part of the victim is set aside to assure the perpetuity of the rite's results. In the second case perishable organs are kept, whereas the *kubandwa* ritual prescribes leaving the bull-calf's horns in a trench filled with bull dung (d'Hertefelt and Coupez, 1964:296). They are 'fathered' by Ryangombe, who sprinkles them twice with water whitened with kaolin. Fixed in the thick layer of dung, they will 'age' and bear witness to the god's goodness (Arnoux, 1913). On the other hand, at the royal court, it is the churn containing the vital organs that is covered with bull dung (Coupez and Kamanzi, 1962:32).

The *kubandwa* democratises in the most radical manner the ritual consumption of the royal divinatory bull-calf, while attributing a more general function to its immolation. In the myth this new ritual is based on a truly symbolic revolution. When Ryangombe accidentally met powerful King Ruganzu Ndori, the two men confronted each other in a long oratory duel. Incapable of rivalling his adversary militarily, he displayed his magical superiority by heaping spells upon the king's warriors. For removing them, he demanded five mother cows, which he immediately sacrificed. He covered himself with their meat and climbed up on their remains (Coupez and Kamanzi, 1962:223–253). In this mythical story, the sacrifice of the *kubandwa* followers is based on a sacrilege. The king always sacrifices a sterile cow to his ancestors, never a cow which has given birth. The same Ruganzu Ndori became enraged when, after having restored the herd's fertility during a particularly dramatic period in the history of Rwanda, he saw a man sacrifice in his honour a cow which was still feeding her calf (Pages, 1933:270). He cut off the culprit's hands so that he could never milk again.

Only the enthronement ritual requires the slaughter of two white cows, nursing, respectively, a calf and a little heifer, to provide skins for the king's personal drums (D'Hertefelt and Coupez, 1964:247). Thus Ryangombe defiantly founds his own ritual practices on a transgression of the rules that govern the court sacrifice. In so doing, he provides his followers with a more effective, mystical counter-royalty. Ryangombe also has the royal divinatory sacrifice make a functional detour. He devotes it wholly to royalty's magical function assuring prosperity and fertility. Consequently, his followers exercise the divinatory function through a new ritual process, possession.

In the eroded hills of Rwanda, where the farmers were often victims of famine, Ryangombe is a troublemaker, just as Dionysus was in the ancient Mediterranean cities. The comparison is not necessarily excessive. In both cases we are dealing with a possession cult which is set up on the fringe of the official ritual system. The Dyonisiac sect runs counter to the sacrificial code used by the City (See p. 20). The *kubandwa* sect takes over and subverts the royal rites. It invites its members, who have broken away from the official royal order, to participate in a truly popular feast, whereas the population is kept at a distance from the great royal rituals, which are generally held in secret. The *kubandwa* initiates have their own secret but anyone can have access to it thanks to an initiation rite that is nothing more than a parody of the enthronement. The followers of *kubandwa* join a new royalty in this 'prodigious effervescence', in which Georges Bataille thought he discovered the profound meaning of 'sacred'. This heretical disciple of Hubert and Mauss enjoyed describing the religious feast and sacrifice as a 'headlong and contagious movement, a consummation for pure glory, which has nothing in common with the vulgar violence of war' (Bataille, 1973:71). The takeover of the royal space by *Ryangombe* and his divine companions, the bull-calf's sacrifice, are partial illustrations of this proposition; yet one cannot forget that here sacrifice is a creative act: the immolated animal, like the dead and reborn god-king, works towards a regeneration of life.

We began our inquiry with the ritual deaths of representatives of wild species, which were associated metaphorically and metonymically with the spirit world (the Lele pangolin) or with a specific divinity (the Zulu hornbill). These 'sacrifices' launched us on a journey leading to the heart of the mystery of sacred royalty. The Kuba king is, in a way, a pangolin but also a dangerous leopard, just as the Swazi king is a rainmaking hornbill but also a lion and a bull. Sacred kings know no limits. In varying degrees, they assume a specific, sacrificial role that is not comparable to the diverse ritual preparations of food in honour of the gods or the ancestors. The death of the pangolin or hornbill is both sacrilegeous and potent, like that of the kings. The death of the Zulu Rainbow Princess, eternal virgin, is, however, just as unthinkable as that of the spirits of nature in the Lele forest. The hornbill and pangolin species which represent them are inexhaustible, as are the royal descendants; far from ending royalty, the sacrifice of a king assures the perpetual regeneration of its power. Frazer's shadow never leaves us.

We shall now turn our attention to West Africa. The theme of the sacrificial death of a demiurge, guarantor of fertility, is at the heart of Dogon myth and ritual practice. In this case, however, it all happens at the beginning of time, when the world was yet to be born.

VI

Sacrifice as the core of myth

An essay on Dogon thought

The Bantu societies we have just studied are not greatly concerned with the origin and formation of the world in which a distant creator placed them. In central Africa the important cosmogonic themes are to be found in the remarkable adventures of the founding heroes of sacred royalty (de Heusch, 1972 and 1982). Yet however rich they are symbolically, these epics, which are basically historical, are in no way comparable to the highly fanciful cosmogenesis developed by the ancient Mande civilisations in West Africa. Among the Dogon and Bambara, these symbolic systems survived the arrival and the rise of Islam.

The great biological, astronomical and historical panorama that constitutes the Dogon myth recounts the difficulties surrounding the creation of man and of the universe after the explosion of the primordial seed. It took years of patience for Marcel Griaule and Germaine Dieterlen to reconstruct this symbolic puzzle from fragments of information and of narrative. These were progressively arranged and structured by the most qualified 'doctors', the guardians of 'limpid speech'. In 1946 the wise man Ogotemmêli, delegated by his peers, introduced Griaule to a first level of knowledge in the course of thirty-three days of discussion (*Dieu d'eau*, 1948). After Griaule's death, Dieterlen, tirelessly continuing this exemplary study, unique in the annals of African ethnography, published a masterly book, *Le Renard pâle* (1965). In this last work Griaule and Dieterlen brilliantly describe the dominant role of sacrifice in the progressive establishment of the Dogon universe. This prodigious myth, which cannot be told briefly, unfolds simultaneously on several levels. At one time I proposed to interpret it as a mythology of the seed and the fish, a mythology of divine ancestors, a mythology of the Blacksmith and historical ancestors (de Heusch, 1971:157–9). Alfred Adler and Michel Cartry undertook, in turn, a reading centred on the themes of unity and fragmentation (Adler and Cartry, 1971). At the risk of offering an oversimplifying schema, I shall now limit myself to the series of sacrificial sequences that constitute so many energising nuclei and essential stages in the complex unfolding of the mythic events.

This scholarly thought was developed and transmitted among a limited group of 'initiates' whom we readily define as theologians. All Dogon have access to it, however, if only by successive stages, the 'knowledge' of it conferring no religious or political power. It does nevertheless illuminate the meaning of the rites that are deeply immersed in the Dogon symbolic universe. For every degree of knowledge there is a correspondingly different version of the myth. From a structuralist's point of view, all the versions merit the same attention as so many transformations of the same system of thought. We shall begin with the succinct description of the richest and most complex version as given in *Le Renard pâle*.

The Dogon Myth (Esoteric Version)

After the failure and destruction of a first creation, developed from a wild seed, God (*Amma*) formulated a new design inside the cosmic egg. He started by 'writing' the universe. He literally drew its blueprint in a series of graphic signs into which he later breathed the Word. He then animated the tiny fonio seed (*Digitaria exilis*) with a vibrating movement. Next he created eight principal seeds on which the eight primordial ancestors would nourish themselves in a world based on agriculture. Amma's egg then transformed itself into a double placenta, foretelling the future division of sky and earth. The first live creature appeared there in the form of a fish, the silurus, a prefiguration of man in a foetal state. Then God created two pairs of androgynous twins dominated by the male principle. The first pair dwell in the upper half of the placenta. Nommo Die ('great Nommo') will stay in the Sky with Amma, whose deputy he is; 'a witness and steward of the Sky's atmosphere, he will be the dispenser of rain ... and the guardian of the spiritual principles of living beings on earth' (Griaule and Dieterlen, 1965:156). Nommo Titiyayne is his assistant. It is he who will assume the role of sacrificer in the ensuing drama. The two male twins in the lower half of the placenta are called, respectively, 'Nommo of the Pond' (or Nommo Semu, the 'sacrificed one') and Ogo. Amma bestowed upon each of these four primordial creatures a corresponding twin sister. But it is as if, at this stage the latter has only a potential existence.

Impatient and presumptuous, Ogo will try to create 'a world for himself' (Adler and Cartry, 1971:50). Upsetting the divine plan, based on twin births, he prematurely tears his placenta and rushes into a space that is still dark. A piece of the placenta tissue which he brought with him becomes the earth. Ogo tries to penetrate it in the hope of finding his twin sister. He thus commits a grave offence, analogous to maternal incest. This union causes the birth of a first race of deformed, monstrous beings, the Yeban, who reproduce through incestuous unions. Ogo rises to the Sky again to try to find the rest of the placenta, i.e., his lost twin sister. Hopeful of repossessing the universe, he manages to steal the white fonio, the germ of the world, and seven other male seeds. However, Amma has kept the corresponding female seeds as well as the sorghum. The agriculture Ogo manages to establish is unsuccessful. Nommo Titiyayne crushes underfoot the first field, which was made from a piece of the placenta, condemning it to rot. But the white fonio's male seed germinates and becomes red, impure. This seed, strictly forbidden to most Dogon, will in future be the cause of many evils.

The offences committed by Ogo, the seed-thief, make a general purification necessary. Amma decides to sacrifice Nommo Semu, Ogo's twin. He starts by dividing in two the four 'corporal souls' of the victim-to-be in order to create 'sexual souls'. Next he instructs Nommo Titiyayne to proceed with the castration. The sacrificer, 'folding the penis over the umbilical cord, slits them both', separating the victim from 'both his placenta and his penis' (Griaule and Dieterlen, 1965:233). Sirius, the first star, 'navel of the world', is born from the castration blood; it is the inverse homologue of the sun, which is formed from the rest of Ogo's placenta. Nommo Semu's genital organ, emptied of its content, is held in reserve; its sperm will fall later on Ogo's dry earth in the form of rain, creating the system of fresh and salt water.

Ogo persists in his solitary revolt. He returns to the sky a second time and approaches his castrated twin. He steals his four 'sexual souls', which he places in his own foreskin. Nommo Titiyayne recovers them by circumcising Ogo with his teeth. Deprived of the physical support of his femininity, permanently separated from his twin sister, Ogo is henceforth doomed to celibacy and sterility. The blood of the wound pollutes Nommo Semu's placenta and causes the appearance of Mars, 'the star of menstruating women'. Later, when men were circumcised, the blood they shed would be considered impure, as if they were menstruating (Griaule and Dieterlen, 1965:249).

Let us consider further these first bloody acts, the preludes to the brutal sacrifice which will follow. Nommo Semu's castration and Ogo's circumcision hold symmetrical positions, as if the second were a weak image of the first. These two procedures are punitive in nature. First, an innocent creature is punished instead of the guilty one. The Dogon allege a shared guilt: 'being of the same essence as Ogo and being his twin, Nommo Semu shared responsibility with him to some extent, and should have at least answered for the theft he allowed to be committed. For this reason the sacrifice was a punishment' (Griaule and Dieterlen, 1965:255). But it is also said that Nommo Semu himself revolted. When Amma ordered Nommo Titiyayne to purify earth by crushing Ogo's placenta, Nommo Semu claimed that this was *his* prerogative because he had been made in the same part of the double placenta as Ogo; it was then that Amma designated him as victim of the reparatory sacrifice (Griaule and Dieterlen, 1965:228).

The birth of Nommo Semu, torn from his placenta as a mutilated being, imposes a painful sense of loss on all future births. This brutal act marks the end of primordial hermaphroditism for 'the victim will be reborn under the aspect of two sexually different beings, man and woman' (Griaule and Dieterlen, 1965:236).

What exactly is the intention of this terrifying God who assails the genitals of a docile victim close at hand, while the true culprit continues to go free, deprived only of his foreskin? The law of the Father, castrator and circumcisor, is even stranger in that by destroying or altering the very principle of reproduction, he assures its functioning. The first elements of space and time (Sun, Sirius, Mars) arose from the tearing of the placenta tissue and the separation of the sexes. This discontinuous universe is born out of violence.

Let us return to our story. After his misadventure, Ogo settles permanently on earth, where Amma has a new punishment in store for him—he deprives him of speech and condemns him to be an animal. Transformed into the Pale Fox, Ogo takes refuge in the wild bush, henceforth his domain. Amma proceeds with the slitting of Nommo's throat. The unfortunate creature is tied to a tree, standing upright in order to prolong his agony; this is the 'punishment' (Griaule and Dieterlen, 1965:285). The tortured prisoner is thirsty and, at his request, Amma allows him to drink from a copper cup. 'Having drunk too much, he vomits a water snake into the cup' (Griaule and Dieterlen, 1965:286). This fabulous animal soon reappears in the myth as a guarantor of agrarian fertility. As the terrestrial avatar of the Nommo who was sacrificed in the sky, he is called *Yuguru*, a word composed of two roots: *yu* (small millet) and *guru* (shell). A play on words contrasts the water snake (*yuguru*) with the Pale Fox (*yurugu*, 'thief of millet') (Griaule and Dieterlen, 1965). Indeed, 'both on earth and in the water, the sacrificed Nommo will be the protector of seeds, "Amma's sperm", and will oppose the one who stole them from the creator' (Griaule and Dieterlen, 1965).

The agony continues. The blood gushing from the slit throat is called 'the menses of the earth'. While losing his own vital power, the sacrificed entity rids the universe of all impurity; he 'makes it drink' (Griaule and Dieterlen, 1965:287). This blood with its strange properties, flows 'like a torrent in a valley' and brings about the appearance of new stars. Amma, using the body of the sacrificial victim, then resumes the work he first began in connection with the infinitely small: he takes out seven internal organs, corresponding to the seven vibrations of the primordial fonio seed. He determines, in this way, 'the morphology of a spatial universe of which the resuscitated victim will become the master and steward'. He finishes dismembering the victim and hurls the parts in the four directions, thus achieving the purification of the Fox's earth. He makes 'Nommo's body pass into the world'. Now all he has to do is gather up the organs in order to assure his 'resurrection' as one pair of mixed twins. Biological evolution is then finished. It has gone from 'the fish stage to the human stage, and from the hermaphrodite stage to the sexually differentiated stage' (Adler and Cartry, 1971:56).

The second part of the mythic tale begins. It describes the descent from the sky to the earth of the eight ancestors of humanity (four male twins accompanied by their respective twin sisters). They were placed on an ark made of pure soil, in the centre of which stood the reborn Nommo Semu, their 'father'. Made of a soft and moist substance like the original placenta, the ark struck against the Fox's impure earth. The sky closed up and the sun rose for the first time. Nommo's sperm, which had been put aside after the castration, fell in the form of rain, making the first pond. Nommo went to live there, resuming his primitive, silurean form. The Fox ran away to a cave to escape from his twin. Next the castes' ancestors descended from the sky; first the Blacksmith, Nommo's twin, then the Griot and the Shoemaker, with their twin sisters.

It was not long before the celestial sacrifice which made possible the creation of the world is re-enacted on earth. The four male ancestors, Amma Seru, Lebe Seru, Binu Seru and Dyongu Seru and their twin sisters, were created immortal. Each one was a 'witness' for one of the four demiurges who appeared in the original double placenta. Fig 19 shows

Fig. 19

Amma Seru:	Witness for Nommo Die
Lebe Seru:	Witness for Nommo Titiyayne
Binu Seru:	Witness for the sacrificed Nommo
Dyongu Seru:	Witness for Ogo

these relationships (Griaule and Dieterlen, 1965:374). Lebu Seru, who was responsible for agriculture on the earth, purified by the celestial sacrificer Nommo Titiyayne, sowed the first collective field. But he was soon guilty of a transgression 'which endangered the integrity of the grains, fields and the entire society' (Griaule and Dieterlen, 1965:422). In various articles and discussions, Dieterlen comments on this new transgression which is parallel to the one committed by Ogo in the sky. Lebe Seru tried to set apart the impure soil created by Ogo (Dieterlen, 1957:117). (Let us remember that the latter had succeeded in making impure, red fonio grow there.) It so happened that Ogo's twin sister, Yasigui, descended to earth in human form under cover of a solar eclipse (Dieterlen, 1982:19), married Lebe Seru. She ate the harvested fonio crop and treacherously made her husband eat it too. Now impure, her husband was sacrificed by his brothers (Dieterlen 1957:118). With his blood gone he lost his spiritual principles. Unlike Nommo his body was not dismembered, but laid out on the field with the head shaved. For three days the Blacksmith beat his anvil to bring him back to life. Two snakes, Lebe Seru's avatars, appeared. They made a long journey. The first one finally settled in the house of Amma Seru, the eldest; the second chose to stay in the uncultivated part of the ritual field. This is how Amma Seru becomes the first religious chief (*hogon*) of the Dogon. He takes charge of the agrarian cult in honour of Lebe Seru, the first terrestrial sacrificial victim.

A "Blacksmith" version of the sacrificial myth

Griaule recorded a somewhat different version of this last episode during his discussions with Ogotemméli (Griaule, 1948). This account, which can rightly be considered a variant of the esoteric version, should not be overlooked. It brings together, in a single person presented as the seventh of the eight Ancestors, the features characteristic of the myth's various heroes: Ogo, as thief of the seeds, Nommo as sacrificial victim and Lebe as serpent. Ogotemméli also transposes the metaphysic of sacrifice into a sociological code. Conflict between the older and younger brothers—even the quest for power—appears as a last resort. Moreover he presents a 'Blacksmith' version of the myth.

In *Le Renard pâle*, the Blacksmith plays only a subordinate role. He appears on earth after the eight Farmer Ancestors. *Dieu d'eau* ('The water god'), on the other hand, gives him the leading role. On the celestial ark this craftsman has the central position of Nommo. He is also represented as the eldest; he leaves first, followed by the other seven Ancestors (Griaule, 1948:56). It is then that the incident which causes the sacrifice takes place. The eighth Ancestor, upsetting the order of precedence, descended before the seventh, 'Master of the Word'. The latter was angered and, once on the ground, 'turned against the others; he became a big serpent and rushed to the granary to steal the seeds'.The Blacksmith advised his brothers 'to kill the snake, eat it and give him the head', suggesting this anthropophagic killing 'both to get rid of an adversary and to continue God's grand design' (Griaule, 1948:57). The Blacksmith buried the head under the anvil.

This variant introduces a major conflict between the Blacksmith, considered to be the eldest of the Ancestors, and a young one (the seventh), who finds himself ridiculed by his younger brother (the eighth). The seventh seizes the granary. A struggle for power follows and the Blacksmith triumphs. Ogotemméli also mentioned a conflict that would put the Blacksmith in direct opposition to the seventh Ancestor for possession of the seeds. According to this variant, the Blacksmith had them, and his rival broke the bellows skin of the forge in order to scatter the seeds (Griaule, 1948:57).

Now let us consult *Le Renard pâle*. There we find that the Blacksmith descended to earth at the head of the castes, after the arrival of the eight Ancestors and the resuscitated Nommo. The latter, and not the Blacksmith, takes possession of the ground by setting his left foot on it (Griaule and Dieterlen, 1965:441). The Blacksmith, although he is the 'twin of the sacrificed one' (born of the victim's umbilical cord) arrived later, accompanied by his own twin sister and that of Nommo (Griaule and Dieterlen, 1965:446, 489). As to control of the seeds, two contradictory versions are proposed. On the one hand it is asserted that each of the eight Ancestors received one of the cultivated seeds from God (Griaule and Dieterlen, 1965:421, 429); on the other it is said that the Blacksmith brought the cereals in his sledgehammer, and that their souls 'would come and place themselves momentarily in the iron hoe' (Griaule and Dieterlen, 1965:378). A third text confirms this exegesis, which favours the pre-eminence of the Blacksmith over the terrestrial ancestors: 'As Nommo's twin', he belongs to the generation of 'fathers'; it is he who brings the seeds to man (Dieterlen, 1976b:262).

These differences, these variations of the sociological code, no doubt reveal a quarrel over the Blacksmith's social and political status. His eminent role in the cycle of production, as furnisher of hoes, is attested by the title given him, 'Master of the Dogon' (Dieterlen, 1976b:263), even though the true political and religious chief is the Hogon. This role was first assumed by the elder of the ancestors, Amma Seru (and not by the Blacksmith) (Dieterlen, 1957:118).

The account proposed by Ogotemmêli implies an attempted taking of power by the Blacksmith, who is likened to both Nommo and the eldest of the Ancestors. Though the second title may be somewhat doubtful, no one, on the other hand, questions that the Blacksmith has the same nature as Nommo. It is said that he received half of Nommo's 'corporal souls' or that he possesses the latter's male soul. The resuscitated victim only has a female soul (Griaule and Dieterlen, 1965:376–7). Like the twins, the Blacksmith is, in other respects, endowed with an ontological status richer than that of the farmers, for his collarbones contain 'a double endowment of seeds'; this characteristic allows him to take part in a certain number of rites, 'the purpose of all of them being to increase the returns, the wealth, and the prosperity of commerce and barter' (Dieterlen, 1973:211). All blacksmiths claim their due, their 'tribute' from the farmers at harvest time (Griaule, 1948:106).

Let us finish this sociological digression and return to Ogotemmêli's account. If the Blacksmith is the instigator of the sacrifice of the seventh Ancestor, Master of the Word, then the myth does not describe a political assassination. The decapitation and dismemberment of the victim's body constitutes the terrestrial duplication of the Nommo's castration and dismemberment, which was carried out in the sky on God's orders. Ogotemmêli specifies that the seventh Ancestor could not die since he was

Nommo (Griaule, 1948:61). His resurrection is only held in suspense. Ogotemméli has this event coincide with the rebirth of Lebe Seru, as if there had only been one sacrifice. He presents the ancestor Lebe as an old man, descendant of the eighth Ancestor. He appeared to die, but at that time man was immortal (Griaule, 1948:61). His body was buried in the primordial field. When the Blacksmith filled the air with the ringing of his anvil, the previously sacrificed seventh Ancestor reappeared as the Nommo genie; half snake below, half man above. He 'swam the first dance' right up to the old man's grave. He entered it, swallowing the body in order to regenerate it, and vomited a torrent of water. The bones were transformed into coloured stones which he laid out in the form of a skeleton. Later, when men decided to emigrate, they opened Lebe's grave and discovered there 'the system of stones vomited by the seventh Nommo and this genie himself in the form of a snake' (Griaule, 1948:71). The totemic priests henceforth wore these stones around their necks. The body of the second sacrificial victim (Lebe), closely associated with the immortal body of the first (Nommo), serves as a foundation for the organisation of human society and the division of totemic clans, just as Nommo's body, cosmogonically, symbolises the passage from primordial unity to sexual division and then to the multiplicity of the categories in the universe. In *Le Renard pâle*, it is the sacrifice of the celestial Nommo itself which is linked with the constituent elements of the social body. 'Each clan is associated with one of the parts of the body which was cut into pieces; all of them together constitute the whole resuscitated body' (Griaule and Dieterlen, 1965:25).

Let us put these two versions into perspective. In Ogotemméli's account, the sacrifice and dismemberment of the mysterious seventh Ancestor is none other than that of the celestial Nommo, who assumed responsibility for the deeds of his twin Ogo, thief of the seeds. Ogo is presented in the veiled image of the eighth Ancestor. Does he not leave the ark before his elder brother, just as Ogo, the abusive elder, abandoned his placenta before Nommo did? And was not Nommo sacrificed instead of Ogo, the true culprit, just as the seventh was, whereas it is the eighth who was impatient? The second sacrifice, that of Lebe Seru, is eliminated by Ogotemméli; only the mutual rebirth of Nommo (the seventh Ancestor, the Master of the Word) and of a 'descendant' of the eighth Ancestor, called Lebe, remain. In short, *Dieu d'eau* proposes a syncretic version of the two successive purificatory sacrifices. Ogotemméli insists on their total unity. At planting time, the Dogon worship both Nommo and Lebe Seru. They start by sacrificing a goat on Lebe's altar and declaiming: 'May Nommo and Lebe never cease to be the same good thing, may they never separate themselves from the state of being the same thing' (Griaule 1948:73).

Actually the sacrifice's of Nommo and of Lebe take on complementary roles. The first serves a cosmogonic purpose; it creates the universal machine and starts it up; the second ensures the fertility of the soil. Lebe Seru was, in fact, 'originally responsible for the integrity of cultivated land' (Griaule and Dieterlen, 1965:25).

A first attempt to interpret the sacrifice

The sacrifice of Nommo must be perceived from a double perspective— that of an offence on the one hand, that of a loss on the other. We shall see that these two aspects are linked. The bursting of the primordial egg, i.e. the birth of the world, is marked by a double, tragic rupture—first, the one which Ogo initiated, then the one of which Nommo is the victim at the very instant of his birth. Nommo is responsible for the impulse of his twin, Ogo, who transgressed by carrying out the first act of separation, his tearing away from the placenta.

It is not easy to grasp the meaning of this original 'offence' in all its nuances. Ogo is, like Nommo, androgynous with the male dominant. He prematurely split from his placenta before Amma could finish the creation of his twin sister: she was not to be given to him until his birth (Griaule & Dieterlen, 1965:175). Ogo wishes to be a creator, and does not accept being a created being (Adler & Cartry, 1971:950). He hopes to find his twin sister in the piece of placenta he stole to make the earth. Then he commits a grave fault since, in a certain manner, he has lain with his mother. He goes back up to the sky in the vain hope of recovering his lost twin sister. He got hold of the seeds '*id est* his father's sperm' (Adler & Cartry, 1971:51). Later he stole the Nommo's 'sex-souls' and placed them in his foreskin in order to reappropriate the fertilising power of which he had deprived himself. Circumcised by way of 'punishment', he permanently lost his feminine part. Henceforth, the twin sister God had destined for him is definitively out of his reach. Henceforth Ogo is defined as the first 'individual'. His solitude is absolute. A sterile, voiceless male, he wanders through the bush as a Fox. He did however leave on the earth the first mark of civilisation, the cultivation of red fonio.

Nommo's sacrificial destiny is to slow down, to some extent, this dizzying fall, this brutal passage from the harmonious unity represented by androgyny and 'twinness' to the sterile solitude of masculinity. From this point of view, sacrifice establishes a mediation: the sacrificed Nommo loses his androgyny, but not his twin sister. The ancestors who proceed from him will themselves form pairs of mixed twins. The only prohibition separating them is that of incest: each pair exchanges one member with the other. Man's ideal marriage with his own female counterpart is henceforth impossible (Dieterlen, 1957; de Heusch, 1978). The fate of Yasigui, the Fox's twin, is stranger still. Descending very late upon earth, she was to overturn the matrimonial rule established by God by successively marrying Lebe Seru, Dyongu Seru and Binu Seru. Adler and Cartry clearly perceive that

Yasigui is the first extra woman, the one 'whose mere presence upsets the law of the *tête à tête*, of each male linked with his twin sister' (Adler & Cartry, 1971:25).

Nommo's primordial sacrifice is steeped in guilt. It is a 'punishment', a 'purification', a reminder of the Father's law. For Ogo's initial act, joining with a part of his placenta which created the earth, is likened to incest. This first level of interpretation, which has been noted by Griaule and Dieterlen, cannot be questioned. However, Adler and Cartry point out that the analysis cannot stop there. Ogo wished to create a world for himself. What we call incest may be only the 'disguised representation' of an absolute excess which is expressed by that 'look behind the veil, the envelope of the placenta' (Adler and Cartry, 1971:19). But does not this desire to control the entire universe also characterise the project of a sacred royalty which is so often established around the incestuous figure? We shall have to ask whether Ogo is not, in the myth, a failed and dethroned king whose circumcision is but an aborted sacrifice, inseparable from the sacrifice-castration of his twin. The latter is ultimately called upon to assume the quasi-royal role of Master of the Word, of germination and fertility, in a regenerated universe.

Now let us turn to Ogo's positive aspects. His incestuous impulse is creative. It accomplished the separation of earth and sky, foreshadowed in the division of the placenta into two. This urge of Ogo's precipitated the birth of the world. Of course the impulsion was already present in the vibrations of that microcosm, the original fonio seed. Yet it is the supreme transgression by Ogo, a rebel against the father's law and plan, which realises it. While the universe is still in gestation, Ogo travels around it and manages to imitate 'Amma's spiral-vibratory movement' (Griaule and Dieterlen, 1965:179). The restlessness of Ogo, the first troublemaker, only points up the empirical evidence that life is tension, conflict, desire, rupture. This eagerness, this ferment of disorder—life—this urge which possesses Ogo can in no way be likened to the Christian principle of evil. 'One must never forget', Dieterlen comments discerningly, 'that the Fox is an agent of exploration and of development' (Dieterlen, 1976c:85). Ogo's bold stroke induced God to 'follow the trend', so to speak. By sacrificing his innocent and passive double, Amma dramatically introduced the principle of differentiation into the biological, cosmogonic, and social schema with extraordinary violence. From this point of view, sacrifice appears to be less a punishment than a vital necessity. It is the price paid so that the signs of difference inscribed in the primordial egg are brought into being, so that the passage from the 'one' to the 'many' takes place. Nommo's sacrifice truly brings about the birth of a discontinuous world, in which every being is committed first to a sexual identity, then to a social one.

Castration, circumcision and menstrual blood

However, an enigma arises here. The androgynous Nommo is reborn as a man (*vir*) with a twin sister. Yet, if it was only a matter of suppressing the femininity of the dominantly male Nommo, why castrate him? The question of masculinity and femininity is crucial[1].

Germaine Dieterlen believes that the answer is clear: the castration of the androgynous Nommo also affected the clitoris; he would therefore be, properly speaking, asexual (personal communication). But the clitoris is, itself, the organ of woman's masculine principle, the obstacle to procreation (see below). For my part, I have concluded that the androgyn has indeed been radically feminised. Obviously I thus depart from the explicit Dogon dogma, according to which God keeps the kernels of the testicles in reserve so that later on the first rain will gush from them. But it is as if there were an unspoken message in this cosmogonic commentary. In order for the world to be set in place, for the mediating rain to be established between the sky and the dry earth, for the sexes to be separated and distinct, God begins by tearing out all the male organs from the body of Nommo, the agent of differentiation.

A curious commentary by the Dogon recorded by Griaule and Dieterlen is a clear affirmation that the castrated Nommo is a *feminised* creature. When he was resuscitated, 'Amma gave him only his female soul', keeping the male soul for the Blacksmith (Griaule and Dieterlen, 1965:376–7).

Once again the mysterious Blacksmith is back, this time because of his overwhelming masculinity. He sprang from the umbilical cord of the victim, whose penis was severed at the same time. He came to earth with the latter's penis and testicles, which he used to make the pipe and bellows of the first forge. The Blacksmith, Nommo's twin, in fact appears to be the *male counterpart* of the feminised Nommo. Does not one of the versions of the myth go so far as to substitute him for the resuscitated Nommo on the celestial ark? The contradiction between the two versions of the ark's descent melts away if one concedes that the sacrificed androgyn is transformed into a woman and is deprived of his male potency in favour of the Blacksmith. Otherwise, we cannot understand why castration would constitute the inaugural act of sacrifice. Commenting on the transfer of the sacrifice victim's male soul into the body of his 'twin', the Blacksmith, Griaule and Dieterlen write: 'Thus the Nommo demonstrates that with a female soul he is, nevertheless, all-powerful' (Griaule and Dieterlen, 1965:377).

However, this incidental remark points up the entire problematic with regard to sacrifice. It is as if the sacrificed androgynous Nommo could not undertake the creation of the world without acquiring the reproductive power of woman. Even though Nommo is called the 'father' of the first ancestors, no trace of sexual union with his twin sister Yasa can be found. She is not even on the ark with her brother. Significantly, she will descend

---

[1] It was treated from another viewpoint by Danuta Liberski, in an unpublished thesis (1978).

to earth later, with the Blacksmith who is accompanied by his own twin sister (Dieterlen, 1957:110). Yasa's fate is most curious. The Blacksmith cuts her arm to make a hammer and he also severs her hand to use it as tongs (Dieterlen, 1981:432). However, according to an even more indelicate version (personal communication by G. Dieterlen) the Blacksmith places Yasa's severed hand on the outside of the blast pipe. Thus Yasa masturbates her brother's castrated male penis to activate the forge's fire. When the Blacksmith strikes the iron, the two great Nommo genies left in the sky mate; the hammer represents the male genie, the anvil the female genie (Griaule, 1948:103). The complementary couple formed by the sacrified Nommo and his twin sister intervenes in this sexual process in a very strange way: through the contact of a severed hand and a severed penis. This extraordinary metonymical figure tickles the imagination. In any case it suggests that the Blacksmith is the great manipulator of the sacrificial victim's sexual organs. Even after having resumed their initial form as fish, Nommo and Yasa do not live together. The former stays in a pond formed by the first rain, the latter in a deep hole formed by the fall of the primordial anvil and filled with water (Dieterlen, 1982:19).

If we take all the implications of Nommo's castration seriously, one of Ogotemmêli's strange declarations becomes clear. In the series of terrestrial ancestors, the seventh and eighth, he asserts, are feminine (Griaule, 1948:75). Now the seventh Ancestor underwent a sacrificial fate similar to that of Nommo, whom he truly embodies. The seventh is the 'Master of Words; he is the Master of the World, capable of doing all things' (Griaule, 1948:72). As for Lebe, the second sacrificial victim, 'he is a new word created by two women' (Griaule, 1948:75). In order to understand this enigmatic text, we must realise that the Dogon liken birth, like germination, to verbal expression, 'an externalisation of the Word' (Dieterlen, 1973:218). But the Nommo-snake, who ensures Lebe's rebirth, is none other than the seventh Ancestor who, Ogotemmêli states elsewhere, is a woman. Lebe himself is descended from a woman, the eighth Ancestor. In a study published a year before *Dieu d'eau*, Griaule confidently wrote that the seventh Ancestor, who later became the water genie, was female, and that the eighth was 'made of two twin femininities' (Griaule, 1947a:450).

We conclude that the feminisation of the two last ancestors, those who play a crucial role in the version of the sacrifice proposed by Ogotemmêli, is only a way of disguising the transformation of the celestial Nommo into a female creature, a procedure which can be discerned in the account of the castration in *Le Renard pâle*. An observation by Calame-Griaule confirms this interpretation. Even though Nommo is always depicted in the form of an androgyn, or of a pair of twins, the Dogon say that he possesses a special female aspect (Calame-Griaule, 1962:91).

A further mythic preoccupation is clarified by this perspective—the repeated reference to menstrual blood. Nommo's castration makes 'bad blood' shoot forth, blood that is likened to menses that prevent the formation of a child. However, it flows over the original placenta and vivifies it (Griaule and Dieterlen, 1965:234–5). The blood from throat-slitting, called 'menses of the earth', contains 'the life of the world' (Griaule and Dieterlen, 1965:286). Sacrifice is, then, a beneficent cosmic menstruation. On the other hand, the blood of Ogo's circumcision falls on the placenta at the spot where the wave of blood released by Nommo's castration stopped. It gives birth to Mars, 'the star of menstruating women', visible on earth during the first menses of Yasigui, the Fox's twin, (Griaule and Dieterlen, 1965:248–9). The blood of the circumcision thus extends the 'bad blood' of the castration. Both are related to sterility. Griaule and Dieterlen recall in this connection that the circumcision rite will later assimilate men and impure (menstruating) women. They do not, however, comment on the strange ambiguity with which the latter are invested in Dogon thought. Let us take the risk of interpreting it by introducing the opposing values that the myth gives to the original placenta itself.

The Dogon position on this is astonishing. The splitting of Ogo's placenta introduces the opposition between sterility and fecundity. The part of it he seizes is the very substance of the original earth; imperfect, impure. From the second part Amma created the sun, which he placed beyond the rebel's reach. In fact he placed this burning tissue beneath Nommo's moist placenta at the precise moment of the latter's birth-castration. Thus the encounter of the Sun and Sirius was accomplished for the first time (Griaule and Dieterlen, 1965:235). The original placenta contained the power of the four elements, but a new stage is reached here: the obvious differentiation between fire and water. It may well be this primordial state of living matter which the Dogon refer to when they maintain that blood, as the source of life, contains these fundamental but opposed elements[2]. The earth just created by Ogo with a piece of placenta quickly lost its humidity: it became 'sandy and heavy' (Griaule and Dieterlen, 1965:185). Ogo burrowed into it, vainly searching for his lost twin sister. When he returned to the sky, he approached the rest of his celestial placenta and burnt his hand on it. He nevertheless succeeded in tearing off a small piece in which he hid the stolen cereals (Griaule and Dieterlen, 1965:200–01) Returning to earth, he sowed the seeds. But God ordered two insects to empty this first field. The ant gathered up seven of the eight seeds, leaving only the fonio, while the termite dried up the holes in which they had been planted.

In the course of these various vicissitudes it is apparent that Ogo's earth, which had retained some of the moisture of the original placenta from which it emerged, is doomed to drought. In order to complete this process, Nommo Titiyayne, the sacrificer, stamps out the rest of the moist placenta

---

[2]This hypothesis is in reply to a question posed by Germaine Dieterlen in the course of a conversation.

in which the fonio had been planted. But that unique seed will germinate 'in spite of the efforts to prevent it, in the placenta's putrefaction and its bloody moisture'. After that, the earth 'dried out and became progressively arid and sterile' (Griaule and Dieterlen, 1965:200). Paralleling this, when God condemns Ogo to take the form of the Fox, the sun's heat 'burns' him, 'in order to keep him from acting, to dry him out'. Ogo's fate, then, is to pass from the moist to the dry, from the cultivated area to that of the bush and the night. In effect, the Fox is forever fleeing the sun (Dieterlen, personal communication). Conversely, Nommo's action brings about the harmonious synthesis of water and celestial fire: 'the sun's rays, as "placenta blood", will act upon the seeds that are planted in the ground and watered by the rain, and will develop agriculture and the growth of vegetation' (Griaule and Dieterlen, 1965:200).

Let us pause to consider this moist and bloody placenta which constitutes the first cultivated field, doomed to decay. In wiping it out, Nommo Titiyane, the executor of God's great deeds, introduces into it the seed of death (see below). Now this placenta, in the process of decay, resembles menstrual blood. The first signifies the suppression of fertility, the second that of procreation, of female fecundity. The voice of the Fox, a sterile creature, is described as 'rotten', like 'the tone of voice of menstruating women' Calame-Griaule, 1965:55). The category of 'rottenness' thus allows the Dogon to associate menstrual blood, the debasement of the placenta, and drying up. Cosmogonically, the 'rottenness' results from the disappearance of water. Biologically, 'rottenness' is the negation of reproduction.

In this anthropo-cosmogony menstrual blood holds a key position. It allows Dogon thought to surmount the opposition between sterility and fertility introduced by the Fox's deeds. This theme runs through sacrificial speculation. Let us consider, successively, the two aspects of the killing of Nommo. The castration released a first flux likened to menstrual or 'bad blood', because it bars reproduction. Yet in this tragic moment Nommo recuperated the solar part of Ogo's placenta; the blood flows on this double fertile placenta. Subsequently, the slitting of the victim's throat caused the discharge of a second flux 'compared with the menses which precede procreation' (Griaule & Dieterlen, 1965:286). Sacrifice as manipulation of the genitals and the throat constitutes, in a certain way, the dialectic reversal of menstruation, the transformation of sterility into fertility. This is why the myth ends with the victim's rebirth. After his resurrection Nommo, starting his descent, literally took possession of the sun. He approached it, touched it and became 'red as fire' (Griaule and Dieterlen, 1965:441). When the ark landed on earth, at night—the dry earth of the Fox—it raised a whirlwind of dust. Immediately thereafter, the sun rose for the first time. Its rising and its setting testify to 'Nommo's presence on the Fox's earth' (Griaule and Dieterlen, 1965:441). Three days later, the rain fell. Then the ark started to slide over the mud, and Nommo, changed into a horse, pulled it like a canoe towards the first pond (Dieterlen, personal communication; see also Griaule and Dieterlen, 1965:444). The earth was ready for the cultivation which the ancestors will undertake.

Sacrifice has remedied the dramatic disjunction of the sky and the earth, brought on by the Fox's haste: 'the sun and the earth became twins' (Griaule and Dieterlen, 1965:198). Nommo's castration-menstruation is a symmetrical and inverse figure of Ogo's circumcision. The latter kept his penis but, deprived of his foreskin, he was literally incapable of pursuing the creative project he had undertaken using his own placenta, *id est* his own feminine part. Indeed, to the Dogon the prepuce is the locus of femininity in the male child; he remains a kind of androgyn, an ambiguous entity, before the ritual wound establishes him in his own sex group (Griaule, 1948, chapter 24). Men and women have 'sexual souls'; these eight spiritual principles (*kikinu*) are grouped in twin couples of opposite sex. Thus two masculine 'sexual souls' correspond to two female, and it is the same for 'corporal souls' (Calame-Griaule, 1965:36). The four sexual *kikinu* are divide into a pair called 'intelligent' and another pair called 'stupid'. The sexual *kikinu* 'intelligent male' and its female counterpart live in the pancreas which governs 'the physical and affective harmony between men and women' (Calame-Griaule, 1965: 37). On the other hand the locus of the two 'stupid' sexual *kikinu*, male and female, is the sexual organ itself, and their action is related to the spleen. It is apparently upon these two principles that circumcision and excision act, reducing respectively man's femininity and woman's masculinity (Calame-Griaule, 1965: 40). As noted by Liberski, these two homologous operations do not suppress fundamental androgyny (Liberski, 1978). We should particularly note that every man (*vir*) always keeps with him his 'intelligent' and 'male' *kikinu* whereas his 'intelligent' and 'female' *kikinu* is 'kept reserved in the waters of the family pond'; the pattern is reversed for the woman (Calame-Griaule, 1965:38).

However, Ogo's circumcision presents a more radical aspect. Our hero had placed the four 'sex-souls' he had stolen from Nommo in his foreskin. Circumcised, he is permanently sterile. He is condemned to celibacy, whereas the circumcision rite, on the contrary, opens the way to exogamic marriage for mankind. In other words, far from foreshadowing the rite, the myth reverses its meaning. Yet, even stranger, Nommo's castration confers upon him the reproductive power of which Ogo is deprived, whereas this radical ablation would seem to be the very negation of it.

The fundamental opposition of the myth can be summarised in Fig. 20.

Fig. 20

Ogo	*Nommo*
Sterile male	Fertile woman

In the myth the circumcision appears, then, as a failed sacrifice. Mars, the planet of menstruating women, sprang from Ogo's wound. Let us construct a simple geometrical figure to illustrate this symbolic language. Starting with menstrual blood, we trace two axes: that of fertility, renewal of life, on one side; that of sterility on the other. Sacrifice will be placed on the first axis; circumcision on the second. The last two points are joined to form a triangle (Fig. 21).

Fig. 21

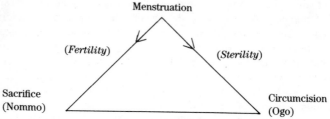

Rooted in the primordial and ambivalent image of menstruation, sacrifice and circumcision are, from various points of view, opposed to each other. Sacrifice, a total annihilation of being, causes the dismemberment of an androgynous body and its rebirth in an immortal twin body, symbol of fertility. Circumcision, a partial loss, is in the myth a radical separation of the twin couple, an affirmation of masculine sterility.

Yet the same operation carried out upon children on the threshold of adolescence, shares henceforth in sacrifice; it is no longer a failed act. Ogotemmêli states it clearly: 'The flow of the circumcision blood is comparable to the offering of a victim upon the altar. And it is the earth who comes to drink' (Griaule, 1948:188). This blood is also called 'men's menses' (Griaule & Dieterlen, 1965:249).

The ritual of circumcision brings together the characteristics of menstruation and sacrifice. It blurs the dividing lines within the myth; indeed it narrows the gap that the myth had dug between Ogo and Nommo. The rite also inverts the dialectic of the myth. The ablation of the foreskin forever separates Ogo from any feminine complement whereas the preliminary act of sacrifice (castration) deprives Nommo of his virility. As for the circumcised youths, they find their femininity relegated to the background in order to acquire the full reproductive force of masculinity. Their temporary assimilation to menstruating women refers to the symbolic common denominator of circumcision and sacrifice. But the opposition between fertility and sterility is overcome.

The Dogon present the clitoral excision of girls as a concept which is homologous and symmetrical to the circumcision of boys (Griaule, 1948,

Chapter 24). We should complete the preceding schema by adding a supplementary triangle (represented by dashes) (Fig. 22).

Fig. 22

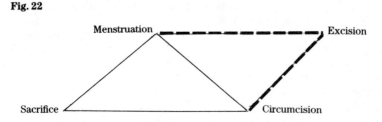

Let us explore the relations between excision, menstruation and circumcision set up by the myth.

It is remarkable that feminine mutilation is practically ignored in the canonic version of the myth found in *Le Renard pâle*. All we learn is that it was practised for the first time on the sun, which constitutes the 'good' part of Ogo's placenta (Griaule and Dieterlen, 1965:250). Its severed foreskin was metamorphosed into a lizard which settled on the female star. This animal, which shared Ogo's aggressiveness, circumcised the sun. It all happened as if this were the Fox's vengeance, following the circumcision.

On the other hand, in *Dieu d'eau* Ogotemmêli presents excision as the inaugural act of creation. In this version of the myth, God is cast as a technician. He becomes a potter in order to fashion a roll of clay into a woman-earth. Her genitals were made of an anthill. However a clitoris termite-mound barred the entry. God knocked it down. From this imperfect, 'defective' union was born the Pale Fox. Nommo covered the earth's genitals with a skirt of fibres full of water and 'words'. Yet the Fox, 'the deceived and deceitful son of god' wished to possess his mother. He penetrated the termite-mound and the fibres were tinted by menstrual blood. It is thus that the earth became impure (Griaule 1948:24–31).[3] In a complementary note in another essay Griaule associates the origin of circumcision with these events. It is the mother earth's vagina which had 'kept [the fox's] female soul as if it had teeth, as if it had cut off the foreskin, the support of this soul' (Griaule, 1947a:447).

From this mythic perspective, the sexually excised Earth, deprived of its maleness,[4] also performs the first male circumcision while she herself undergoes her first menstruation. These three bloody manifestations appear in a single diachronic sequence under the sign of the Fox. The sequence of events is reversed in the 'celestial' version of the myth.

---

[3] In *Dieu d'eau*, Griaule mistakenly identified the fox as a jackal. This error was corrected later.

[4] The clitoris symbolises her masculinity (Griaule, 1947a:447).

Nommo's sacrifice-menstruation takes place first; it is followed by Ogo's circumcision, which itself is the cause of the sun's sexual excision.

Despite this primordial androgyny, the Dogon do not consider the male principle and the female principle to be on the same level; these two principles are graded in rank, as Calame-Griaule so aptly noted (1965).[5] We should note, however, that the apparent superiority of men is contradicted on several occasions. The sovereign God, the father figure, castrates one of his sons so that he may give birth to a purified universe, rid of the disorder introduced by the total male, Ogo the Fox. Circumcision, which partakes of sacrifice,is the ransom paid to femininity; it is men's menstruation. Contrary to male chauvinist appearances, despite the 'quarrel between the Sky and the Earth' and the final submission of the latter to the former (Griaule, 1938:55–8), Dogon myth credits woman with phenomenal power, symbolised by menstruation.

While sacrifice proclaims the absolute supremacy of the female principle in the act of world creation (a truly bloody lying-in), the excision of the clitoris takes Earth's masculine power away from her. It is indeed in terms of power that Griaule comments on this event. The presence of the termite-mound clitoris obstructs God's (male) sexual desire; but God 'emerges as victor from this contest . . . : he does away with the *rebellious* [my emphasis] termite-mound'. Later, the excised earth undergoes the assault of her incestuous son, the Fox; she 'recognises her assailant's strength and admits defeat'. Griaule concludes: 'In this way were pre-figured the balanced struggles between men and women which nevertheless end in male victory' (Griaule, 1947a:446–7)..

While stressing the decisive symbolic function of menstrual blood in the myth, while showing that men try to appropriate the reproductive power of women for themselves in sacrifice and in circumcision, I have avoided any psychoanalytical interpretation. I have no intention of following Bruno Bettelheim's theory. As we know, this author challenges Freud's position that circumcision introduces a threat of castration in order to impose the father's law. Bettelheim claims that young boys feel the unconscious desire to identify with girls, the desire to bleed menstrual blood like them, in order to be able to give life (Bettelheim, 1971). Other African societies liken newly circumcised boys to menstruating girls. However, it appears that in many cases in southern Africa for example menstrual blood is resented as an obstacle to male fertility. The circumcision ritual confronts the young men with a menstrual fire which they must face and fight like an enemy (de Heusch, 1982, chapter X). As for the Ndembu of Zambia, they contrast menstrual blood, blood caused by war, and blood caused by hunting in pairs. Circumcision blood is placed half way between the first and the second (de Heusch, 1972:275). In the entire Bantu area, clitoral excision is

[5] See the excellent commentary on this subject by Liberski (1978).

unknown. Therefore all the symbolic relationships we have just established for the Dogon could not be extrapolated to the whole of Africa. In the Bantu societies we have previously analysed, sacrifice is itself situated on a totally different register.

The third human sacrifice and the origin of death

Menstrual blood, which provides one of the myth's main articulations, is a biological model which justifies thinking in terms of discontinuity, periodicity, the alternation of sterility and fecundity, life and its negation and its eternal dialectical renewal. Nommo's menstrual blood regenerates the primordial celestial placenta. On the other hand, the degraded placenta matter, used in forming the Earth, lies at the origin of a stunted humanity, among whom death is soon to appear. When Ogo 'incestuously' plunges into her, the Earth-mother becomes pregnant. She brings into the world the Yeban genies, 'small creatures with big heads, discoloured bodies and frail members who, ashamed of their condition, hide in holes in the earth'. They couple with each other and give birth to the Andambulu, who gradually people the underground (Griaule and Dieterlen, 1965:187). Later, Ogo steals a second part of the celestial placenta in order to turn it into the first cultivated field; Nommo Titiyayne stamps it out with his foot, condemning it to rot. Now, in the course of this destructive act, which also brought drought, this genie, God's representative, also crushes the sexual member of a male Andambulu, who promptly dies. 'So it was that the seed of destruction which developed on earth through the rottenness of the placenta had its replica in the emergence of death among the Andambulu' (Griaule and Dieterlen, 1965:210). The latter were the first to celebrate funeral rites (Griaule, 1938:47–61). In the world of men, the ancestor Dyongu Seru, Ogo's 'witness', is the one responsible for the loss of immortality (Griaule and Dieterlen, 1957:119; Dieterlen, 1976c:84–5; Dieterlen, 1980). From the very moment of his creation he appeared similar to Ogo. Amma only gave him two 'sex souls' The other two having been 'left to the Fox' (Griaule and Dieterlen, 1965:374). This Dyongu Seru suffers from the same sexual incompleteness as the latter. It is his misfortune to be conjoined with Yasigui, the Fox's twin sister. She plays no role in the previously detailed cosmogonic events. Here she is in the foreground of the myth, as a *femme fatale*. It will be recalled that she was first married to Lebe Seru, and treacherously made him eat red fonio, the forbidden seed. The poor wretch, having become impure, was sacrificed, but was reborn as two serpents. Now a widow, Yasigui married Dyongu Seru. Having fathered only single children, he hoped by this marriage to have twins. He set himself apart from his brothers, who kept a collective field, by taking a private field. He used land south of the fonio field started by the Fox, and enlarged it. He stole seeds from the granaries which were reserved for

Nommo. He also drew on the granaries of Lebe's field and of the collective field. Finally, Dyongu Seru captured a silurus, the representative of the water god, and buried it alive in the fonio hole.

These trangressions brought on chain reaction catastrophes. Nommo's pond, the source of life, dried up. Having become impure and dangerous to the community, Dyongu Seru was sacrificed in the fonio field. He was decapitated. His body, cut into seven pieces, was distributed among the seven parcels of another field, called 'the field of the ancestors'. When the flesh decomposed, the skeleton, starting with the head, was exhumed. According to one version, the latter was buried in the bush (Dieterlen, 1957:119). According to the other, it served to make an altar intended to protect the village (Dieterlen, 1980). The bones were carried to a cave. A cow's throat was slit to finish the purification of the field and Nommo was asked to resuscitate the silurus. Dyongu Seru himself came back to life as a snake, just as Lebe Seru had. However, he was missing one of the eight spiritual principles (*kikinu*). His first wife gave birth to an only child, while the twins carried by Yasigui turned into an albino within her. The snake wandered from pond to pond searching for the missing soul. Human fertility was still halted. Then it was decided to sever the penis of the snake, Dyongu Seru's avatar, who died once and for all. His genitals, thrown into the pond, served as bait to catch siluruses, symbols of future foetuses. Dieterlen notes: 'These fish will be given to young women when they married, as carriers of re-acquired fertility' (Dieterlen, 1976:85). But man lost the capability to have twins at the same time that he lost immortality. Dyongu Seru's funeral was celebrated by carving the serpentine Big Mask, which served as a support for his vital force.

Let us place these events within one entire mythic panorama. Let us compare the various treatments dealt out to the three sacrificial victims. (Fig. 23).

Fig. 23

Nommo	Lebe	Dyongu Seru
Initial castration	Shaved head	Head cut off
Dismembered body	Body buried intact	Body dismembered Condemned to rot Bones exhumed
Rebirth as twins	Rebirth as two snakes	Rebirth as one snake
Immortality	Immortality	Final castration — death

From a diachronic point of view, the Dogon myth can be read as a progressive fall from sacrifice to death. The three treatments of the body summed up above have the same cathartic function, yet they are opposed to each other, in pairs, in at least one respect. It is as if the last sacrifice tried to repeat Nommo's initial sacrifice (characterised by dismemberment and castration) but failed; it ends in a double loss (the end of 'twinness' and of immortality). It brings to its tragic end the primordial androgyn's sexual severing, the division of the being which was begun by Nommo's castration.

Let us explore more extensively the interplay of corresponding factors among the three sacrificial victims who were responsible for the actual state of the world and the status of the individual. The preceding schema brings out the central, mediating position of Lebe Seru's agrarian sacrifice. His body remains intact after the killing. Lebe Seru symbolises 'the integrity of the cultivated land' (Griaule and Dieterlen, 1965:25).

On the other hand, Dyongu Seru, like the Fox, can be defined as a bush creature. This aberrant and solitary agricultural entrepreneur is primarily a hunter and a healer (Griaule and Dieterlen, 1965:25, 423). The Ancestors' heroic account sharply contrasts Lebe's cultivated land, reinvigorated by Nommo (master of water) with the Fox's sterile and dry bushland. The fields are where the Ancestors' 'word', made of water, is inscribed (Griaule, 1948:94). Collective agricultural effort 'extends civilisation beyond inhabited places', constantly encroaching on the Fox's land. Yet, by a strange contradiction, it is the Fox who was the first civilising hero, the first farmer. Dyongu Seru, throwing himself into the working of the fields, irrespective of prohibitions and social rules, prolonged the Fox's solitary course. The bad seed left by the latter is responsible for death. It grew in a field made of unclean placenta and was itself impure like menstrual blood; 'fonio and menses', Ogotemmêli pithily states, 'are one' (Griaule, 1948:178). Yet threshing the red fonio is an operation comparable both to menstruation and sacrifice: 'it is like a man slitting a victim's throat on the altar; it is like a woman making the earth drink her blood' (ibidi.182–3). It is as if the purifying treatment imposed upon the fox's seed replayed Nommo's sacrifice-menstruation. This cursed seed is forbidden to most men. Only a few men characterised by a statuary or temporary impurity, an existential incompleteness, can freely eat it. Let us examine this more closely.

As a farmer made of the same substance as seed, man is a 'living' being (*inne omo*) because he possesses in his collarbones the symbols of the eight cereals given by God. However, Dogon society is composed of a certain number of 'impure' (*puru*) men; due to a difference in social status, they have only seven, instead of eight, seeds in their collarbones (Dieterlen, 1957:113). More exactly, the eighth seed is replaced by *Digitaria exilis*, the Fox's seed (Dieterlen, 1973:211). This is the case for caste members, griots, leather workers, woodworkers and basketmakers, who are not included in the main rituals (Dieterlen, 1973:212). Menstruating women have the same status during their five days of withdrawal; they are deprived of the femal sorghum, which is replaced by the *Digitaria*. Moreover, each family includes a certain number of 'impure' men, identified by divination; they are freed of all the prohibitions concerning death. They must wash the body, carry it to the necropolis and eat the flesh of animals offered at the funeral.

Let us return to the preceding schema and explore the mystery of castration. The first sacrificial victim, Nommo, undergoes it just as does the third victim, Dyongu Seru. However, this operation does not occupy the same position in the two schemas. Nommo's *initial* castration is associated with the very birth of an immortal god, called on to regenerate the universe. The *final* castration of Dyongu Seru, on the other hand, introduces the principle of death. It is also because one of their ancestors' sexual organs had been crushed, that death appeared among the Andambulu.

We have stated at length the reasons which lead us to believe that the inaugural act of this epic implies the femininisation of Nommo, who is condemned to be sacrificed. We have also seen that the Blacksmith Ancestor, his 'twin', assumed the masculinity of the castrated Nommo, who was changed into a silurus. Now we have Dyongu Seru directly attacking this fish. What does this new incident of conflict between the Fox and Nommo mean? Why are Dyongu Seru's genitals finally thrown in the water, i.e., offered to the Nommo-silurus?

Does not the dénouement of this mythic panorama, featured by three sacrifices, signify that the last sacrifice has fulfilled the first? The final castration of Dyongu Seru in the form of a snake restores to Nommo the male sex organ which was torn from him at the beginning of time so that he could assume the female reproductive function. In this perspective, Dyongu Seru, the bush creature (hunter), one of the Fox's creatures, pays back to Nommo the initial debt owed by Ogo.

For it was indeed in Ogo's place (he was the true culprit) that Nommo, an innocent victim, was castrated, then sacrificed. Dyongu Seru's final castration now appears as the last harmonic chord of a complex, involved, but perfectly coherent, myth. This time castration indeed signifies death. However, this event reintroduces the god-fish into the cycle of life which he helped to create. By entrusting Dyongu Seru's genitals to Nommo, the ancestors did more than re-establish fertility; they restored to the water genie the male principle, which he had lost through sacrifice. After this, children emerging from the pond are born singly and are mortal, but they are endowed with a double identity, male and female, just like the primordial silurus. The new-born may have lost 'twinness' but he has gained symbolic androgyny, which the rites of adolescence partially abolish. The captured silurus is indeed the foetus, considered to be like a fresh bisexual fish (Griaule, 1955:305). It would be hard to find a better way of saying that children are the reproduction of the androgynous Nommo, of Nommo before the sacrificial severing, before the separation of the sexes.

The offering of Dyongu Seru's male sex to the water genie appears to be one of the central problems of the myth; this theme, which is somewhat hidden, gives it a tension at least as strong as the Fox's sterile agitation when he is deprived of his female double. As decisive proof, we have the central episode of the Sigui, the great ritual of the world's regeneration, which is celebrated by the Dogon every sixty years for commemorating Dyongu Seru's death. All males take part in it, whatever their age. They are dressed 'in a manner resembling fish', resembling creatures at the foetal stage (Dieterlen, 1971:4). During a drinking session, they sit on red T-shaped benches, which explicitly symbolise 'the male genital of human-ity's father' whereas the half gourd from which they drink the Sigui-beer is a womb, the image of the primordial egg (Dieterlen, 1971:5).

The celebration of the Sigui, is the ultimate collective victory over death, which was introduced by Dyongu Seru. During the drinking, the male generations form a continuous tight chain, from newborns to elders. A new great Serpentine Mask, which supported Dyongu Seru's life force, is carved. The rite is celebrated under the sign of the 'star of the fonio'. Indeed, this 'companion' of Sirius is the representation in the sky of the little fonio seed which was the universal womb before it was perverted by the Fox. The men-siluruses seated on Nommo's phallus thus form the clasp of the long mythic loop which began with the castration-birth of the water genie and ended in the castration-death of Dyongu Seru, representing the Fox. For eight years, the ritual was sent on from one region to another, following a route which evoked that of Dyongu Seru (Dieterlen, 1971:6). In a manner of speaking, the Sigui is the resurrection of the first dead man or at least his emergence into the temporal world for another sixty years. The whole male segment of society celebrates this rediscovered eternity by displaying its own continuity, its collective being, with all age differences abolished.[6]

I would even dare say that this prodigious cyclical negation of time, of the rupture of death—which no sacrifice can remedy—also re-enacts the restitution of Nommo's phallus. The men as a group reaffirm their superiority to women, as the feminisation of the primordial androgyny appears in myth to be the only response to the quest of that lonely male, the Fox. The assembled male social body ostentatiously displays the continui-ty of its intact existence, in contrast to the dismembered body of the first dead man, Dyongu Seru. Each participant identifies with the resuscitated Nommo, finally in possession of his phallus. By carving a new mask in honour of Dyongu Seru, the men, grouped in a compact body, carry out a

---

[6] During the years 1967 to 1974 Jean Rouch, along with Dieterlen, made a striking film of this ritual, which had not been celebrated since 1907.

striking 'drawing together' of the first and third sacrificial victims. Time seems to be suspended.

Blood's vital force

The Dogon say that Nommo 'showed men their first example of sacrifice' (Griaule and Dieterlen, 1965:359). All ritual immolations are inspired by this model, 'whatever the place, the purpose, the officiants, or the procedure'. The ritual always starts with slitting the throat of a young chick or a pullet, which 'represents' Nommo's castration. The libation of gruel is a reminder of the discharge of the primordial seeds. Then a second animal is immolated to commemorate Nommo's sacrifice, properly speaking. The sharing of the body among the participants and the throwing of the liver on the altar re-enact, respectively, the dismemberment and the rebirth of the genie.

Griaule examines the technique of animal sacrifice in a study written in 1940 and republished in 1976. He reminds us that the blood of every living creature carries a life force (*nyama*) 'which tends to make the support with which it is temporarily provided persist in its being' (Griaule, 1976:51). By freeing the animal victim's *nyama*, the sacrifice sets off an energy circuit which, through a complex network, links the sacrifier, the alerted power, the altar and the victim. Its death releases 'a force whose propulsion stimulates action in other forces; these through their reactions and their interactions, benefit the sacrifier and the supernatural power' (Griaule, 1976:53).

Ogotemméli enthusiastically describes the effects of sacrifice, which he likens to a linguistic communication. 'The Word is for everyone in this world; it must be exchanged; it must come and go, for it is good to give and to receive the forces of life' (Griaule, 1948:165).

Later fieldwork brought to light the complementary cathartic role of sacrifice. It will be recalled that every living being (*omo*) has in his collarbones the symbols of the eight cereal seeds, the basic food. Any transgression compromises the stability of the system; it is said that 'the seeds fight' (Dieterlen, 1973:210). The individual affected by this condition is in a state of impurity (*puru*), in danger of death. This notion does not really imply a 'pollution', but more a loss of vital energy. The seeds leave when the *nyama* leaves (Dieterlen, 1976a:46). Only a sacrifice can restore the organism's integrity, can again make man complete, 'alive' (*omo*). This new interpretation conforms with the mythic paradigm since Nommo's sacrifice was itself 'purifying and reorganising' in reply to the Fox's disturbing behaviour (Dieterlen, 1976a:47).

Let us return to the beginning of our investigation. By criticising Evans-Pritchard's interpretation of Nuer sacrifice, we revealed the inadequacy of the notions of 'sin' and 'pollution'. Although the Nuer do not seem to have developed as refined a theory of the individual as that of the Dogon, we arrived at a conclusion close to that of Dieterlen. Among the Nuer, any infraction of the symbolic code, any transgression, brings on a weakening of the individual which is manifested through sickness (see Chapter I). On considering the same issue with regard to the Lele, we showed the need to carefully distinguish the notion of pollution (*hama*) from that of prohibition. What happens among the Dogon? Ogo's behaviour is the paradigm of all transgressions. The troublesome Fox is a being partly deprived of his spiritual principles. The tone of his voice is 'rotten', like that of menstruating women (Calame-Griaule, 1965:102). Menstrual blood is both rotten and '*puru*', being empty of *nyama* 'because it did not form a foetus' (Calame-Griaule, 1965:55). The semantic shift from the notion of loss, of spiritual incompleteness (*puru*), towards the notion of 'rot' indicates that the being is in danger, for 'anything which hinders fertility is a step towards death' (Calame-Griaule, 1965:55).

These Dogon variations on 'pollution' are as we can see, totally foreign to the Christian conception of sin. The so called 'purifying' sacrifice palliates a deficiency (Dieterlen, 1976a:45). It has a conjunctive power (it brings the life force back to the body), whereas Nuer sacrifice effects the disjunction of the sacrifier from the spirit who attacked him ('to get rid of the Spirit', in Evans-Pritchard's expression).

The status of domestic animals

Dieterlen stresses an essential fact: the *nyama* of domestic animals, liberated by sacrifice and put into general circulation for man's benefit, is contrasted with the *nyama* of animals killed in a hunt or that of men killed in war. In the last two cases, the victim's life force displays a formidable aggressiveness. 'Liberated by the sacrifice, but guided by the prayer accompanying the immolation, the victim's *nyama* becomes the agent of transfer' (Dieterlen, 1976a:44). Sacrifice is nourished by the hope of maintaining life through the tireless repetition, under the most varied conditions, of Nommo's primordial immolation. The very term used to designate sacrifice (*bulu*) is a derivative of the verb *bulo*, which means 'to bring back to life, to resuscitate' (Dieterlen, 1976a:47).

One may ask why domestic animals are the means selected for this vital purpose. To my knowledge there is no definitive answer to this question in the various exegeses of the Dogon mythos. But a brief tale will clarify their status (Griaule, 1938:50–1). In past times all the animals lived in the bush and were dependent on the *Yeban* —those malformed genie born of the Fox—except for aquatic creatures and certain birds which were placed under Nommo's jurisdiction. As the cultivated area spread out, limiting the hunting space, men followed the Blacksmith's advice and began to capture a certain number of mammals belonging to the *Yeban* and to shut them up in their dwellings. 'Through their contact with men and because of the potash water they were given to drink, the *Yeban* genie considered these animals impure *(puru)* ... Due to this acquired impurity, the captured animals could no longer return to the genie and they became domestic animals'.

This brief account points up the broadening of the impurity concept. The domestic animals, uprooted from their place of origin, the Fox's bush, have taken on an ambiguous status. This status is a symmetrical reversal of the 'impure' men who do not belong entirely to the human world because they carry in their collarbones the Fox's seed, the fonio.

Four domestic species, however—the chicken, the sheep, the horse and the cat—'came from Nommo' while the goat and the donkey are 'from the Fox's side' because of their evil nature (Calame-Griaule, 1965:520). The sheep, Nommo's peaceful representative, is the opposite of the restless goat, which, like the Fox, enjoys wandering around the bush (Calame-Griaule, 1965:134, 464). The same division is to be found in the *Equidae* species, between the noble horse and the donkey, a beast of burden associated with the Fox. The cat, protector of granaries, endowed with absolute purity, represents Nommo; it is radically opposed to that impure animal, the dog, which eats absolutely everything and represents the Fox (Calame-Griaule, 1965:132, 265, 464–7). The esoteric version confirms this popular interpretation; the first dog is born from the Fox's amniotic fluid (Dieterlen, discussion on May 11, 1978).

Speaking generally, 'the placenta of domestic and wild animals recalls that of the Fox' (Calame-Griaule, 1965:173). The placenta from cows, ewes, bitches, female donkeys, etc., is hung on a tree in the bush or on a post in the courtyard where it dries 'like that of the Fox'. The placenta, the 'twin' of the domestic mammals, thus belongs to the world of the bush. There does exist, however, a very great contrast between the Fox's animals and Nommo's (Fig. 24).

Fig. 24

Nommo	Fox
Sheep	Goat
Horse	Donkey
Cat	Dog

The first animal sacrifice was that of a cow; it was carried out after the ritual killing of the ancestor Dyongu Seru (Dieterlen, 1980). Now, according to the myth, a mysterious white cow 'of the death' appeared in the 'hole' formed in the original celestial placenta by the springing up of the sun, as if the alternation of day and night foreshadowed man's death (Griaule and Dieterlen, 1965:224). But we do not know the exact position of cattle in the sacrificial system. Basically, the Dogon raise goats and sheep. It is these animals who make victims *par excellence*. They have specific symbolic characteristics. The goat, the Fox's representative, hates rain, unlike the sheep (Calame-Griaule, 1965:134). We shall find these respective allegiances again in the agrarian rites.

Sacrifice and agriculture

Just before seeding and the rainy season the Dogon begin a complex ritual whose very name (*bulu*) ('to make relive') designates sacrifice. It is carried out in honour of the ancestor Lebe Seru, the patron of agriculture and the first terrestrial sacrificial victim. Two altars are dedicated to him. The first, called 'Lebe's terrace' can be seen on the principal square of *Ogol du Haut* in Sanga. It consists of a 'navel of grey earth' representing 'in a certain manner Lebe's tomb' (Griaule, 1948:160). It is forbidden to approach it for this earthen platform is 'the image of the sky where the primordial sacrifice took place' (Griaule and Dieterlen, 1965:32–3). Lebe's main altar is the one 'inside'. It lies in the sanctuary of the religious leader—the *hogon*—in a room no one may enter except the *hogon* and his sacrificer (idem:501).

Back in 1936 Lifszyc and Paulme noted in Sanga the existence of the 'exterior' altar. These authors stressed that for the Dogon, the true Lebe is an enormous serpent which no one must ever see, on pain of death; at night he comes to lick his priest, the *hogon* all over his body (Lifszyc, D and Paulme, D., 1935:96). In fact Lebe's two altars must be correlated with the two immortal snakes, reincarnations of the ancestor Lebe after his sacrifice. Indeed, according to G. Dieterlen, there is a Lebe snake 'of the interior' (*de Lebe*), guardian of the *hogon's* altar, and a snake 'of the exterior' (*para Lebe*) which watches over the fields and harvests (Dieterlen, 1982:21). For her part, Calame-Griaule writes that 'the Lebe comports two complementary parts: the Lebe of the interior, totally pure, and that of the exterior, which is impure and recalls Lebe Seru's mythical death and the earth's sterility during the dry season' (Calame-Griaule, 1965:299).

In 1946, Ogotemmêli described to Griaule the sacrifice which takes place on the exterior altar in Sanga at the end of the agrarian ritual (Griaule, 1948:160). A goat's throat is slit in the presence of the Blacksmith. He faces the oldest of the 'impure' men and strikes the ground with his anvil. The vital force contained within the altar enters the victim's liver, which is cooked and eaten by the 'impure' old man. In a hushed voice Ogotemmêli reveals that the old man thus gives his own life: 'he is emptied of his own life to fill himself with that of the Ancestor' (*ibid:*161–2).

What does this mysterious language mean? The old man symbolically assumes the fate of the ancestor Lebe who was sacrificed long ago to purify the earth of the Fox's transgression, to conjure drought and sterility. As he is 'impure' he has in his collarbones the seed of red fonio grown by the Fox (see p. 146). The sacrifice of a goat is indeed under the sign of the master of disorder. But what happens on the 'interior' altar, the one that is directly entrusted to the *hogon*? To find out, let us accompany Gertrude Dieterlen to the *hogon* of the Aru.

Dogon society is not ruled by a single sovereign. Each tribe has one, or several *hogons* whose political and ritual authority is exercised over a territorial segment. But the sole *hogon* of the Aru tribe, representing the ancestral lineage of Lebe Seru, is considered the supreme leader of all the Dogon. He is elected from among the young men of his territorial group (Griaule and Dieterlen, 1965:32). Amma's representative on earth, 'the personification of the universe', he is also 'Lebe Seru's successor' (Griaule and Dieterlen, 1954:99). Bearing the title 'Amma's Witness', the *hogon* of Aru 'is the Great celestial Nommo, master of the celestial water and guardian of the spiritual principles of the cereals' (Dieterlen, 1982:33). He has in his collarbones twice as many seeds as ordinary men.

During his enthronement, the *hogon* withdraws into a cave which is associated with fecundity and the multiplying of totemic clans (Dieterlen, 1982:83–9). He will remain there seven days, wearing a white loincloth, which represents, through the intermediary of 'weaving', the revelation of the 'word' to men. From that moment, his female soul, which normally resides in the family pond with Nommo, comes to rejoin his male soul. He thus acquires immortality. The future *hogon* is thought to be required to remain flat on his stomach on the ground of the cave 'as if he had plunged into the primordial pond in which the resuscitated Nommo remains' (Dieterlen, 1982:84).

In the evening of the seventh day of the retreat, he must eat white fonio, the primordial seed, the seed of the universe; from this he thus acquires 'a great weight'. He will be constrained to observe a great many prohibitions with the utmost rigour. After his head has been shaved, a head-dress (which represents the sky) is put on him, and boots (which represent the earth) are put on his feet. He seats himself, 'like Amma', on a platform facing east. His wife is shaved in her turn and, dressed in loincloths and scarves with long fringes dyed a deep indigo (the colour which denotes terrestrial water and rain), is made to resemble the twin sister of the Nommo of the Pond. The *hogon's* essential duty is to take charge of the rainfall pattern, ordering the rites which he deems necessary (Dieterlen, 1982:94). This ritual chief is indeed a sacred king, as we have defined it in the preceding chapter, even though his political power is not that of a chief of state.

Let us examine from this perspective the ritual eating of white fonio. Dieterlen relates that this act reminds us 'that after the serious upheavals brought about by the Fox the Nommo was entrusted with this primordial seed' (Dieterlen 1982:86). Yet there is more. The *hogon* acquires the very 'substance' of the white fonio which is henceforth part of his collarbones *ibid.* Is this not a way of saying that the enthronement confers upon him God's creative force which the Fox vainly tried to appropriate by stealing this same fonio? Because he has twice as many seeds in his collarbones, the *hogon* is a potentially dangerous man for the other dignitaries: entry to a granary is forbidden to him (*ibid:*33).

The hidden face of this personage, whose mystic 'weight' sentences him almost to immobility, is less well known. But in an article which has not been sufficiently discussed, Griaule suggests that the *hogon* also shares the Fox's disturbing movement, his transgression. 'Like *Yurugu* (the Fox), the *hogon* is considered to be obliged to couple with his mother. Also, after his enthronement he is separated from her. He maintains a relationship with her, feeds her, but only through the intermediation of his own sisters, who are both his daughters, since he is their mother's pseudo-husband, and his wives, for they are like twin sisters with whom, according to the myth, he is supposed to be united' (Griaule, 1954:45). This identification of the Aru *hogon* with the Fox explains why that dignitary is chosen from among the young men. The Dogon say: 'The Hogon who is taken when young, that is like the way [in which] the thing ended between the Fox and his mother', alluding to the incest the Fox committed in penetrating his own placenta (Dieterlen, 1982:35). The Dogon offer two different etymologies for the word *hogon*. The first refers to ogo, 'the umbilical cord'; it underscores the fact that the *hogon* (ogone) is the 'centre, the umbilicus of the social body' (Dieterlen, 1982:31). But in the second, the same term is said to derive from ogo-ine, 'rich man'. Well, that is the true name of the Fox (Calame-Griaule, 1965:148). The feminine soul acquired by the *hogon* during his enthronement raises a few questions. Is this bisexuality guaranteeing his immortality, the symbolic equivalent of the androgyny characterising the primordial genies before the splitting of the egg of the world? In any case, the Hogon's feminine part is ambiguous because he shares some of the characteristics of the Fox. Calame-Griaule asserts that he is 'at the same time pure, like cultivated earth and a fertile mother, and impure, like the sterile bush and a menstruating woman' (Calame-Griaule, 1965:299).

A Synthesis of the sky and the earth, those two elements which were separated from the original placenta, the *hogon* is, in fact, like other sacred African chiefs, a twinned royal figure (de Heusch, 1982). He unites in his person the complementary powers of the male twins lodged in the lower part of the divine placenta; he holds his investiture from the Nommo of the Pond, but he is secretly identified, as we have just seen, with Ogo, the fomenter of 'incestuous' trouble. He is also likened to the Great Celestial Nommo (*Nommo Die*) who occupies the upper part of the original placenta and who sends the rain. It is indeed because he symbolises the totality of the universe that he represents Amma on earth. This extreme mystic power, which confers on the *hogon* of Aru the absolute mastery of the universe, no doubt explains why, like a sacred (and even a 'divine') king, he is surrounded with prohibitions, sentenced to remain in the agglomeration of buildings in which his dwelling is placed. He stays there, seated, on a platform outside his house, for the major part of the day, in imitation of Amma (Griaule and Dieterlen, 1965:503).

But as we saw in the preceding chapter, the acquisition of this ambivalent status, characteristic of sacred royalty, usually implies the premature death of its possessor. Well, the *hogon* of Aru, chosen from among the young men, considers himself to be granted a very long life. We have already encountered this problematic among the Rukuba of Nigeria (see p. 100). In that case, substituted human victims guaranteed the sacred chief's old age; he himself was symbolically put to death at the time of his enthronement. Everything indicates that it is the same with the Dogon. 'The enthronement', Dieterlen writes, 'is clearly likened to a new birth' (Dieterlen, 1982:88). The designated candidate takes a new name and will live separated from his mother. What is more, three years after his enthronement, an albino will be sacrificed (Dieterlen, 1976c:88). We shall return to this dramatic rite, which confirms the *hogon's* accession to supreme religious power.

Master of nature's rhythms, the *hogon* of Aru, the prisoner of his duty, is obliged to remain in his dwelling after having managed the annual ceremonies which precede planting, the *bulu*.

The ultimate, most important purpose of this very complex ritual, is to ask the two great Celestial Nommos, through the intermediary of the Nommo of the Pond (the sacrificed one who has been revived), to send back the 'souls' of the seeds along with the rain; these have been entrusted to those tutelary genies during the offering of the first fruits which took place at the time of the preceding harvest (Dieterlen, 1982:91). At the beginning of the dry season the *hogon* got rid of the female soul which was conferred on him at his enthronement. He entrusted it to the snake, the 'interior' Lebe, the guardian of the altar, and he thus finds himself theoretically free to travel. It is exactly at the time of the *bulu* rite that he regains his female soul; he will keep it throughout the rainy season; it is settled in the ritual headcovering made of millet straw (Dieterlen, 1982:33). The period of immobility imposed on the Hogon thus coincides with that in which he exercises control over the rain. It may not be too venturesome to suggest that the freedom of movement which is theoretically granted him during the dry season (when he is without his female soul) places him symbolically on the side of the Fox, a wandering male creature lacking his female counterpart.

No doubt that is what enables Calame-Griaule to underline the ambiguity of the *hogon* associated both with the cultivated earth and the sterile bush (Calame-Griaule, 1965:299). Although the Fox is theoretically the 'enemy' whom the Aru official should fight (Dieterlen, 1982:165), it will be recalled that the *hogon* is the representative of Lebe, that is, of the Ancestor who broke a prohibition under pressure from the Fox. The duplication of Lebe (pure in the interior of the *hogon's* dwelling and impure outside it) reminds us of that contradiction, which is also that of sacred royalty as an institution articulating opposing spaces. The Lebe of the 'interior' and that of the 'exterior' call for two different and complementary types of sacrifice. The animal sacrificed inside the *hogon's* house to obtain the rain indispensable for germination' is always *a sheep* (Dieterlen, 1982:92). Now this animal is the Nommo's preferred representative (Calame-Griaule, 1965:134; Griaule, 1948:130). Thus the sacrifice of the sheep carried out in the *hogon's* presence reactualises the primordial celestial sacrifice. A similar rite apparently takes place in the *hogon* of Sanga's house where the priest himself eats the victim's liver (Griaule, 1948:163). Unfortunately Ogotemmêli does not mention the species; however we do know that here, the ritual of seeding ends with the sacrifice of a *goat* carried out on the Lebe's 'exterior' altar for purification purposes. An 'impure' man who eats the animal's liver is symbolically put to death as Lebe Seru, the first terrestrial sacrificial victim. Yet it is the *hogon* who perpetuates the cult of this ancestor. It is as if the 'impure' man, symbolically sacrificed under the sign of the Fox, was the inverted figure of the *hogon*, the most exemplary 'pure' man. The former has in his collarbones the Fox's seed, the red fonio, the latter, Amma's seed, white fonio. In any case, this hypothesis which, for lack of any complementary information, must be left in suspense, conforms to the sacrificial logic of sacred royalty.

The sacrifice of the albino

To make the *hogon's* mystic power secure, a human sacrifice used to take place three years after his enthronement—the sacrifice of an albino. It occasioned an anthropophagic meal (Dieterlen, 1976c:88). This extremely serious event, which was kept secret, takes us back to a climactic element of the myth. The immolation of an albino concludes the series of human sacrifices whose victims were, successively, Nommo, Lebe and Dyongu Seru. Let us resume the account of the terrestrial ancestors' saga which we interrupted after Dyongu Seru's death.

The union of Dyongu Seru and Yasigui, the Fox's twin sister, resulted in the conception of an albino instead of the expected twins. But Yasigui did not stop there. After her second husband's death, she went on to marry the third Ancestor, Binu Seru, Nommo's 'witness'. By him she had three sons, and she did not hesitate to couple incestuously with the youngest. In punishment, Nommo drowned her in the pond, and the albino met the same fate (Dieterlen, 1957:129). The myth, which began with the Fox's incestuous deed, coupling with the Earth mother, his own placenta, ends with the incest of his twin sister, coupling with her own son. The albino expiates all the previous offences.

Why does the enthronement of the *hogon*, require, after three years, the repetition of this last mythic sacrifice? We suggest that the albino is a substitute victim; he represents the *hogon* himself. The sacrifice of an albino is the accursed sealing of a new contract; it grants survival to the sacred chief while simultaneously ridding both the tilled land and society of the Fox's impurity. In the Dogon schema, the albino is the reverse image of the Nommo twin couple. The sacrifice of the albino is strictly equivalent to the periodic ejection of the repulsive old man who, among the Rukuba, takes over the monstrous aspect of sacred power after having been identified with the chief (see Chapter V).

From another viewpoint, the albino represents Nommo at the time of his arrival on earth; it was then that he became 'white' after having been burnt on contact with the sun during his descent (Griaule and Dieterlen, 1965:441). The albino is 'the witness of Nommo's burns'. From this one will deduce that the Nommo albino bears the mark of the Fox's burning placenta (solar fire) on his body. To sacrifice the albino, then, is also to sacrifice Nommo in his capacity as mediator between the celestial and earthy part of the original placenta. The other version of the myth shows the albino as the doomed son of the Fox's twin sister; he is the monstrous product of the fusion of the two twins in Yasigui's breast.

Let us look at the neighbouring Bambara. An albino was sacrificed during the enthronement of the kings of Segu. This was repeated every year (Cissé, 1980). The victim's blood was poured over the king's shaved head. Another procedure consisted of strangling the albino; his urine and excrement, mixed with water, were used to wash the sovereign. But the Bambara also sacrificed the king himself if his reign lasted too long or if he was incompetent. He was then executed in the same manner as the albino.

Inversely, the *hogon* is immortal. Yet he only permanently acquires his power over the world at the cost of a substitute human sacrifice: the immolation is that of his own caricature, the deformed image of the twin model. The *hogon* and the *albino* form a couple, as do the Rukuba chief and the weak old man who serves as foil after a few years (see p. 100).

The Dogon mythic paradigm can be read as the consummate theology of sacred kingship. Its two opposite and complementary aspects appear in the twin couple Nommo-Ogo. Like so many legendary heroes, Ogo sets himself up as king of the universe. By tearing off a part of the celestial placenta he accomplishes the founding act of civilisation (the invention of agriculture) through transgression. Banished from the land he was the first to plant, Ogo continues to rule over the uncultivated bush. The sun and the moon are witnesses of his placenta (Griaule and Dieterlen, 1965:204). The sun's rays 'feed' the seeds planted in the fields (Griaule and Dieterlen, 1965:251). The celestial fire, which is Ogo's female part, thus completes the action of the water provided by Nommo. Ogo and his twin brother do indeed exercise a co-sovereignty over the universe. In this couple, Nommo assumes the purifying, sacrificial function; he expiates Ogo's offence; he takes charge of the beneficial aspects of sacred kingship: the cultivated land, the word.

Ogo, now the Fox, is in charge of funeral ceremonies, from which the *hogon* is strictly excluded. Responsible for death, the Fox also was the first to introduce mourning rituals. One must go back in mythical time to the episode, mentioned earlier, in which the Fox incestuously couples with the Earth Mother, causing the appearance of the first menstrual flow. It reddened the damp fibre clothes covering the maternal vagina, the anthill (see p. 141). The ant (representing the earth herself) spread the skirt in the sun to dry it. When the Fox saw it he exclaimed: 'I see a red thing; is it fire, or the sun, or an astonishing thing?' The ant replied: 'No, it is not sun, it is not fire, it is as cool as water'. The Fox asked her to borrow the skirt. He donned it and went up on the terrace where he danced in honour of his dead father. Did he make fun of Amma? Is he celebrating the death of God? It seems more likely that he is commemorating the final split between heaven and earth. In any case, a fibre skirt and various masks make up men's attire when they come to dance in the village, to perform the end of the mourning rites (*dama*), permanently warding off the souls of the dead. Tinting the fibres red is a decisive element in the funeral ritual. The day when this technical procedure takes place is called 'men's menstruation' (Griaule, 1938:354). But before putting on the skirt, the dancers must sprinkle it with a little water. 'Pouring water on the dance skirt is good for women', says Ogotemmêli. 'It is like putting moisture on their sexual organs, which helps them to conceive' (Griaule, 1948:202). Without beating about the bush, Ogotemmêli concludes: 'When the men put on the fibres, it is as if they were putting the moisture of the women's sexual organs on themselves' (Griaule, 1948:203).

One could not better express the fact that, in the funeral rites, the men force themselves to pursue to the point of absurdity the quest for fertility undertaken by the Fox: the sterile male, transforming himself into fertile woman, in imitation of the sacrificed Nommo. The red paint which they put on the masks they will wear is indeed the blood from the castration of the water genie (Griaule and Dieterlen, 1965:236).

But the masks were first painted black, and the dancers' costumes also are required to include a skirt made of fibres of the same colour, the symbol of water. They wear one skirt with long fibres and one with short fibres. The first is almost always black, the second is either black, yellow, or red, 'but quite often the dancer wears two skirts of different colours, the red one placed over the other one' (Griaule, 1938:396). The masked dancers whose role is to ward off death, to limit its spread, thus display at the same time the symbols of the Fox and of Nommo. During their showing in the village a mysterious bark mask (*azagay*) keeps the women and children away. It was described to Griaule as the oldest of all masks. (Griaule, 1938:396). Many years later Dieterlen learned that this primordial vegetal mask represented the Fox himself, the Fox covered with part of his twin Nommo's sacrificial body. It is made of bark (which covers the dancer's head), from a sacred tree (*Lannea acida*), thought to be the symbol ('witness') of the sacrificed Nommo's head. The remarkable feature of the bark is its bright red colour, like a bloody, torn skin (Dieterlen, personal note). The Fox and Nommo compose a Janus figure of royalty.

It is remarkable that the Dogon do not disavow the actions of the Fox, which are linked to so many catastrophes. He is the ultimate 'agent of enquiry and of development' (Dieterlen, 1976:85), as if transgression was the indispensable means of connecting social and cultural order with cosmic order. But such is precisely the fundamental ritual role of sacred kingship.

Nommo and Lebe can be introduced into the great universal pantheon made up of gods who die and are reborn, the authoritative inventory of which was begun by Frazer. But these complex entities do not permit a reduction to spirits of vegetation; one cannot be satisfied with deciphering the natural rhythms which pervade them. On this point, Frazer's thesis is decidedly too simplistic. It does not take into account the extraordinary complexity of symbolic thought which produced the prodigious mythology of the seed, which we have explored in an effort to point up certain main structural axes. I have been content to investigate the central, incisive idea of sacrifice, while stripping this labyrinthine, proliferating concept of a great part of its richness.

Nor does Dogon metaphysics permit itself to be imprisoned within the evolutionist schema proposed by Hubert and Mauss. Starting with the hypothesis that 'sacrifice is repeated periodically because the rhythm of nature requires this regular recurrence, these authors credit the 'creators of myth' with having provided 'firstly a status and a history, and consequently, a more continuous life to the intermittent, dull and passive personality which was born from the regular occurence of sacrifices. From that premise they deduce that 'myth, then, shows the god emerging alive from the test only in order to submit him to it afresh. His life is thus composed of an uninterrupted chain of sufferings and resurrections' (Hubert and Mauss, 1964:81–89).

Dogon mythology does not fit in with that approach, even though fabled power is here brought to its zenith. The successive 'passions' of Nommo, of Lebe and of Dyongu Seru do not conform exactly to an agrarian scenario. They constitute so many responses to a disturbance which threatens cosmic order. The Dogon have deliberately adopted the viewpoint of Sirius. This star, the world's umbilicus, was the first to be born of sacrificial blood. In addition, the preferred models which are used to account for the appearance and the renewal of life are biological in nature. Ontogenesis reproduces mythic phylogenesis, which begins with the fish stage;

menstruation, the provisional suspension of fertility and the threat of death, provide the key of the *natura naturans*. Menstrual blood is the primal source of cosmic rhythms.

It could be objected that the agricultural code dominates this mythology devised by and for farmers. God created the world in the form of a minute seed animated by vibrations, and the sacrifice of a 'water god' proceeded to permit its bursting forth, its expansion. The seeds which the Dogon cultivate are part of the very essence of their being since they are settled in their collarbones. There is no denying that Dogon religion is inseparable from the mode of production which it undertakes to maintain. But neither economic necessities nor ecological constraints serve to explain why the founding act should be precisely a human sacrifice conceived as the menstruation of a castrated androgyn. Symbolic religious order is at the heart of Dogon society. It underlies the economy as well as the politics. It circumscribes the power zone even though it confers no privilege whatever on those privy to the knowledge. No doubt individual perception apprehends it differently, with more of less indifference, depending on the level of awareness.

But this thought should by no means be considered an esoteric doctrine reserved to a few initiates. There does not exist, here, an intellectual elite separate from the mass of the faithful and endowed with a clerical power. Many of Griaule's detractors have questioned the interest of the Dogon's intellectual speculations, which seemed to them to be floating in a sociological void. As if lineage, family, existed independently of the system of representations which they arrived at in order to explain existence, as if empirical social reality could be analytically disassociated from the symbolic. It is trivial to object that the thought of the Dogon 'doctors' is not the same as that of ignorant men. In 1948 Griaule already foresaw this argument and and answered it forcefully: 'One would not undertake to charge the Christian dogma of the transubstantiation with esotericism on the pretext that the man in the street does not know the word and has only glimmerings of the thing itself' (Griaule, 1948:9). Who would dare deny that Christianity, a religion of sacrifice, has, from its formation and throughout the centuries, established the ultimate reference point of our own social system, beyond the various modes of production which have marked its development?

The development of Dogon society is among the most uncertain. Pursuing the tireless research begun by Griaule, Dieterlen observed in 1982 that the responsible Dogon religious individuals were experiencing more and more difficulties in passing on their heritage. But this crisis itself could indeed be interpreted as the expression of a religious scruple. The social and economic changes are such that no candidate 'can be sure of fulfilling his office without being placed, without his knowledge, in the position of committing errors prejudicial to many of those under his jurisdiction and to his own integrity; the 'Word' which he must take upon himself then becomes 'nonsense' lacking power or effect' (Dieterlen, 1982:206).

VII

The Dogon's neighbours

The Bambara: a new light on human sacrifice

The systematic studies carried out over the past thirty years by Dieterlen, de Ganay, Zahan and Cissé have shown that, like many other populations of West Africa, the Bambara share in the religious heritage of the ancient Mandé civilisations. Dieterlen quickly noticed that there are many correspondences between the Dogon and the Bambara origin myths (Dieterlen, 1951:56). We do not intend to give a complete account of this different metaphysical system. We shall limit ourselves to a broad outline—which follows Dieterlen's initial presentation (Dieterlen, 1951:1–33)—in order to show that these sacrificial patterns constitute a remarkable transformation of those we have just analysed among the Dogon.

Dieterlen warned us that the creation myths 'must be understood as a totality, a sophia, and not as a sequence of fixed etiological accounts' (Dieterlen, 1951:1).

This raises many questions about the status of myth, and we shall have to leave them unanswered. For the Dogon's highly personalised god (*Amma*), the Bambara *sophia* substitutes an abstract, mechanical entity, which is at the same time both thought and action, and is conceived as a genetic vibration: *Gla*. However, one must not forget that among the Dogon creation also starts with the appearance of 'a type of atom' animated by the same vibrating motion (Dieterlen, 1951:3). Gla, 'full of his emptiness and his emptiness full of himself', emitted a voice from which his double sprang (Dieterlen, 1951:3). After a series of processes (from the inaudible to rumbling, to whirling), the egg of the world (*miri*) appeared. It thereupon split in two. Something heavy and globule-shaped fell downwards; it will become the genie Pemba, who will form the earth after having wandered around space in a swirling movement. A vibration which was to become Faro, Master of Sky and Terrestrial Waters, was projected upwards. Pemba moulded a female creature, Musokoroni, with whom he coupled. Life started to proliferate. From their embraces an abundance of plants and animals were born. Pemba himself grew roots and became the first tree, the Balanza (acacia). During this time, the human species was born of Faro. Mankind took refuge under the Pemba-tree, which was green even in dry seasons, and they worshipped it. They were immortal but naked, and had no language. They received their food from the sky. Pemba extracted a tribute from them: all women must lie with him, give him their sap. Gnawed by jealousy, Musokoroni became furious. She began circumcising and sexually excising humans with her nails and teeth. Her own violence provoked her first menstrual period. Disorder set in and the earth became impure. Aided by Faro, Pemba pursued Musokoroni throughout the universe but she refused to submit. At the end of a long life she went mad, and died destitute.

By coupling with women, the Tree gave birth to a multitude of new beings, both plants and animals. Worn out by this work, Pemba increased his demands. Men had to feed him with their own blood, by slitting their wrists. Women were forced to offer him menstrual blood. In exchange, humanity remained immortal. Pemba made men and women younger when they reached the age of fifty-nine; he also gave them fire.

However these blood offerings exhausted the humans, who came to know hunger. Faro than taught them to eat wild tomatoes. He also decided to put an end to Pemba's intemperate rule. The two genies fought and Faro won. Then began the benevolent reign of the water genie.

Abandoned by his former subjects, the Pemba tree cursed them and humanity came to know sickness and death. Faro brought them the rain, and bestowed upon them speech but declared that he could not shield them from their mortal destiny. The various species ceased to reproduce at random. Thenceforth women, impregnated by Faro, gave birth only to human beings, twins and no longer individuals. Yet men turned away from him to follow Teliko, the air genie, Faro's rival. Faro threw him against a crag after Teliko had tried to cross the sea, and deprived him of his virility. He punished men by ending twin births. He also condemned them to manual labour by giving them articulated extremities. Through the Blacksmith, he gave them eight cereals. He classified men, animals and vegetables in separate categories. Animated by a vibratory power, he reorganised the universe. Primarily, he created the seven stories of the sky, lodging himself on the seventh, whence he sends the beneficial rain. The sun, for which Faro 'pulls the rope' is an avatar of Pemba. The empty space separating earth and sky, remained Teliko's domain.

This concise summary is sufficient to permit a first conclusion. The reader will have easily recognised Nommo's features in the figure of Faro, the water genie. He might also suspect that the Pemba-Musokoroni couple have something to do with the Fox and his twin sister. However, the respective relations between these principal protagonists are far from identical. First, Faro alone assumes the sovereignty attributed to Amma in the Dogon myth. Faro is unique; an androgyn, he does not undergo the sacrificial rupture which establishes Nommo as a double being, as sexually differentiated twins. 'The opposition of the sexes, which is conveyed in the myth by the corporal separation of Pemba and Musokoroni, by their disagreements and quarrels (the source of all cosmic disorders), is counterbalanced by a harmonious understanding and union, established by Faro as an androgyn' (Dieterlen, 1951:55.)

Let us start by studying this central figure more thoroughly. Faro's head is 'comparable to that of a white woman: the eyes are black and piercing, the hair black, smooth and long like a horse's tail' (Dieterlen, 1951:41). This dominating female factor becomes more specific when Faro gives birth to the first human ancestors: The genie 'gave birth to two female twins on a desert knoll' (Dieterlen 1951:14). A variant of the myth, gathered by de Ganay, presents Faro and Musokoroni as 'female twins within the divine substance' (de Ganay, 1949). Dieterlen admits the pre-eminence of the female form in the representation of Faro (Dieterlen, 1951:42). This is not without importance: an intact, androgynous, undivided and ambisexual being, the Bambara water genie presents the same predominantly female character as the Dogon Nommo *after the sacrificial castration* (see p.135). One of the graphic signs taught to the initiates of the Komo society refers to Faro explicitly as a woman, this time flanked by a male twin, Koni, just as Musokoroni is accompanied by Pemba (Dieterlen and Cissé, 1972:183–5).

This ideogram, concerning the first mythical couple and called the 'portrait of Koni's perfection' obviously calls to mind the Dogon image of the cosmic egg, in whose lower part are lodged two androgyns with male dominance, prefigurations of two sets of twins. However, in Bambara cosmogony, it is androgyn with female dominance (Faro) who takes all the initiative. The mixed twin couple, Pemba ($\triangle$)-Musokoroni(O) rise to confront her. Here again the Dogon myth is transformed. Whereas Ogo (the Fox) leaves his female twin, Yasigui, and is doomed to sterility, Pemba couples voluptuously, passionately, with his companion Musokoroni, engendering a profusion of animal and vegetable species. What is more, this great erotomaniac has sex with all women, to the point of exhaustion. This very excess of sexuality brings on the break-up of the initial couple: Musokoroni leaves Pemba because she is jealous, and starts causing trouble. The Dogon schema defining the Fox's relationship with his female twin is thus reversed.

Musokoroni is the active, mobile agent of disorder, whereas Pemba literally took root after his initial vibrating movement. In Dogon myth, on the contrary, Ogo (the Fox) is perpetually on the move while his companion Yasigui stays in the sky, waiting to come and upset the social order established by the first ancestors. The physical aspect of Musokoroni is comparable to the Fox's: 'This creature had two long, pointed ears and an animal's chest; the rest of its body was human, but had a tail' (Dieterlen,

1951:16). Like the Fox, Musokoroni taught men the first agricultural techniques (Dieterlen, 1951:39). The first seed she cultivated was the one which, according to the Dogon, was planted by the Fox: the red fonio (*Digitaria exilis*) (Dieterlen and Cissé, 1972:35).

In another remarkable transformation, the genie of terrestrial waters (Faro) begins by collaborating with Pemba who, as a tree on solid ground, symbolises *natura naturans*. Mankind, Faro's descendants, are themselves part of this epoch of wild nature, since they are naked and communicate only by grunts. Spontaneously, they place themselves under the Pemba-tree's protection. This first phase of the myth presents the reign of undifferentiated nature, before civilisation. Although men had fire, they did not need to farm or cook. But the excesses of Pemba, the terrifying ruler, who fed on men and women's blood, brought on a new reign, marked by the appearance of language, work and death.

The advent of Faro requires a human sacrifice. When the insatiable Pemba was at the height of his power, a woman who was exhausted from giving menstrual blood fainted one night while passing through a wild tomato field. 'When she regained her senses, Faro put into her head the idea of eating the fruit. It became blood inside her body and after her strength returned, she got up and went to bathe in the Niger. The famine in the area was so great that sand was the only food. She was seized by Faro, who slit her nose and navel and opened her stomach. He ate the red pulp he found there. He counted the seeds and found a multiple of seven. Each tomato bore within it both blood and the principle of twin births (3+4), which are the basic elements that make up a human being. Faro placed the life principle in this fruit. Men and women, on learning this, ate it in order to be regenerated and to continue to feed the balanza (acacia) which, in exchange, made them young again' (Dieterlen, 1951:22).

However, Faro could not endure this sharing and he soon proclaimed himself the only master, since he had given men water and the fruit of life. Pemba uprooted himself and confronted Faro. 'The struggle was as sharp as their words, as brutal as hate', but Faro was the victor (Dieterlen, 1951:22). First women, then men turned away from Pemba to worship Faro, who, in exchange for their lost immortality, granted them twin births, whereas during Pemba's reign women bore only single children (Dieterlen, 1951:25). Let us consider this data. The new law imposed by Faro is indeed strange. At first, the androgyn maintains, at the price of a sacrifice, the uncertain immortality of men, who pay Pemba a perpetual blood debt. When mankind breaks away from the latter in order to recognize Faro's supremacy, they become mortal but acquire 'twinship', the prefiguration of which was in the blood of the sacrificial victim, nourished with tomato juice.

Sacrifice is the foundation of existence. Death is the very price of life paid Faro, who continues to demand human victims. To the first of the eight old men who have reached the end of their lives Faro says, 'You are going to die'. The man went to the bank of a swift stream and found himself unable to move. In the hope of reviving him, his friends threw his body into the water. The second old man jumped in to rescue him. 'But his body, the navel and nose slit, floated to the surface of the water, which was reddened by blood. The body was then carried to a baobab tree and placed in a crack in the trunk. Eight days later, the third old man drowned while swimming; at that spot the water became red. The fourth old man, on seeing that, concluded that Faro demanded sacrifices. He was the first priest of the cult he set up, which from that time on men dedicated to the genie' (Dieterlen, 1951:25).

'The supreme sacrifice demanded by Faro was that of an albino. It took place whenever the realm was in danger' (Dieterlen, 1951:94). 'When the King had governmental difficulties, the victim was cut in half, at the stomach . . . His cries, gestures and excrement were believed to transmit a *nyama* ('vital force') which could do away with the difficulty the king faced' (Dieterlen, 1951:95). The cries, directed to Faro, could not be heard by human ears. The lower half of the body, put in the Niger, was given over to the water genie. Some of the river water was poured on the throne; the victim's head was hidden under its seat.

The victim's blood possessed an active potential for magic; in times of war it was dried in the sun and, 'before an assault, was hurled in the direction of the city to be captured' (Dieterlen, 1951:96). The Bambara say that the king 'found his sacrifice preceding him' when he advanced with his army (Dieterlen, 1951:96).

At the end of the last chapter we suggested that the albino was the king's double; the king himself had to be sacrificed in extreme circumstances. Strange affinities linked the king, Faro and the albino. The seventh sky where Faro dwells is 'the seat of domination, especially of all royalty' (Dieterlen, 1951:29). On earth, the king obviously represented Faro; his wickerwork head-dress evoked the vibratory movement of 'Faro creating everything in the universe' (Dieterlen, 1951:40). Although at first an immaterial creature, a pure 'voice', Faro borrowed human shape from Teliko, an albino. While flying over the sea in order to dominate the world, Teliko was fed on his own substance. 'He gnawed his own flesh, and his bones were soon bare. The marrow was coming out. It changed into red copper that fell into the sea and fed Faro' (Dieterlen, 1951:41). Whenever Teliko came down to the level of the water, a fish-dog (sic), Faro's messenger, sang to attract him. Faro caught and took possession of him, but left his genitals to the fish. Ever since, Faro's body has been made up of albino flesh and copper half and half.

Thus Faro seems to have acquired a human shape thanks to the self-sacrifice of an albino, incorporating his substance after castrating him. In the Dogon myth, Nommo acquired a twin body after undergoing castration and then sacrifice. The inversion is complete, for the albino is the very antithesis of twins in Dogon thought: the first Albino resulted from the transformation of a pair of twins in Yasigui's womb (see p.155). The same idea prevails in Bambara thought: the albino started out as twins who fused into one person, a doomed, diminished creature, because his parents have transgressed, supposedly by having had sexual intercourse in the middle of the day. Consequently, the twins originally granted by Faro are merged within the womb, and their skin is bleached (Dieterlen, 1951:88).

Let us compare the Bambara and Dogon myths (Fig. 25).

Fig. 25

Nommo	*Faro*
Androgynous genie, victim of the first sacrifice	Androgynous sacrificer genie.
Changed into twins with opposite genders after being castrated.	Took his physical form from the flesh of an albino that he castrated.

This contrast invites us to reconsider Faro's sexual ambiguity. From the very beginning this divinity is presented as a feminine creature, doubled by a male twin who lives in his shadow (Koni); the latter 'owes all his fame to his wife Faro who was considered to be the best among wives and among mothers' 'Dieterlen & Cissé; 1972:185). We shall henceforth refer to Faro as a woman. Yet in a contradictory way, Faro has the essential characteristics of an androgyn. At the beginning of her reign, this strange creature bestowed twin births upon humanity, yet as soon as she had assimilated the substance of the castrated albino, she hastened to put an end to this situation.

The problematic of sacrifices now appears in a different light. Faro, by sacrificing Teliko, identifies with the victim who provided her with his body. Any albino is 'of the same essence as Faro' and has extraordinary magical powers. 'Whoever possesses his skull will have a big family and be prosperous; his hair will bring wealth; his bone marrow will bestow gold and copper. If you sit upon the spot where his bones are buried, your every wish will be granted. His excrement, mixed with the seeds, will increase the year's harvest' (Dieterlen, 1951:88). Cissé identifies different sorts of albinos. Teliko is a *zoroble*, a creature with red lips and gums, a black body and blond hair. An albino with a completely red body is called *ngombele*. As for Faro, she is sometimes white and sometimes black. Her eyes redden whenever she inflicts punishment. When she took Teliko's substance for herself, she did not take his skin; instead, she used it to make a war drum (Cissé, personal communication).

The capture of the albino's body secured absolute power, wealth and strength for Faro or for the king, her representative on earth. But the king only sacrificed albinos while waiting to be immolated, like a monster. This familiar problematic will be explored later on.

Bambara sacrificial practice is organised around Faro and the ancestors. Men no longer exhaust themselves by giving blood to the Pemba tree in exchange for immortality. In each family Pemba is represented by wooden stumps called *pembele*. These venerable objects receive the defunct vital forces (*nyama*) while awaiting new births (Dieterlen, 1951:37). Sacrificial loci multiply and are diversified. There the blood of domestic animal is shed to maintain the life of man, now mortal. Emptied of his spiritual principles, the victim 'nourishes' the altar. Roughly cut stones refer to the mythical stone associated with the place where Faro gave birth to the first twin girls (*Ibid*:90). The objects *boli* made up of 'an amalgam of elements representing the parts of the universe' are issued from ' globules' left in space when Faro descended to earth (*Ibid*:92). Via the blood shed upon these various altars, an energy circuit is set up between the sacrifier and the propitiated force. In this respect the sacrificial mechanism is comparable to that described among the Dogon, as Dieterlen points out (*Ibid*:90). However, we have just seen that the founding myth is not the same. Much unlike Nommo, whose body was given to the world to help in its genesis, Faro merely gives another form to the initial blood debt claimed by Pemba. He demands in particular the sacrifice of albinos, under the control of his representative the king, who is himself the ultimate sacrificial victim.

The sacrifice of the celestial ram *Bambara)*

The question becomes more complicated upon examining another version of the myth related by Youssouf Cissé (paper, 1980). A celestial supreme god rises against Pemba and Musokoroni. This primeval couple of terrestrial twins provoked God's anger when he coupled with a donkey and she with a dog. (This episode conveys the state of confusion reigning in nature and mankind, expressed differently in the preceding version, by asserting that the tree coupled with women to engender, in disorder, all kinds of animal and vegetable species.) To end the pollution of the earth provoked by Pemba and Musokoroni's 'beastiality' God resorted to a sacrifice. In the sky, he created a white ram. The ends of his legs, as well as the neck and head, were black; on his forehead however was a white star. God slit the primeval ram's throat using a flash of lightning as a knife and dismembered it without flaying it. The animal's blood purified the universe, literally 'laundering' it; it rid it of a nauseating smell caused by sexual perversion. The remains were thrown head first into space, the legs in the direction of the four cardinal points. The ram bore the 'signs of the world', an ideogrammatical writing comparable to that inscribed by Dogon cosmogony in the cosmic egg before the appearance of word and action. According to Y. Cissé, the majority of sacrifices later carried out by men referred to this founding graphic reality.

Yet God eventually carries out a second sacrifice, this time an awesome one, a sacrifice of destruction, to end Musokoroni's acts. Endeavouring to seize control of the universe, she sent the winged folk to God in the hopes of obtaining knowledge and the secret of eternal youth. These birds, insects and butterflies were gigantic. Furious, God went to the fifth level of the sky and blasted Musokoroni's envoys with lightning. It destroyed most of the species; those who survived did so only in a smaller or shrivelled-up form. The hornbill, its wings, feet and back bone broken, submitted. He gathered the signs of the world in his big beak. The vulture, who, like the turtle dove, had remained faithful to Faro, brought the surviving birds under God's rule. Musokoroni gave birth to a corrupt humanity, little bush creatures (similar to the Dogon Andambulu, descended from the Fox). God also made the pond where Faro lived, overflow, causing a great flood. Faro's followers, who included various animal species, hid in an ark which drifted for seven days. Then the rain washed the sky. This was the beginning of the reign of Faro, the water genie, associated with the Blacksmith. The ram, sacrificed to the sky, came back to life, and became the ancestor of the ovine species.

Perhaps Noah's adventures interfere here with the traditional Mande cosmogony which, after all, could have easily adopted this biblical episode. We must not forget West Africa's—and especially the Bambara's—very ancient contact with Islam. We must not however lose sight of the fact that a celestial ark, a granary made of pure earth, containing the ancestors, seeds and living species, is the instrument of the second creation in Dogon cosmogony. The flood theme is found in Dieterlen's version, though somewhat in the background: 'following the treason of Musokoroni and those who listened to her, impurity was transmitted to the earth: the water covering it became troubled, changed colour and became 'difficult'. It either dried up or, on the contrary, flooded the countryside, drowning living creatures' (Dieterlen, 1951:44–5).

When Cissé wrote down the esoteric version that he had presented orally, he enlarged it, adding new events (Cissé, 1981). Let us examine this text before drawing further conclusions.

In the sky God created twins of opposite sexes: Musokoroni and her younger brother Pemba. Musokoroni rebelled against her creator and, after pushing Pemba ahead of her, jumped into the cosmos. They twirled down to earth along their unwinding umbilical cord. But the cord broke, and the pair lost contact with God. They started dancing obscenely. Their later acts were all so violent that the Creator had to intervene through a series of sacrifices.

God uprooted Musokoroni's and Pemba's tree. Hurled down from above, it split into pieces. Each piece became double, thereby giving birth to twins, who soon became giants. They were so tall that 'they only had to raise their arms in order to grasp the stars' (Cissé, 1981:42). Provoked beyond measure by Musokoroni's sarcasm and her children's actions, God made heaven collide with earth. The giants perished in multitudes. Those who were not vaporised plunged into the depths of the earth or changed into dwarfs. This was the first sacrifice made by God.

However, the 'true sacrifice' involved a ram to purify the universe. Musokoroni and Pemba came out of the cataclysm unharmed. Motivated by resentment and hate, Musokoroni coupled with her twin brother. She sank into lust. 'She made love with the earth, with tree trunks, with thorns, with the wind, with hot sunbeams, with stones, with red ants' (Cissé, 1981:44). Pemba was also seized by lewd frenzy. In a mad spell, Musokoroni tore her brother's foreskin with her teeth and her own clitoris with her fingernails. These acts were so brutal that they could not lie together. They had to separate. Musokoroni copulated with a dog and Pemba with a she-donkey. These unnatural acts raised an unbearable stench. To purify the universe God used the dense matter in heaven to make a white ram with black spots and then sacrificed it with a stroke of lightning. He thereupon sent a second pair of mixed twins, Faro and her brother, Bemba, to earth. They came down from heaven in a gold canoe that contained the 'signs' of all living beings. They settled near a ficus tree by a pond. Meanwhile Musokoroni was inciting the dwarfs to revolt. She taught them the secrets of plants and of divination. However, she grew more and more decrepit, becoming 'hunch-backed and wizened'. Her body was covered with nauseating pustules, her fingers were crooked her hair sparse and spiky. Faro, on the contrary, was shining with beauty and youth. Mad with jealousy, Musokoroni persuaded the men around Faro to leave her. She also persuaded 'flying beings' to go up to heaven and find out the secret of eternal youth, of 'nonaging'. Some of these winged creatures were enormous. When they reached the fourth sky, God, from the fifth sky, poured out upon them an incandescent sunny matter. Several species became extinct. The survivors suffered serious burns, and became smaller. Only the vulture and the turtle-dove came through unharmed. This hecatomb was God's third sacrifice. The vulture was given the tasks of picking up the dead and bringing the wounded back to earth where the hyenas were allowed to devour them.

Musokoroni grew stubborn. 'Using all kinds of cosmetics to make herself, if not beautiful, at least attractive and desirable, she daily drew into her lair more and more young men from Faro's camp.' They became—for a few minutes only—her lovers, for she killed all those who penetrated her and immediately threw their bodies out to the dogs (Cissé, 1981:56–7). So God sent a flood. He made water spurt out of the earth and rain pour from heaven. This new cataclysm engulfed all Musokoroni's 'children' except the dwarfs, who walled themselves up in a cave. Even Musokoroni drowned. This was the fourth sacrifice. Using her canoe, Faro saved the human beings and animals that had remained faithful. Faro's era began. God revived the ram he had sacrificed in heaven. He made it emerge from the pond water. It mounted nine ewes and then was sacrificed again, this time by Faro. 'Since then, it is said, any true sacrifice presupposes the resurrection of the victim' (Cissé, 1981:59). A comparison of Cissé's oral version with the foregoing reveals, at the source, the very process that causes variations in a myth. Initiated into major Bambara cults, Cissé first presents us with a condensed version and then with an elaborated one. More than one conclusion can be drawn from this exemplary lesson.

The 'bad sacrifice' was repeated a second time in the 'written' version. In the first instance, it was directed against Musokoroni's human descendants, the giants who became dwarfs. These are the exact counterparts of the Yeban and Andambulu, the Fox's stunted progeny in the Dogon myth. The subsequent destruction of the winged beings, themselves initially giants, reproduced this event in the animal world. Like the human giants, these monstrous insects and winged creatures established an excessive conjuncture between Heaven and Earth. The two successive 'sacrifices', exterminated them or shrunk their sizes. Their destructive finality was again revealed in the flood that carried off Musokoroni herself. But the 'true sacrifice' was that of the celestial ram, repeated, in turn, on earth.

Cissé explicitly confirms two points of our thesis. First of all, the driving force in these disturbances was Musokoroni, the feminine element in the primordial pair of twins. Pemba, the younger brother, was hurled by his older sister into space. On earth, he merely followed his sister's baneful destiny. Faro, Musokoroni's counterpart in the other primordial pair of twins, was also a woman. Cissé pairs her with a male companion, Bemba (not to be confused with Pemba). Bemba, a very pale character, is but another name for the mysterious Koni, who appears as the male principal alongside Faro in other traditions.

It is easy to verify that the myth presented by Cissé constitutes a structural variant of the Dieterlen text. Faro has been pushed into the background; and a supreme God, similar to the Dogon's, has assumed sovereignty over the Universe. The fifth sky from which he struck down the rebellious animals was, according to the most common tradition, the seat from which Faro sentenced those who transgressed. This 'red sky' was the site of combats and of victory (Dieterlen, 1951:28). It was clearly a place of terrifying power. It was associated with blood, with fire and with hot, injurious winds (Dieterlen, 1951:28). The rebellion of the winged creatures, who tried to pry into God's secrets, must be set alongside the revolt of Teliko, the albino, who pursued the same aim for himself. In fact, Teliko, genie of the air with a 'hot body worn by the wind', arrogantly decided to journey to the ends of the world by rising into the sky above the sea (Dieterlen, 1951:25). The fight between Faro and Teliko, a flying creature, is a replica of the combat between God and the inhabitants of the air. Teliko lost his vital substance and was thrown onto a rock and castrated. Faro also smashed his right arm (Dieterlen, 1951:25). In Cissé's version, God reduced the number of winged species as well as their sizes. In Dieterlen's version, Faro, after her victory over Teliko, intervened in order to limit the anarchic proliferation of the living species that had been born from the Pemba-tree's embraces with women. She classified living beings by separating them into clear-cut categories (Dieterlen, 1951:29). She also put a stop to twin births in the human species (Dieterlen, 1951:26). She replaced an overly generous, continuous nature with a discontinuous natural order. After the 'bad' sacrifice, expressing God's wrath, men knew hunger and had to till the soil in order to eat (Cissé, 1980). After the sacrifice of Teliko, the airborne albino, Faro gave men articulated limbs to allow them to work the land (Dieterlen, 1951:26).

In the version gathered by Dieterlen, Faro unquestionably holds the position which Cissé accords to God. The latter wields lightning to punish the rebel birds, just as being struck by lightning is proof of Faro's revenge when she is angry (Dieterlen, 1951:44). We need not worry about which one is the canonical version. I shall merely point out that the sacrifice of the winged creatures carried out by God in the sky is the exact equivalent of the primeval sacrifice of the albino genie, Teliko, carried out by Faro on earth. All subsequent albino sacrifices explicitly belong to the category of 'bad sacrifices'. Cissé himself emphasises that this dreaded ritual act helps to establish a sovereign's political authority, just as the violent sacrifice of the winged creatures clearly established that of God over the universe (Cissé 1980). The fifth sky from which God attacked the hordes rising towards him, is the same one to which the king sacrifices before leaving to destroy the enemy. It is called the 'Red Sky' (Dieterlen, 1951:28). Now we have seen that one of the sacrificial procedures which help to rout the enemy is to throw dried albino blood towards them (see p.165). This cursed blood obviously does not have the same property as does the blood of 'good sacrifice', which releases a positive vital energy.

The version of the myth noted by Cissé proposes a new division of the sacrificial sphere. The albino sacrifices required by Faro resemble the sacrifices carried out in the shadows by those who practise black magic. In this perspective God, like the king, is involved in sorcery, at least in one respect. It is note-worthy that Bambara sorcerers notably sacrifice insects, thus reiterating God's act of destruction. On the other hand, most of the blood rites which are carried out on the altars are modelled on 'good sacrifice'. They repeat the purifying and regenerating sacrifice of the ram, carried out by the same divinity. This second model presents the domestic animal as an ideal victim, like the celestial ram. The blood shed on the altars (*boli*) gives life to the primordial 'signs' borne by the ram. It purifies and reinforces them. In order to realise this objective, domestic animals are accorded a very meticulous classification based on the colourings and markings on their hide (Cissé, 1980).

This 'good sacrifice' model apparently has nothing to do with the sacrifice of a god. Let us look a little closer, however. We might wonder whether the celestial ram, sacrificed, then resuscitated by God, is not in fact Faro's double; more exactly, Faro's male double, since the female aspect of the androgyn has appeared to be predominant. The white fleece evokes the actual colour of the water genie. The ram is also resusitated in the water. The black spots which mark the head (but not the forehead) and the feet can be related to the double physical aspect of Faro, sometimes 'white', sometimes 'black'. She keeps her secrets in a mysterious 'black water' (Dieterlen, 1951:45). We must not forget that the celestial ram bears all of the 'signs of the world', i.e., absolute knowledge, which only Faro possesses infallibly (Dieterlen and Cissé, 1972:26). Faro's black water is the third in a series of seven aquatic dwellings, which have their equivalent in the seven levels of the sky (Dieterlen and Cissé, 1972:26). Faro takes on the form of a golden-fleeced ram when she travels underground along veins of gold (Dieterlen and Cissé, 1972:44), and Cissé also tells us that the blood that flowed during the sacrifice of the celestial ram rendered the entire universe 'as pure as gold'. This celestial ram is also said to be a leaping gazelle (Cissé, 1980), and one of the animal forms which Faro likes to assume is precisely that of a gazelle (Dieterlen, 1951:44).

How can we fail to conclude that the ram sacrificed by God in the sky was an avatar of Faro? At the heart of the myth, as among the Dogon, a god who would be reborn was put to death. Commenting on this episode, Cissé states that the ram was reborn in the pond and then sacrificed again at Faro's order *in order to establish her authority* (Cissé, in personal communication). The course of events suggests that the water genie sacrificed her masculine counterpart in order to accede to royalty, as though she carried out a substitute sacrifice at the time of her enthrone- ment. The sacrifices of albinos can also be interpreted as the slaying of Faro herself since these creatures are 'of the same essence' as her.

These two sacrifices in fact constituted the founding acts of earthly kingship. The sovereign, Faro's representative, had two opposite but complementary functions: as war leader he sacrificed albinos, and as land leader, he controlled the 'good sacrifice' of the ram (Cissé, in personal communication).

This double aspect of kingship, sometimes terrifying and sometimes benevolent, recalls Faro's ambivalence. The twin nature of this androgy- nous genie becomes clearer. As a woman, Faro had a twin brother Bemba, who remained inactive. Her real masculine counterpart was the celestial ram, the victim of the purifying sacrifice. She, on the other hand, was an all-powerful sacrificer, who vanquished Pemba and Teliko and founded the sacred monarchy. Her anger was to be seen in the red glare of her eyes. The sacrifice of the ram—of the male principal—had no other purpose than to ceaselessly regenerate her female reproductive function, her eminent quality of being eternally young and beautiful compared to her decrepit rival, Musokoroni. Maybe we can now better understand the reasons that the Bambara give so much importance to the femininity of this terrifying divinity. Do they not say that this formidable warrior, made up of albino flesh, is 'the best among wives and mothers' (see p.166)?

This version of the myth strikingly resembles the Dogon's: the divine androgyn who died in the sky and was reborn in the form of twins of opposite sexes (Nommo) has been replaced, in the Bambara sacrificial scene by an animal—the ram—filled with celestial matter, whose sacrifice preceded the descent to earth of a pair of twins, Faro and Bemba, often assimilated into a unique, androgynous being. This similarity is confirmed by the transformation of Nommo into a ram, which is often found in Dogon oral literature (Calame-Griaule, 1965:403). Dieterlen emphasizes that the sheep was one of the reborn Nommo's avatars (during a May 11, 1978 meeting of the Laboratoire Associé No. 221). Ogotemmêli described Nommo to Griaule as a golden ram that can be seen moving in the sky before every storm during the rainy season (Griaule, 1948:131).

Teliko's position needs a last explanation. This genie of the air, after suffering defeat at the hands of Faro, governs over an 'empty space separating heaven and earth' (Dieterlen, 1951:29). He is none other than the albino double of the twin couple Pemba-Musokoroni, responsible for disorders. Y. Cissé establishes precise correlations between them (Cissé, paper, 1980). Musokoroni is associated with the 'blowing of hot air that burns everything' Her condition was heat; her colour red. But Teliko is also materialised as a fast moving ball of fire. Like Pemba, he is the drying wind. The bad tendencies of the one were attributed to the other. Clearly, Musokoroni, Pemba and Teliko are one and the same personage, the principle of drought, denoted in the Dogon myth by the Fox.

The Bambara myth dealing with the struggle for cosmic supremacy clearly does not continue in the same way as the Dogon. However the same theme does run through the replication pattern. The Dogon God had one opponent, the Fox. Faro, who literally assumed divine power, fought against Pemba and then Teliko. Faro herself was replicated, as a white ram and as a woman with black or white skin made from albino flesh. Under his animal form, the genie was a sacrificial victim; in the second, a sacrificer. This duality was, as we have seen central to the Bambara sacred kingship (Fig. 26).

Fig. 26

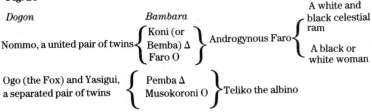

Whereas in the Dogon myth there is strong and constant opposition between Nommo and the Fox, the Bambara myth describes a literal transubstantiation based on cannibalism. Faro fed on Teliko's marrow transformed into copper, and identified with the victim by taking its flesh. Before setting up her own dominion, Faro collaborated with Pemba, who had an insatiable appetite for human blood (Dieterlen's version). This exhausting tribute, required to feed Pemba and provide for humanity's immortality, gave way, when Faro took power, to the bloody levy of albinos in a population now fated to die.

These transformations of the Dogon myth accompany the development of sacred kingship, which no doubt explains them. Considerable political differences separate the *hogon*, a religious chief confined to his abode, and the Bambara sovereign, a military chief who is head of a centralised state. The Bambara king's power 'has no limit' (Dieterlen and Cissé, 1972:99). He openly assumes Faro's position on earth.The sacrifice of albinos which he observes, 'totally inmoved' guarantees him success in war and riches (Dieterlen, 1951:95).

Of course, the Dogon's water genie could also get angry. Like Faro, Nommo drowns those who have broke his prohibitions and slit their noses and navels (Dieterlen and de Ganay, 1942). In Dogon mythology however, Nommo was not violent, like Faro. Faro was a terrifying monarch who, as sacrificer, took over control of the world, whereas Nommo was a sacrificial victim whose reign never fully overcame that of the rebellious Fox. The sovereign takeover of the universe under the sign of Faro requires that the king, her representative, assume the roles of both sacrificer and victim. If he is Faro, the slayer of albinos, he is also potentially the albino destined for a sacrificial death, like all sacred monarchs.

Dog sacrifice among the Minyanka

In Bambara as well as in Dogon thought, graphic symbols, the ideogrammatic expressions of the divine plan, represent the foundation of the universe. Bambara culture has strongly influenced a peasant lineage society whose 'Voltaic' language does not belong to the Mandé linguistic group, namely the Minyanka of Mali. Several of their ritual institutions come directly from the Bambara; among them are the initiate societies, Komo and Nya (Dieterlen, 1951:142). The Minyanka stand out, however, because of the exceptional importance they accord the Nya sacrificial cult. Though the Komo is placed under the sign of Faro, we shall show that in Minyanka country the followers of Nya are of the Musokoroni persuasion. This analysis is based on the work of three Belgian researchers, Philippe Jespers, Danielle Jonckers, and Jean-Paul Colleyn.

There is a primary and obvious symbolic contrast between the Komo and the Nya. The former's mysterious power is conveyed through the medium of a mask, the latter's through the mouth of a possessed person. (Jespers, unpublished paper, May 11, 1978). The Nya cult is but one aspect of the many ritual practices of the Minyanka. The altar of the Supreme Being (Kle) regularly receives libations of beer, millet porridge, and the blood of white chickens (Jonckers, 1976:93, 97). Animal sacrifices performed on very diverse altars fall into the general category of 'gift' (*kara*). By examining the specific role of blood we shall see, however, that animal sacrifice is a type of communication far more complex than mere exchange. Among the recipients are the following: the ancestors, the anvil (given to men by the mythic Vulture), the village's Foundation Jug, Tyele ('the Old Woman'), and Fari, the water genie (Jonckers, 1976:92–3). These last two names designate characters which are familiar from Bambara mythology: Musokoroni and Faro. The members of initiate groups also sacrifice on portable altars (*yapere*) made from various materials constituting a sort of summary of the world (Jonckers, 1976:94). The sacrificed animals are chickens, goats, sheep, cattle and, surprisingly, dogs (Jonckers, 1976:96).

The choice of the victim is determined by liturgical tradition, by divination, by the word of a possessed person, by the mask of the Komo initiate group, or by children. Thus Jespers tells us sacrifice is directly connected to 'a word that comes from afar', from a mythic world preceding our own. (Jespers, unpublished paper, May 11, 1978). This diversified divinatory mechanism, which cannot be dissociated from sacrifice, is based on an extraordinarily subtle code, a truly bizarre classificatory system. It carries differentiation to absurd lengths by introducing into the small world of the barnyard forty types of chickens, some of which are purely imaginary (Jespers, unpublished papers, May 11, 1978). It is as if Minyanka culture endeavours to render most meaningful the seemingly banal domestic species to which other African cultures (the Thonga, for example) pay little attention, or none at all (the Lele). The only purpose of this procedure is to determine with the utmost precision the sacrificial agent which best suits a given situation, according to a system of cosmological correspondences. The Nya cult demands a veritable slaughter of dogs. It is this particular aspect of the Minyanka sacrificial system that we shall examine. The word *Nya* designates both one of the main initiate groups and the extraordinary magic force located in the particularly fearsome fetishes. A source of fertility, these *yapere* also protect the villagers against sorcerers' attacks (Jonckers, 1976:93). Jespers analyses the mechanism of these unusual sacrifices in relation to the origin myth (Jespers, 1976).

It is thanks to the dog that men were able to snatch away from the bush those most prestigious *yapere* which make up the Nya. Formerly, they were held captive by the 'red monkeys' (*cercopithecus*). An etiological tale shows that 'the Nya's knowledge came from the violent killing of its former possessors, who lived in the bush' (Jespers, 1976:176).

'One day, a hunter and his dog surprised a group of red monkeys stealing peanuts from a field near the village. The dog quickly put all the monkeys to flight, except for one which, bent under the weight of three sacks, could not escape his attacker. The dog ripped open his throat. Upon their return to the village, the dog betrayed the secret of the sacks' contents, and immediately died.' This is why, the narrator adds, 'today, dogs' throats are slit for the Nya'. In the version recorded by Colleyn, the dog was slain by the men he initiated with the knowledge; the hunter was killed by Nya as the result of an excessive state of possession (Colleyn, personal communication).

The Nya's mythic descent is indeed complicated. The magic force contained in the Nya's three sacks goes back to humanity's first ancestors.

A chain of dramatic events links them with the world of the living: the dog dies for betraying the Nya's secrets to men, after having itself killed the former owner. What is more, during the transmission of the secrets from one village to another, the new 'owner of the Nya' is supposed to die shortly afterwards just like the primeval hunter; some pieces of his body are then included in the sacks containing the fetishes (Jespers, 1976:139). Jespers fully understands that 'a murder pact' is at the base of the institution; 'here, sacrifice refers back to time immemorial when man snatched the *yapere* away from the mythic beast of the bush' (Jespers, 1976:139).

From a comparative point of view one cannot fail to be struck once again by the astonishing parallels which are discernible between this sacrificial complex and the ideology of sacred kingship. To be sure, the Minyanka do not have this institution. Yet it is as if the initiate groups of the Nya collectively exercise a magical force of the same essence as royalty—a dangerous power, outside society, rooted in nature and directly connected with cosmic forces. More than one African myth attributes to a hunter-hero the introduction of the magic principle of kingship. Like a sacred king, the initial human 'owner' of the Nya is doomed to a rapid end, and later on, the dog becomes a substitute victim. This sacrificial animal, presents a very specific ambivalence: though he is scorned, his infallible sense of smell assures, 'so to speak the link between the domestic and the savage world' (Jespers, 1976:138). Although it is a fertility instrument and a protection against sorcery, the Nya itself is steeped in murder. As we shall see it belongs to the descent line of Musokoroni, whom the Minyanka worship under the name of Tyele (Jonckers, 1976:93) or Tyelere ('The Little Old Lady') (Jespers, 1976:194).

The Nya, that magical, sovereign force closely linked with sorcery, is acquired at the cost of the death of he who had obtained it. It is maintained in the heart of society at the cost of a perpetual blood debt; the Nya is most certainly the 'fetishised' equivalent of a royal power. It is as if the Minyanka had, at least partially, taken up the cause of Musokoroni, or that of the Dogon Fox, in order to assure themselves collective control over the universe. All the *yapere* fetishes contained in the Nya's three sacks refer to secret graphic signs which designate the ancestral cosmic forces. Jespers, who began to analyse them shows how these ideograms are brought into play in the sacrifices dedicated to the Nya.

The annual Nya ceremonies are held just before planting and just after harvest. The three heavy sacks are carried by possessed people called 'the Nya's horses' to the sanctuary in the bush. They enter it backwards and put down their load on the east side, facing three big jars located on the west side. They thus set the boundaries of a cosmic space which conforms to the plan of divine creation. The *yapere*, taken out of the bags, are placed in the jars according to precise arrangement which constitutes 'a logical classifying procedure for the powers of the universe' (Jespers, 1976:112). The bags vary in size. The big one (called 'the bag of the soul of the sky and of the earth') and the middle sized one (called 'the bag of the soul of humans and of animals') contain eighty-five *yapere*; the small one (called 'the bag of the soul of all things') contains eighty-six, *id est* one extra (Jespers, 1976:113). The latter is the dwelling place of a pair of particularly powerful genies, the twin ancestors of humanity. These twins are sacred monsters; they were born after a prolonged pregnancy (ten months). They are attached to a single trunk and their body is scarred by leprosy. They are gifted with extraordinary intelligence. These twins are worshipped in the village's sacred wood, but they can also come and lodge in the Nya's little bag where the *yapere* which support them is made 'of a warthog's tusk and two pieces of gold, a symbol of the divine intangibility which animates them' (Jespers, 1976:115). In all rituals the twin ancestors undertake the mediation between Kle (God) and man.

Each of the eighty-six *yapere* contained in the small bag is related to one of the eighty-six graphic signs engraved on a small rectangular wooden board hidden in the Nya's house, out of sight. Each *yapere*, during its fabrication, is connected with the corresponding sign in the course of a rite which ensures 'a kind of transmutation of the sign's essence into the very nature of the *yapere*' (Jespers, 1976:117). In this sequence, the first sign is in the form of a Greek cross symbolising the union of the first ancestors, the 'Earth Mother' (Tyelere) and 'Sky Father' (Nyolere); it is materialised by a *yapere* made of a warthog's tusk containing a grain of gold (Nyolere) and a root of a bastard mahogany (cailcidrat) (Tyelere) (Jespers, 1976:119). Nyolere and Tyelere gave birth to the pair of deformed monstrous twins, described above. It is the power of the twin ancestors (and not that of their parents) which, as we shall see, constitutes the ultimate agent of the vital forces brought into play in the sacrifice. Like the primeval Twins, the Nya possesses the power of the leper (Jespers, 1976:132).

Let us go back to the sacrificial jar. The sacrificer first takes out all of the *yapere* contained in the big bag, one by one, then places them in the first jar which is in front of him. He starts with the *yapere* related to the sign of the union of sky and earth, which we have just described, but this he lays at the foot of the jar; it will surmount all the others at the end of this procedure. Thus the most remote ancestors are on the top of the jar 'as mediators between the Sky and the Earth' (Jespers, 1976:121). The most important *yapere* are laid out 'according to a cosmogonic axis which goes from the nadir (the bottom of the jar) to the zenith (the top of the jar)' (Jespers, 1976:126). The other *yapere* are grouped according to various 'roads' in such a way that, at the end of this transfer the jar forms 'the compact expression of a complete division of the forces ruling the universe' (Jespers, 1976:127).

The sacrificer repeats the process with the contents of the second bag which he transfers into the second jar. When the small bag has been emptied into the third jar, the warthog's tusk and the two pieces of gold, used as supports for the monstrous twins, are placed on top of the jar, capping the *yapere* of their parents (Tyelere and Nyolere). By uttering an incantation, the sacrificer confers all power over the bush and village on the twin genies (Jespers, 1976:129). Jespers comment knowledgeably on this reversal of the order of the mythic generations, which sets up the pair of monstrous twins as the true sovereigns of the universe, rather than their parents. He shows particularly how the twins contrast in every way with the rest of Tyelere's children, all creatures who lack something. Indeed, the 'Little Old Lady' later gives birth to pigeon-toed dwarfs, one-legged creatures, and deaf beings, who all become genies of the bush (Jespers, 1976:132). Though the primordial parents (the sky and the earth) cooperate with Kle (God) in order to assure fertility, they could always compromise divine creation, as they did in the beginning (Jespers, 1976:133). Born prematurely (the reverse of their twin children), Nyolere and Tyelere are, in fact, 'agitated, visible creatures, indulging in sorcery for a long mythic period of time' (Jespers, 1976:131). The Minyanka affirm that the Nya can accept the sacrifice of destructive sorcerers (Jespers, 1976:133).

Let us follow Jespers in his study of the mechanics of the sacrifice (Jespers, 1976:134–6). Here, in three jars, are all of the *yapere*, classified according to a strict order. A dog is now clubbed to death outside the sanctuary while the sacrificer slits a small chicken's throat as he says a prayer. Hanging the dog upside down over the first jar, 'he opens a large hole, the length of its throat', then turns it round and round, until all the blood has drained out.

Colleyn, for his part, describes this immolation as follows: 'The dog is bled over the altars; its throat is slit and it is held above them. When the blood stops flowing, two initiates take, respectively, the left front paw and the right rear one, swing the dog three times over the altars, and then throw it over the wall. They thus make sure that the *nyama* (the vital principle) has left the animal's body and gone into the altars' (Colleyn, personal communication). The sacrificer sees to it that all the *yapere* are thoroughly soaked.

However, there is one *yapere* which cannot under any circumstances receive sacrificial blood, it is one which serves as a dwelling place for the twin genies on top of the third jar. Here is the initiates' interpretation: 'After having poured the blood on all of the Nya's *yapere*—except the twins' *yapere*—we usually left the sanctuary . . . On returning, what did we see? The twins had gone down to the bottom of the jar, then had come back to the surface, sucking in all the blood from the *yapere* on the way. By doing this they had transformed the dog's heavy blood, at the top, into a light blood, which they then sent back to the dog with the *nyama*, the Nya's vital force'. Commenting on this interpretation, Jespers explains the mechanism: the circulation of blood is controlled by the twins' *yapere*; it is used to eliminate the impurity of the dog, a scorned animal. He reminds us that the twins' *yapere* contains two pieces of gold, 'symbols of Kle's intangible purity' (Jespers, 1976:135). The victim's blood undergoes a veritable transmutation in status; it goes from the realm of impurity (heaviness) to that of an absolute purity (lightness). Light blood is the 'vehicle of the Nya's vital force' (Jespers, 1976:136). The victim 'stores' it and the initiates benefit from it in their turn, by eating the animal.

Let us examine all this more closely. We must not forget that the dog represents man, the ultimate victim demanded by the Nya. Even though there is no evidence of this practice, the Minyanka say that, before the colonial period, they sacrificed a madman instead of a dog (Jespers, May 11, 1978). Dog or madman, the victim occupies a marginal position in the village, which benefits totally from this contribution of energy that comes from the bush powers. The victim is thus in a mediatory situation. The sacrifice imposes on it an ontological transformation; emptied of its own vital forces, it is filled with a light vital force, as pure as gold. Jespers considers that it undergoes a 'consecration' and that it goes from the 'profane' sphere to the 'sacred'. I do not think, myself, that Hubert and Mauss's model quite fits this transfer of energy.

Let us examine the myth—relating to the fabrication of the Nya's sack. Napelege (literally 'Little Old Man') went with his brother to his pastures in the bush. Suddenly he saw big globules (*kulukuta*) vibrating and whirling as they fell from the sky towards the earth. He ran all over the place in order to gather them. When he had done so, he had so many that he knew neither where nor how to keep them. Kle then gave him a sign: in Napelege's pastures was an antelope with a torques that had been labouring for several days. By this sign Napelege understood that he would have to intervene. He opened its belly and let out two small twin antelopes. He then recovered the ejected placenta and consecrated it as Nya's first sack.

The antelope's prolonged pregnancy corresponds exactly with that of the Earth Mother, Tyelere, in the myth about the origin of the twins:

'Tyelere ('the Little Old Lady') spent her pregnancy in the bush and could not manage to deliver the child. Her brother Nyolere ('the Little Old Beginning') questioned the chain [which hung from the sky], who let him know that this foretold the birth of twins, who would be far superior to them. Indeed Tyelere gave birth to abnormally shaped twins. Born late, they were Siamese twins and their body was tumefied by leprosy. However, they were gifted with an astonishing intelligence. Quickly, Nanya, the male twin (literally, 'the man who has come') hatched a plan to leave their parents: he played dead and told his sister to cry for him, which she did. 'I did not want to leave', she said, 'and now you tell me that we are leaving. They want to bury you dead, and bury me alive'. Confused, Nyolere decided to bury them anyway, in the bush. Yet he had hardly begun to dig a grave when a bolt of lightning from Kle blinded him. The twins took advantage of this to flee and to settle in a thick wood in the bush (the future sacred wood)' (Jespers, 1976:130).

There are evident analogies between these two stories about delayed pregnancy in which the principal actor is either 'the little old man' or 'the little old man of the beginning' *id est* the primordial ancestor Nyolere. It is as if the placenta of the two antelopes—used as an envelope for the first Nya sack is symbolically substituted for the placenta of the twin Ancestors, who in fact reside in this sack. However the second myth lays bare the conflict opposing the first generation of ancestors (Tyelere and Nyolere) against the second (the monstrous twins). Jespers notes that this story belongs to a cycle of tales or myths 'in which the twins always have the upper hand over their parents' generation, either by killing them or leaving them' (Jespers, 1976:130). In the present case the twins mimic their own death in order to assure their control over the world as soon as they have left (with difficulty) their placenta.

This symbolic mechanism becomes clearer if placed within the homogenous structural whole that the Dogon and Bambara myths constitute. Let us begin with the first. Ogo was born prematurely from Amma's egg, a gigantic cosmic placenta from which the Nommo twins were born normally. As for the Minyanka twins, they could not manage to tear themselves from their mother's womb. Nommo died, sacrificed by God (Amma) when extracted from the placenta; his divided body became the very substance of the universe. On the contrary, the Minyanka twin Ancestors pretended they were dying and God saved them when their father was preparing to bury them. Conceived as an androgyn, the sacrificed Nommo was reborn in two separate beings, man and woman. The Minyanka twins form an indivisible being with a single trunk. The Dogon myth expresses the change from primordial unity to diversity by the division into 'parcels' of the initial placenta. Nya initiates endeavour, on the other hand, to keep all the elements of creation in a compact 'placenta' (the sacks as the universe) placed under the signs of the twins, who are inseparable and, like gold, unalterable.

In order to understand this transformation, let us consider the Fox. He prematurely tore himself from his placenta, which he used to create the earth, and he incestuously coupled with her, confusing the sequence of the generations. The Minyanka twins follow an inverse procedure to reach the same end: to affirm their superiority over the ascendant generation. First, they are literally prisoners of their placenta. After having been freed, they avoid all contact with their parents. They are successful in taking power from the second generation, whereas the Fox rebels in vain against the father's law while appropriating the maternal placentary substance.

A remarkable opposition underlies the conflict between the two generations in the Minyanka myth: if the twins, the second generation, are more powerful than their parents, it is primarily because they have had an abnormally long gestation (ten months) whereas the latter were born prematurely. We shall borrow Piérre Smith's expressions 'over-conceived children' to refer to the terms of this opposition which seems to be relevant in various civilisations (Smith, 1979). Let us resume the comparison of the Dogon Fox and the Minyanka twins from this perspective. Ogo (The Fox), who was born prematurely and who abruptly left his twin sister, can properly be considered an 'under-conceived' creature (as a matter of fact he will always be incomplete) whereas the Minyanka heroes who remain attached to one another (forming a couple that is both twin and androgyn) have all the characteristics of 'over-conceived' and superpowerful children. The Dogon Fox's failure and the Minyanka Twins' success can be explained by these fundamental ontological characteristics provided that all the facets of this problem are considered.

In the Minyanka system, it is the primordial parents (Tyelere and Nyolere) who are defined as 'under-conceived' in relation to their 'over-conceived' twin children. Their congenital weakness makes them 'agitated, unstable creatures indulging in sorcery for a long mythic period' (Jesper, 1976:131). These features liken them more closely to the Dogon Fox, who is characterised by incompleteness and permanent dissatisfaction. Like the Fox, Tyelere and Nyolere, give birth to stunted, deformed, incomplete bush creatures.

I summarise these diverse features in Fig. 27.

Fig. 27

Dogon myth	*Minyanka myth*
Normally-conceived Nommo (Separated twins)	Over-conceived twin ancestors (inseparable)
Under-conceived Ogo, source of disorder	Under-conceived Nyolere and Tyelere, source of disorder
Ogo tries to upset the sequence of the generations by coupling with the Earth Mother	The twin ancestors upset the sequence of the generations by leaving their parents

| The male Nommo sacrificed in the sky at birth is reborn and becomes mankind's ancestor | The twin ancestors feign death and rebirth on earth |

This figure clearly shows how Minyanka thought operates an original synthesis between terms that are antagonistic in Dogon thought. The overdue twins are analogous, from one point of view, to Nommo, the monitor of creation, and from another, to the Fox. Unlike the Minyanka twin ancestors who were born from Tyelere's exceptionally long pregnancy, Nommo is not located in a filiation—considered to be impure—with the Earth Mother. Nommo originates from the celestial father; he comes from Amma's 'breast'. At his birth he is sacrificed to assert the latter's omnipotence. The twin ancestors underwent a parody of death in order to ensure their dominion over the universe which their parents had created. The Minyanka have no hesitation about treating Nya's sacks like a 'fetishised' original placenta that has become the receptacle of their own magical powers. Such audacity clearly locates the Nya's action half way between creative magic and sorcery. Oral literature, in fact, refers to Nya as the supreme sorcerer (Colleyn, personal communication).

In Dogon myth, the upsetting of the hierarchical order of generations is condemned by God (the Fox loses the power of speech, is doomed to sterility and wandering); in Minyanka myth it is willed by God. It is Kle's lightning which blinds the father Nyolere just as he begins to bury his children.

The twins' seizure of power over the sky and earth, over their parents, is expressed forcefully during the sacrifice. It will be remembered that the various *yapere* are placed under the twin ancestors' authority when they are put into the third jar. Life's bounty belongs to the inseparable twins; imperfection to their parents. Yet this mythic and ritual derangement of family and moral order suggests that the Nya initiates, to a certain degree, a break with society's, fundamental rules. Human sacrifice, like that of the dog, is a transgression or a perversion, even though the Minyanka justify themselves by an ultimate appeal to God's supreme authority. In a certain way, the Nya's sacrificial machinery seems like a systematic misappropriation of the sky and earth's power on behalf of men, through the intermediary of those ambivalent creatures, the twins, who are perfect androgyns but physically repulsive. All this strengthens our first hypothesis: the Nya is a royal machination. Thirsting for human blood, he unceasingly is regenerated in order to give men the illusion that they control the obscure forces of nature and the primeval powers. The Minyanka maintain that at the end of her long peregrination during which she bore the future monstrous bush genies, Tyelere was reconciled with her first children, the twins. They came to the aid of their parents but demanded from them a blood sacrifice in the sacred wood. This 'sacrificial pact' thenceforth assigned different locations to the two hostile generations: Nyolere and Tyelere occupied the 'red hill', the foundation site of the first village, and the twins the sacred wood from which their influence emanates (Jespers, 1976:132–3).[1]

We must still reveal, briefly how the Minyanka myth and problematic of sacrifice are linked with Bambara cosmogony. This is all the more necessary since the Minyanka do not hesitate to use the Bambara names of Pemba and Musokoroni for Nyolere and Tyelere (Jespers, 1976:131).

Faro appears sometimes as a female creature with a male twin (Bemba or Koni) at her side, and sometimes as an androgyn who looks like an albino. These two personages can be compared to the leprous Siamese twins in Minyanka cosmogony. Like Faro, the terrifying but benevolent deity, they are associated with gold and demand human sacrifices. They are rivals of Musokoroni (alias Tyelere) and Pemba (alias Nyolere). Faro and her twin appeared on earth after this first pair of twins. In a way they belonged to the next generation, just like the twins, the Minyanka mythical ancestors (Cissé version). However, the latter are Tyelere's children, while the bambara Musokoroni has no human line of descent. The originality of the 'Minyanka solution' rests upon this transformation. Jesper wisely comments:

'This solution implies, in the accounts, that the mother, at the end of a slow and painful gestation, bears a pair of monstrous twins who leave her at birth. In fact, it is as if the twins' deformity was the price paid by mythic thought to grant her this descent line, which she lacks in all other versions. Yet, at the same time, this thought confers a positive meaning upon the twins' deformity: in all the rites, they incarnate the means of mediation between Kle (God) and men' (Jespers, 1976:31).

Signs, placenta, and chicken blood (The Gurmantche)

We have just seen how the original placenta and the life signs it bears appear to be central, symbolic representations in Dogon myth. They reveal one of the keys to sacrifice. These concerns are found in the sacrifices offered by the Gurmantche (Upper Volta) to a large number of fetishised powers, the *buli*, though they seem to be shifted to a different level. We can only outline briefly here the discerning research carried out by Michel Cartry during the past several years among this population—which has no apparent cultural or linguistic link with the societies that developed in the domain of the ancient Mandé. The three preliminary articles which Cartry devoted to sacrificial procedure and representation pose a series of particularly complex problems (Cartry, 1976, 1978 and 1981).

He begins by stating that the 'sacrifiable' species constitutes a closed group composed of fowls, sheep, goats and cattle (rarely sacrificed) and

---

[1] Many other aspects of Minyanka sacrificial rites deserve attention: I shall leave this in the capable hands of Jespers, Jonckers and Colleyn.

exclude the dog, the cat, the donkey and the horse. The dog and cat, like certain wild animals, are only sacrificed within the context of sorcery (Cartry, 1976:157–8; 1978:17). Within each species, the victim must have precise characteristics. Among mammals (the 'four-legged' animals) the male cannot have been castrated; among the sheep and cattle a female is never chosen; among goats only a pubescent, nulliparous female or an intact he-goat can be considered (Cartry, 1976:160). The collective sacrifices are controlled by a 'liturgical code' based on this 'determination of species' (Cartry, 1976:153). In individual sacrifices divination determines the different types of animals which fit the circumstances.

This basic list calls for an explanation which we shall make later. Here, we shall simply state, along with Cartry, that sacrifice implies a loss, a reduction of the 'Having'. But what is the nature of this loss? Cartry's fundamental thesis, inspired by Georges Bataille, is that the sacrificial destruction of a domestic animal, an 'enslaved' creature, transformed into a 'thing', 'will reveal [to man] his intimate essence' (Cartry, 1976:174). In another article he endeavours to penetrate this secret by following step by step the 'vacillation' of the victim's status (1978). Cartry discusses more precisely, the specific sacrifice of the chicken. The choice of a particular animal from this species is highly refined. Geomancy, a veritable divinatory mechanism, is responsible for furnishing a type of very precise 'record card'. The diviner uses ideographic writing. He begins by drawing the geomantic signs. After consulting them, he inscribes 'the words of the earth' on a piece of calabash, this time using a totally different type of writing. For this new procedure, he has two series of abstract signs available. The first designates the powers to whom the client must address himself; the second relates to the sacrificial animals. The Gurmantche diviner possesses no fewer than nineteen separate signs to 'signify' to his client the type of chicken he should sacrifice, whereas goats, sheep and cattle are represented only by generic signs (Cartry, 1978:32–3). The relations of 'signification' between the animal 'inscribed' on the piece of calabash and the real animal which is later to be sacrificed are highly complex. Though certain signs refer to a sub-species which exists empirically (a white, red, crested chicken, etc.) others designate phantas-mogorical categories such as chickens with 'white' 'red' or 'black' hearts (Cartry, 1978:37). Moreover, the animal sacrificed may not necessarily have 'the characteristics indicated by the inscribed sign'. For example, though the sign theoretically calls for a white chicken with black spots, one will often see the sacrifier holding just any chicken (Cartry, 1978:43).

What is the reason for this discrepancy between the message of the sacrificial writing and ritual practice? Certainly not uncertainty or substitution. An egg can never be substituted for a chicken. It is the divinatory mechanism which authoritatively determines this decisive choice. Indeed, the Gurmantche carefully distinguish the sacrifice, in which the animal is killed at the same time as the ritual destruction of the egg (*padita*) and the sacrificial rite when only this last operation takes place (*padipienli*). Commenting on Lévi-Strauss's opinion of the apparent indifference of the sacrificial victim, Cartry remarks that for the Gurmant-che this problem must be expressed differently: 'It matters little what the animal is since here it is part of the essence of sacrifice that it is the sacrificer's word which bestows on it the characteristics indicated on the sign' (Cartry, 1978:43). We shall see that it all happens as if the victim, removed from the 'fowl' species, was caught in a dialectic of 'writing' and of speech which imposes upon it 'a change of status' (Cartry, 1978:41–58).

Suppose the sacrifier takes his chicken to the *bulo* altar (the constituent 'fetish' of a supernatural force). He starts by praying to God as well as to the ancestor who first owned the altar. He has been careful to bring along the piece of calabash given him by the diviner. He 'reads' the first sign in the series dealing with victims, for example: 'a chicken with a crest'. To the *bulo* he points out that the chicken in his hand is the one explicitly required by the sign, even if this is not true. He then indulges in subtle plays on words 'based on the name of the sign-chicken' (Cartry, 1978:44). He thus expresses the actual finality of the sacrifice while passing the knife over the chicken's head without hurting it. He literally attaches the formulations to the chicken's body, which then becomes 'the bearer of the sign's attributes' (Cartry, 1978:45). After this 'inscription' the sacrificer addresses the *bulo*. He calls upon him 'to convey words, which have now become a body, since they were placed on the chicken's body after being taken from the sign' (Cartry, 1978:46).

Then the victim is sacrificed. Cartry proposes to show that the dismemberment and cooking complete the process of transforming an animal into a sign. The sacrificer sprinkles the altar with blood and starts plucking out the feathers; he puts them in the blood, to which they stick, or plants them all around the *bulo* to 'arm' it. Then he breaks the piece of calabash bearing the sign with gestures which become more and more rapid, 'as if he was driven by some kind of desperate eagerness to destroy'. He sticks its fragments on the altar, treating them like the dismembered body of an enemy (Cartry, 1978:49). During this stage the sacrificer 'separates and frees' the inscribed signs, to which he had previously 'attached' his own destiny. After an interruption the partly plucked chicken is passed through the flames. Children then finish the plucking and begin dismembering the animal in a prescribed way. They tear off the wings and legs, tear out the digestive organs and subject them all to a complex treatment before completely roasting the animal. Once the children's work is finished, the sacrificer intervenes again. After a meticulous description which we cannot reproduce here, Cartry shows that the animal, first treated piece by piece, is then reassembled before being put 'in the mouth of the *bulo*', which will present it to God, not as an offering but as an 'animal-sign'.

Why must this animal-sign be killed? 'Why is it not sufficient to leave it in

a kind of "sacred reserve", living among the living yet living apart—set aside'
(Cartry, 1978:53)? Here Cartry examines more closely the notion of loss,
mentioned earlier. Sacrificial death goes back to the representations of
birth. The Gurmantche say that the sacrificer 'kneeling on both knees' is
'like a woman giving birth'. The blood she gives to the earth is like the blood
of a sacrifice (*parli*). The woman in child-birth resembles a dead woman.
Yet to consider her a victim of sacrifice 'would be superficial'. The true
victim 'is that part of himself which the child loses at birth . . . the placenta.
By separating the living child from his placenta, the midwife's knife
condemns to a kind of death this "companion" who was delivered in blood
by the mother' (Cartry, 1978:54).

Though sacrifice may 're-edit' an original act, in this case it is not that of
the birth of the world, as among the Dogon, but rather 'something that
happens at every birth: the inevitable death of what was, for the child, a part
of himself' (Cartry, 1978:54).

Another study by Cartry (1979) explains this symbolic logic. There we
learn that the placenta is a twin, and that any child born singly retains a
mysterious, almost twinlike bond with the little deformed creatures of the
territory of the bush, the *fua-pola*. The newborn creatures belong to the
bush; they have a certain common affinity with these genies, and mothers
fear that the latter may kidnap them (Cartry, 1979:272). The purpose of the
rites of passage is to sever this equivocal bond, to integrate the child within
the village. The twins are, as far as they are concerned, *nu-pola* (lit. 'pola
men') towards whom the Gurmantche adopt an ambivalent attitude. They
make them undergo a test at birth in order to determine whether they are
'good' or 'bad' twins. They are sprinkled with water, and if they remain
silent, it is a sign that they definitely belong to the bush area, like the
fua-pola. They are a threat to their mother and father's life. They are
allowed to die. Even the surviving, accepted twins are thought to be
marginal creatures, closely associated with the dangerous *fua-pola*
(Cartry, 1979: 276–7).

The *fua-pola* are themselves twinlike creatures; they always travel in
pairs, and they each wear a kind of net bag which covers their head and part
of their body (Cartry, 1979:280–1). This covering is expressly perceived as
twins' placenta (Cartry, 1979:283). This placenta which imprisons them
condemns them to eternally roam in the bush area and excludes them from
the village 'territory', (Cartry, 1979:285). From this, one can better
understand the meaning the Gurmantche give to the separation of a child
from his placenta: it is indeed a first mark of 'territorialisation' in the human
area. By plunging the placenta into a pot filled with water, the Gurmantche
act as if they wish to keep it alive, although acknowledging, by the act itself,
that 'it is doomed to a certain type of death' (Cartry, 1979:284). At birth, the
child has lost his twin companion, unlike the *pola* genies who are never
separated from their placenta. He is thus projected into a world of death
whereas the *fua-pola* are immortal.

However, we must still discover why the *pola* who are able to 'escape the placentary mutilation' are nevertheless 'wandering and greedy' (Cartry, 1979:287). Let us begin by noting that the Gurmantche reverse the positive value which the Mandé people—and especially the Dogon—attribute to twins. It is as if the twins, having become alarming creatures of the bush, covered with their placentary tissue, had passed over to the side of the perverse Fox. The *pola* can be compared to those monstrous dwarfs born of the Fox (the Andambulu) which inhabit the bush. They have the same characteristics as the Fox: they are unstable, always moving, and have an 'avidity for life' (Cartry, 1979:285, 286). But the Andambulu are single creatures, deprived of the 'twinness' of Nommo, the water genie; whereas the pigeon-footed *pola* are characterised as twins who never leave their placentary envelope.

The comparison with the Dogon is all the more legitimate in that the Gurmantche, like the former, liken the human foetus to a fish—the silurus (Cartry, 1979:270). Cartry perfectly describes the newborn's double adherence to two 'territories': water on one hand, the bush on the other. This topology might be clearer if one considers the set of symbolic systems which we have presented in this chapter. Whereas the Dogon make water the very territory of 'twinness', placed under the sign of the Nommo pair, and reserve the realm of the bush for the solitary Fox the Gurmantche take a reverse position. In Gurmantche thought, 'twinness' is the very character-istic (strange, dangerous) of the little bush genie which threaten the newborn creatures. The latter have to leave their placenta, their 'twin', in order to fully settle into the human domain.

If, as Cartry suggests, sacrifice does indeed reiterate the brutal act of birth, it is, however, fundamentally different. The separation of the newborn from his placenta inaugurates the difficult process of fixation within the space of the village. On the other hand, the chicken sacrifice—which may or not be followed by other sacrifices—re-establishes contact with the place of origins, the calabash of the world in which the primordial signes of life are written.

Rituals are effective only if they refer to the 'signs of the beginning' (*kikildiani*) that God drew within himself. A Gurmantche diviner ex-plained. 'God or the Great Mother of the World has written up the world within his/her belly for us. He/she has so written in order to tell us that lives are fitted into each other but that they soon fall apart'. An old woman said, 'Everything that exists in the world . . . has its sign of the beginning' (Cartry, 1981:210). These signs are in motion. They control the descent of *tagama*, 'the power to create and procreate' (Cartry, 1981:211). During rituals, 'the actors make contact with this universe of first signs and adjust their gestures, words and acts to it' (Cartry, 1981:211). During the aforemen-tioned sacrifices, the diviner has to 'find the attachment' of the individual client's signs of destiny with the world's first signs by consulting the earth (Cartry, 1981:212). Beginning with this message, he 'draws up his prescription'. Before carving these second signs upon a piece of calabash, 'he must scrape and smooth it in order to make visible, in its grooves, the first signs of the world's belly' (Cartry, 1981:212). This piece of calabash is 'a fragment of the original celestial matrix', but the Gurmantche add, 'It is the life of the sacrifier' (Cartry, 1981:212–3). By destroying it so furiously, the sacrifier does not commit symbolic suicide—this would be lax interpretation. Nor does he desperately attempt to re-establish an attachment to the primordial calabash from which all life has come loose. Through the broken up piece of calabash, he first comes in touch with his own placenta, represented by the cut-up chicken, on the *bulo* altar. The two parts of his being, severed by the midwife's knife at birth, are thus brought back together . . . but in pieces. The bits of calabash are actually 'stuck' with the victim's blood onto the *bulo* (Cartry, 1978:49). Let us recall that preliminary rites 'assigned' to the animal the signs read from the piece of calabash (see p.185). The sacrificer, who is also usually the sacrifier, has thus been tied to the sacrificed animal 'all the tighter in as much as the signs of the calabash are a replication of the signs of his placenta' (Cartry, 1978:54). For the Gurmantche, the placenta is the 'place where the signs of the beginning are drawn' (*ibid*). Sacrifices are tangled up into the following aporia: the sacrifier can re-establish an attachment to a genetic 'place' (the calabash of the world) only through a victim, which represents his own placenta (his twin) sacrificed at birth. Beyond their immediate, contingent finality, sacrifices seem to reassert that death is the price of life, the price to be paid as the immutable signs from the calabash of the world materialise into a real placenta.

The procedures for eating and for 'sticking pieces together' take on great importance. The *bulo's* 'mouth', which receives the parcelled body of the animal and the bits of the broken up calabash, is the obligatory relayer of the sacrifier's words on their way toward the Creator. Both Grandmother and Grandfather of the world according to ritual terminology (Cartry, private discussion), this Supreme Being preceded the separation into sexes. The cutting and breaking into pieces of sacrificial substances suggest that the original unity cannot be restored. The pieces of the animal's body are given up to the enigmatic, gaping *bulo's* mouth. Is the act of 'sticking them together' onto the *bulo* an ultimate, derisive attempt to re-establish the original 'attachment' to the 'world's belly', the place where all things are 'embedded'? The question is left open.

Gurmantche sacrifices apparently vary from the system of thought exemplified by the Dogon. Dogon sacrifices are made in remembrance of the severance of a primordial spirit (Nommo) from his placenta and of his death, dismemberment and resurrection as mankind's ancestor. Gurmantche sacrifices refer to no mythological paradigm of this sort. They do, however, forcefully reiterate the birth of the sacrifier whose placenta died as fated. Dogon ritual celebrates the transition from primordial unity to diversity and fragmentation. Gurmantche ritual proceeds in the opposite direction: from fragmentation (the cutting up of the sacrificial victim) back to the unity of the primordial calabash. In one respect, the Gurmantche procedure is like the Dogon's: the signs of the beginning, which God drew in the original placenta, must be activated.

Gurmantche sacrificial ritual also recalls that of the Minyanka. Both invoke fetish powers that are covered with blood in order to magically attack and defend. The Gurmantche sacrificer continually talks about an 'enemy'. When he plucks the chicken's feathers, he sticks some of them onto the *bulo* but places others on the ground as he conjures the fetish to 'stab' the enemy's eyes so as to make him blind (Cartry, 1978: 48). Destructive fervour, one of the major characteristics of this ceremony, is apparently directed against a surrounding, hostile world. Cartry observes that, by placing feathers around the *bulo*, the sacrificer 'arms' it and bounds its 'territory' (Cartry, 1978: 49).

The *bulo*'s mouth is surrounded by a magic trap that will swallow up those who attack the sacrifier. This functional aspect is not to be separated from the previously explained symbolic logic. The combination of these two aspects is, in fact, evident: the sacrifier is weakened like a newborn babe that has just lost its twin companion, its placenta. During the first few days after birth, danger threatens from all sides. The infant must be armed and attached, through rites, to the village's territory from which the *pola* spirits endeavour to snatch it away. When it is taken outside for the first time, its mother fastens a knife to its back in order to protect it from the *pola* (Cartry, 1978:27). This act is to be likened to the defensive arms that the Gurmantche sacrifier gives to the *bulo* by surrounding it with feathers—an action also aimed at a mysterious 'enemy'.

How surprising to learn that a chicken used to be sacrificed at childbirth! The midwife cut the fowl's throat and poured its blood onto the 'hole of childbirth' (Cartry, 1979:272). However this rite for further separating the newborn babe from its placenta is not a *padita*, a sacrifice of the sort that we have just analysed. It reinforces the separation of the newborn babe from the placenta.

A final problem cannot be avoided. Why, in a *padita*, is the immolation of one or more chickens, whether or not followed by that of other animals, always preceded by the 'sacrifice' of an egg?

Pursuing his long and patient research, Cartry reverts to this important sequence in the *padita* sacrificial ritual, which he had postponed examining. Two kinds of signs of sacrificial animals are carved upon the piece of calabash. Some are crossed with a bar, others not. Only the former entail immolations (Cartry, 1978:25). The first series of inscriptions always contains signs of chickens; and within it, the first two are never barred (Cartry, 1981:199). What does this mean? While reading the first unbarred sign, the sacrificer holds a chicken egg in his hand. He gradually pours out its substance upon the altar according to a strictly observed sequence. He presents it to the *bulo* as though it were a chicken—the chicken designated by the corresponding sign. After these words, he rhythmically strikes the ground with his knife handle as he invokes, respectively, God and the earth. 'With the point of his knife, he breaks the eggshell at the top, makes an opening and takes from the egg's substance a small bit that he throws over the *bulo*. At the very same time as he is making this gesture, he once again appeals to the *bulo*. What does he tell it? While offering it bits of the egg, he invites it to take the chicken corresponding to the first sign' (Cartry, 1981:201).

The second act now begins. The sacrificer reads from the piece of calabash the second unbarred sign, also of a chicken. He acts as before. He once again takes a little of the same egg's substance, until it is used up, unless he has to deal with a third unbarred chicken sign. In this case, he has to keep part of the egg in reserve. Only after having finished sacrificing the egg in accordance with the unbarred signs does he go on to immolate the real chickens (and eventually goats or sheep) that correspond to barred signs.

The situation is summarised in Fig. 28.

Fig. 28

Nonbarred signs	*Barred signs*
Sacrifice of a single egg	Sacrifice of one or more animals

The *padita* type of sacrifice described in the foregoing always entails the sacrifice of an egg before the immolation of animals. But a second type of 'sacrifice of attachment' exists, *padipienli*. This time, only the egg is 'immolated'; no animal takes part at the scene of the sacrifice. Nevertheless, chickens are indeed killed in the egg; invisible chickens (Cartry, 1981:204). There are at least two sorts, which are never identical (Cartry, 1981:214).

What does this immolation mean? 'To break the egg, empty it and spread its substance over the *bulo* are all gestures that the actors in the ritual experience as an act of violence, a violence against life. Our informants explicitly stated, "As for the egg, it's a serious thing . . . we are attacking life . . . we are killing". The sacrificer's prayer confirms that breaking the egg brings one near the boundary that a murderer crosses. Before breaking the shell, the officiant must ask "pardon for the knife". The same formula is used when he immolates the first animal' (Cartry, 1981:203).

Cartry adds that this rite 'does not symbolically replace the successive sacrifices of two chicken embryos' (Cartry, 1981:214). The aim of sacrificing an egg is to stop life—reproduction—itself (Cartry, 1981:215).

Since the sacrifice is sometimes limited to this one destruction (the *padipienli* sacrifice), the very meaning of all real immolations can be sought herein. We can now understand the Gurmantche's choice of victims among all domestic species (see p.184).

'Totally excluded from the list of animals fit for sacrifice are those of either gender that are unfit for procreation' (Cartry, 1981:215). The reason that she-goats that have borne offspring are rejected in favour of nulliparous ones is that the former have already begun their life of reproduction whereas the latter 'possess the highest potential of creation' (Cartry, 1981:215). The egg has this property in the highest degree since it 'contains the future of a descent-line' (Cartry, 1981:215).

This argument seems quite sound. But what is the purport? M. Cartry has not yet advanced a reply, and I am wary of proposing one in anticipation. It is, however, tempting to liken this single egg (which contains, in the bud, we might say, the multiplicity of beings fit for sacrifice) to the calabash of the world (to which all human lineages were attached). This aggression against a simple chicken egg has a fantastic symbolic effectiveness since, by itself, it brings the ultimate source of all life within reach. By attacking this primary signifier that has no economic value, the Gurmantche sacrificer seems to recognize an unending, standing debt that his assets can never pay off to the insatiable *bulo*'s mouth. In other words man, a mere fragment of the world (represented by the piece of calabash), will never really be able to 'stick' himself back on to the primordial womb.

VIII

The sacrificial debt

It is now time to risk enlarging the comparative perspective. We have considered cosmogonic sacrifice among the Dogon and we have shown that the sacrificial rites of a certain number of neighbouring, and even of distant populations provide many variants of it. During the first part of this work, the same transformational procedure was used in discussing a number of Bantu societies. Certain aspects of the Greek cooking model seemed thus to be applicable. Going beyond the specifics peculiar to African cultures, we may now ask whether the Dogon sacrificial pattern might not be related to a different general model, one which could be found in an entirely different historical landscape. Unquestionably it is to ancient India that we must look.

Vedic sacrifice as practised in Brahman India from 1500 to 500 B.C. is, let us remember, the starting point of Hubert and Mauss's study. For us it will be but a brief, final reference point. I direct the reader to the recent works on this subject by two eminent specialists, Madeleine Biardeau and Charles Malamoud (1975, 1976). Before we consider the major themes discussed in this new research, we must note the remarkable common spirit which animates the founding myth of sacrifice in Vedic Indian and in contemporary Dogon civilisations. The terms used by Olivier Herrenschmidt to characterise the first are perfectly applicable to the latter. Brahman world order is explicitly linked to the primordial sacrifice of a cosmogonic genie, Prajāpati. 'The cosmos is a gigantic man, yet man is also a microcosm' (Herrenschmidt, 2979:173). World order has been 'linked explicitly to sacrifice' (Herrenschmidt, 1979:172). To use Masson-Oursel's expression, the world *is* 'literally a sacrifice' (Masson-Oursel, 1948:82). The original sacrifice is 'not only the point at which the individual is joined with the universal, but also the union of the one with the many, of totality with its components' (Herrenschmidt, 1979:172). Prajāpati 'gave out the sacrifice' (Herrenschmidt, 1979:173). It is 'creative' and 'differentiating' (Herrenschmidt, 1979:174). Like Nommo, Prajāpati 'has the Word as a support';

'sacrifice creates (and maintains) world order, creating (and maintaining) the proper differentiations' (Herrenschmidt, 1979:174).

To translate the complexity of Brahman metaphysics into the complexity of Dogon *'sophia'*—or vice versa—is far from my intention. The presence of the Sovereign Father, the conflicting complementarity between the twin Nommo and the lone and incomplete Fox, are just a few original features of Dogon myth which have no equivalents in Indian thought. The Indian sacrifier implicates his own life. He settles down in the closed, darkened hut symbolising the womb, and silently takes the foetal position. He experiences a warming up which transforms him into a 'cooked' person (Malamoud, 1975). One, or several, ritual fires, likened to the god Agni, 'devour' the oblatory material, which is carried by the smoke up to the gods (Malamoud, 1976a:160; Biardeau, 1976:22). These offerings consist of male domestic animals, cereals or milk products, and *soma*, the stimulating liquor from the 'forest'. Yet they are but 'degraded substitutes' for the sacrifier himself, who, having returned to the foetal state, 'prepares himself to be reborn as a god or as food for the gods' (Malamoud, 1976a:161).

Sacrifice consists entirely of cooked food. 'Anything cooked belongs to the gods' and 'all cooking of food is a sacrifice', for what we eat is 'actually the remains of a meal served to the gods' (Malamoud, 1975:101). Milk is itself considered to be cooked; it is in fact the fire-god Agni's sperm; it is warm when it is milked (Malamoud, 1975:101). *Soma*, which delights the gods, is consumed raw and is the only exception. However, *soma* is a god, 'a royal god, king of the Brahmans' (Malamoud, 1975:106). The sacrifier is driven by an abiding faith in the rite's efficacy; his desire is the propellant of a movement towards the gods, of a 'journey' (Malamoud, 1976a:190). The end result of sacrifice is always individual, 'whatever the expected result may be, and even if it is primarily concerned with assuring world order' (Biardeau, 1976:19). To 'return to his being', to 'repossess his body', the sacrifier must pay fees to the priest organising the rite, who introduced him into the celestial world 'as sperm flows into the womb'. (Malamoud, 1976a: 192–3). The sacrifier and his wife finally carry out an exit rite (Malamoud, 1976a:162–3). Malamoud shows that 'these procedures fit into a general economy of debt and ransom which, in Brahmanism, govern not only men's individual lives, but also the whole organisation of the world, and especially sacrifice. From his birth, man is a debt for which death is the creditor' (Malamoud, 1976a:194).

The schema of Hubert and Mauss based on Sylvain Levi's classic analysis certainly aids the understanding of Brahman sacrifice (Biardeau, 1976:19). Yet one must not forget that the mythical paradigm of the rite is the self-sacrifice of Cosmic Man, the source of all energy (Biardeau, 1976:15); 'the cosmos is the product of a sacrifice; sacrifice is at the foundation of all things' (Biardeau, 1976:16). 'To sacrifice is also to redeem this first sacrifice: the rites carried out by the gods and, later, by man (especially the construction of an altar of fire) are intended to reconstitute the body of Purusa-Prajāpati, which is scattered throughout his creation' (Malamoud, 1975:98–9). He was seized by an inflamed desire which preceded the appearance of the Multiple. His body gave birth to all creatures, and first of all to Agni, the hungry and devouring fire. Prajāpati, emptied, then created a replica of himself that serves as fodder for Agni, and which is indeed sacrifice. In the image of Prajāpati, any sacrifier (who is himself the very substance of sacrifice), constructs the world by heating himself (Malamoud, 1975). The gods' immortality depends on sacrifice, which is said to be Prajāpati himself (Biardeau, 1976:20).

Even this rough summary reveals many differences as compared to Dogon myth and sacrificial rites. However, their cosmogonic implication justifies the comparison. Every sacrifice repeats the creative effects of a man-god's primordial immolation. It is the repayment of an original, congenital debt. The Brahman rite, which is placed entirely under the sign of fire, consists of the cooking of the sacrifier, who dies as an embryo and is reborn as a god, whereas the Dogon rite re-enacts the birth, death and rebirth of a water god. Georges Bataille's excellent phrase applies literally to the first case, but not to the second: 'To sacrifice is to give—as a coal is "given" to the furnace' (Bataille, 1973:67). The contrast is striking: delivered into Agni's devouring mouth, the sacrifier assures the rebirth of Prajapāti by maintaining, through heat, the gods' immortality; the blood of the Dogon sacrificial animal, identified with the immortal Nommo and poured over the altar, renews the universe, engendering the circulation of the humid Word, which is destined for men. The participants in the sacrificial meal eat a victim likened to Nommo's dismembered body in a 'communion' which unites 'all the members of the group concerned' (Griaule and Dieterlen, 1965:359). In Brahman thought, the gods eat the offering and men consume only the leftovers. Yet this consumed food is also 'burned—totally destroyed by the fire of digestion'; in this sacrificial cooking, priests and sacrifiers 'themselves represent the gods' (Biardeau, 1976:22).

The theme of kingship takes on a particular coloration in India, where the religious role belongs to the Brahman, while the king's business is war. the king is, however, the sacrifier *par excellence*. He literally *consumes* (burns) his wealth in the sacrifice. In this way, he undergoes 'a loss of substance which results in the happiness of the kingdom' (Malamoud, 1976a:201). Yet as an officiant, he also receives a 'salary' for his ritual work: he levies the tax so as to consume it. If he oppresses his subjects, he himself will be doomed to become an offering: 'the repression he exerts upon them, the friction to which he subjects them, heats them up and creates a flame which bursts out of them, which devours offerings and which will consume him, the king, and his family' (Malamoud, 1976a:201). In the Brahman sacrificial system, the king holds, by turns, the positions assigned to the sacrifier, the sacrificer, and the victim.

By forcing the contrast somewhat, it could be said that man, rendered divine through the Brahman sacrifice, sacrifices himself to maintain the vital force of the gods, whereas in the Dogon rite an anthropomorphised god, the ancestor of humanity, sacrifices himself for it. The cosmogonic myths seem doomed to waver between the two extremes of this alternative. We shall soon find them again in another form: must one eat the god or be eaten by him? (see p.210). We are aware that Freud considered only the first hypothesis in *Totem and Tabu*. By comparing the sacrificial debt inherent in the Brahman rite with that featured in Gurmantche sacrifice, Michel Cartry reveals another alternative: in the first case, the sacrifier, restored to the foetal stage, is himself the sacrificial substance; in the second, he surrenders his 'companion', his placenta, the part of himself which is 'more than himself' (Cartry, 1978:55).

Most sacrifices we have considered in the three preceding chapters bring us face to face with an ultimate stake: a human life (or its double). The symbolic activity consists most often in masking—even denying—this evidence which is hidden behind the sacrifices of the Gurmantche chicken, the Minyanka dog, the Zulu, Thonga, and Lovedu sheep, and the Swazis' royal black ox. It is the paradigm of human life in its most perfect form (the ancestor god) which the Dogon sacrifice when they immolate domestic animals. To understand the Frazerian mystery of 'gods who die', I thought it necessary to study more thoroughly the sacrifice of sacred kings (real or substitutes), the majestic and formidable incarnation of all cosmic forces. Dogon and Bambara myths can be read as the 'texts' of sacred royalty, and not as the expression of murderous tendencies indigenous to a mankind which is trying desperately to expel violence from society.

Yet the Dogon sacrifice adjusts a fundamental disorder, an offence against the Creator's law. In this respect, the Dogon myth diverges from the Brahman model to resemble, curiously, the Christian myth. There are reasons for asking if the few features they share are superficial or, on the contrary, if they belong to a common symbolic structure, liable to appear in radically different historical environments and to express highly diverse philosophical and moral concerns.

Let us begin by observing, with Herrenschmidt, that ancient Brahman-ism, which is based on the 'efficacy' of sacrifice, guarantor of cosmic order, contrasts in many respects with the Old Testament, where the sacrifices are only 'symbolic'[1] acts within a legislative order (the law), guaranteed by a transcendent god (Herrenschmidt, 1979). What is the position of Christianity in this respect? Herrenschmidt clearly detects its ambiguity. 'From the very beginning, opinions ... diverge: while the Last Supper may foretell a coming event—the sacrifice of Christ—it can be read either as the basis of a rite which will be merely commemorative, symbolic, or as an efficacious act, just like sacrifice, in which the blood, *truly* consumed (or

---

[1] I do not think his use of the term 'symbolic' is quite adequate.

shed) possesses all of its redeeming power' (Herrenschmidt, 1979:186). When confronted with the rise of Protestantism, the Church never ceased to consider Communion as a sacrament and to proclaim the validity of the dogma of transubstantiation. 'Therefore, the Mass is effective because it *re-enacts*, in the strongest sense of the word, Christ's sacrifice' (Herrenschmidt, 1979:188).

Here we can begin a comparison with Dogon problematic. Every sacrifice re-enacts that of a saviour-god (Nommo) destined to be 'resurrected'. Like Christ, Nommo is the Father's consubstantial son (he is born in 'Amma's breast') and the consenting instrument of his will. However, the efficacy of the son's sacrificial death is given different values. Nommo's blood is assuredly more powerful on the energy level, than Christ's, since it floods a gestating universe, and since the god's dismembered body becomes the very substance of the world. Contrary to Christian theology, African thought does not separate matter and spirit, seeds and 'souls'. Nommo's sacrifice takes place in the sky, at the very instant of world creation; Christ's passion takes place on earth, at an intermediate time. Christ's sacrifice transforms the Old Testament alliance between men and God—as expressed through animal sacrifices and obedience to commandments—into a unique sacrificial mediation between heaven and the earth. Its purpose is the saving of souls and not the reorganisation of the world. With these differences clearly established, it is no less remarkable that it is the sacrifice of a son-god, in both cases a man-god, which atones for an offence, a transgression of the Father's law.

The Christian philosophy of sin is highly complex. It has certainly varied through theological developments. On several occasions I have emphasised that it was absurd to rely on it in order to set up an anthropology of transgression and pollution. I shall therefore try to avoid falling into that trap. It is nevertheless true that sacrifice often relates to a philosophy of offence and indebtedness of which 'sin' could well be just one specific aspect.

In Christian thought, the oldest offence committed against the Father's law was the angels' revolt. Curiously, this theme does not appear in the Old Testament. The fall of the angels, delivered unto 'the chains of darkness' while awaiting the Last Judgment, is depicted in 2 Peter 2, IV and Jude 6. As for John (XIV, 30), he refers to the Devil as 'Prince of This World'. Genesis merely places in Eden the mysterious figure of the Serpent; yet Christian tradition equates him with the Spirit of Evil, through whom, according to the Book of Wisdom (2,24) 'death appeared in the world' (Cross ed. 1971:393). In the mythic chronology, the Fall of the Angels, led by the Prince of Shadows, precedes 'Original Sin'.

How could angels, perfect creatures, sin against God? Jacques Maritain poses the question from a Thomist perspective and comes up with an astonishing reply: The angels' sin is 'a disordered act bearing on a thing fundamentally good' (Maritain, 1961:46, cited by Kristeva, 1980:151). This interpretation could be applied to the primordial transgression of the Fox. Originally a perfect creature, he competes with God and tries to steal his secrets, the signs deposited in the cosmic placenta, in order to build a universe 'for himself'. The second offence committed against the Father's order in Christian thought is that of Adam, the first man. Opinions differ as to the nature of this sin and in a very provocative essay, Kristeva reminds us that Hegel saw in it 'a trait that was marvellous, contradictory' (Kristeva, 1980:148). In any case, the Tree of Knowledge planted in the Garden of Eden and the very object of the Interdiction suggests in a way, the divine signs which the Dogon Fox tried to steal so as to equal God, to take the Father's place. The offence relates to a higher political order, where knowledge and power are combined under the sign of absolute sovereignty. Adam's offence is certainly not that of the Rebellious Angel. It is, after all, less serious; it is due more to curiosity. It is even indispensable for the advancement of the divine plan. Adam's descendants will be saved by the later sacrifice of Christ, whereas the Rebel Angel is permanently damned. So why did this second biblical offence become the paradigm of sin, the 'Original Sin'?

The Old Testament sets up a barrier of prohibitions between man and God, a world of pollution, of abomination external to man. Mary Douglas and Jean Soler, following parallel paths, have admirably shown that the rules distinguishing pure meat from impure meat follow a highly developed classificatory pattern (Douglas, 1969; Soler, 1973). Soler writes: 'Paradise is vegetarian' (Soler, 1973:944). After the Flood, men are authorised explicitly to eat 'every moving thing' as well as grass (Genesis, IX, 3), but not the blood (the significance of the animal's vital principle) which belongs to God. The prohibition 'ensures the maintenance of the difference between man and God' (Soler, 1973:945). Finally, Mosaic law introduces the famous opposition between pure species (ruminants with 'hoofed feet' and 'cloven hoofs') and impure species, excluded from this classification, which limits the edible animals to cattle, sheep and those wild animals which resemble them the most. For an animal to be 'sacrifiable', it must, furthermore, be perfect, 'pure', as the priest must also be (Soler, 1973:948–9).

Thus the biblical world established a rift between man and God, which respect for the prohibitions constantly demonstrates and maintains. Kristeva proposes a novel interpretation of the Christian religious revolution (Kristeva, 1980). Jesus advocates a significant reversal of attitudes. He constantly protests against the idea, characteristic of Jewish ritualists, of abomination external to man. He came so as to establish the 'inwardness' of the offence; it is a pollution from within, not from without: 'Not that which goeth into the mouth defileth a man, but that which cometh out of the mouth, this defileth a man' (Matthew, XV, 2). Soler astutely notes that one of the decisive departures introduced by Christianity concerns food.

Mark lifted the old prohibitions by proclaiming that all food was pure (Soler, 1973:954).

Jesus also brought forgiveness, the end of the sacrificial indebtedness: 'The *debt*, by all evidence a Jewish concept, implies a pitiless creditor and forces the subject, man, into the role of a debtor whose unspecified payments will bridge the gap which separates him from God only through a faith that is indefinitely maintained' (Kristeva, 1980:142). The sacrifice of the Son of God, who is also the son of man, assures the payment of the ancient debt. Yet St. Paul, then St. Augustine, worked on the problem of sin as an offence from *within*, a result of free will. Christianity proceeds to identify sin with the very flesh of man, in particular with sexuality. Henceforth, original sin is also the desiring of woman—sexual enjoyment. One of the interpretive lines in Adamic transgression places it 'in the sequence: femininity-desire-nutrition-abjection' (Kristeva, 1980:148). I would point out in passing the subsequent necessity to purify Christ's mother, through the proclamation of the dogma of the Immaculate Conception.

This long journey through history has taken us quite a distance from the offence of the Fox, who, conversely, suffers from being separated from his female companion, from his perfect 'twinness', from losing his fertility. The corruption of his desire lay in wanting to rule over the world alone, in stealing God's secret. Yet the original historical synthesis which the Christian myth establishes, at the crossroads of Judaism and Greco-Roman thought, re-establishes in a very interesting way the armature of the Dogon myth.

Let us recall the principal points of the Dogon myth. The immolation of a god makes reparation for the disorder that a rebellious creature, hungry for power and knowledge, brought into the universe when he prematurely tore himself loose from the original placenta, an act that threatened to make future humanity incomplete. Changed into the Fox, this trickster hero instigated human revolt. In the Judeo-Christian myth, God created man perfect, in his image, but a deceptive demiurge hidden in the Tree of Eden inspired the original sin. In both cases, sacrifices were made to redress this first disruption. Consented to (or willed) by the Father, sacrifice restored the purity of the soul blemished by the original sin (or restored lost fertility, the integrity of one's vital principles). The salvation promised to Christians is in the next world. For the Dogon, it is here and now, upon the cultivated earth that has been purified by the sacrifice of a god.

Only careful self-censorship explains why the name of Jesus does not appear in Frazer's index of gods who die, whereas we do find 'sacrifices of children in Jerusalem' listed there. Let us take at face value the image of Christ the King, co-sovereign of the universe, along with the Father, and let us ask whether this royal theme does not shed even more light on the structural relationship of these two schemas. Let me propose the following as one of many possible readings of Christian theology. While drawing inspiration from the metaphysics of Good and Evil that constitutes its philosophical foundations, Christianity bases itself on the universal symbolism of sacred kingship. But it imposes a division upon it by its anti-thesis between the Prince of Darkness and Christ the King, as between fire and water, between flesh and spirit, damnation and eternal life. The slight aperture established by Dogon thought between the twin genies Nommo and Ogo, whose relationship is one of antagonistic complementarity, here becomes a bottomless abyss. Satan, into whose fiefdom Adam places himself by committing 'original sin', is the principle of disorder, always active even though ceaselessly expelled from the world of man.

In iconography Satan is depicted as a goat, whereas the sheep is a metaphor for Christ. In English, one metonym for the Devil is 'Cloven Hoof'. Even though, I repeat, the Fox is not the Evil One, it is nevertheless interesting to note that the goat belongs to him, just as the sheep is Nommo's animal. This mythic 'underworld' which Satan succeeded in creating by tearing himself away from the Father's law just like a cunning Fox is the equivalent of the dark domain which is traditionally associated with witchcraft in Europe. When the Church became worried by the persistence of ancient folklore, it developed around the Rebel Angel a veritable anti-theology of the Sorcerer King, practising execrable sacrifices as counters to Christ the King's redeeming sacrifice, re-enacted on the altars during the Eucharist.

Mutatis mutandis, I have tried to develop a comparable reduplication of sacred kingship in the complementary figures of Dogon myth. To be sure, the Fox does not take on the Devil's role, nor even that of witchcraft. He plays a positive role in universal dialectic. Yet the cursed part of cosmic kingship which he assumes is at the origin of all later disorders, and the heart of man cannot escape an irreducible 'temptation' by the Fox, the first civilising hero. His offence against God, which deprived him of human form and speech is, after all, the equivalent of the 'Angel's sin' as defined in the purest Thomist tradition. The ancestor Dyongu Seru follows the Fox's path by later transgressing an agricultural interdiction while Adam, on the prompting of the snake, breaks an interdiction concerning gathering.

The offence against God is atoned for by the 'purifying' sacrifice of a son of a god, unceasingly repeated in the form of a substitute, in which the animal in one case and the bread and wine in the other, undergo a veritable 'transubstantiation'. This structural configuration is original enough to suggest that the unexpected parallel between Christ and Nommo deserves our attention, despite all the differences between their respective conceptions of life. It is certainly not Islam which introduced such a mythic schema on the banks of the Niger. The myth's metaphysical framework, like the speculations about blood is purely African; I have already described its multiple transformations in Mali.

Like the Brahman myth, the Dogon myth sends sacrifice back to the question of origins. The Dogon's (but not the Brahman's) sacrifice, as in Christian myth, also revolves around the question of a fault. The tearing of the primordial placenta is naturally situated on an ethical and philosophical register very different from Judeo-Christian speculations. Dogon sacrifice does not conjure up evil. It celebrates unceasingly the beneficial results of the death and rebirth of a god, the ancestor of mankind. Though it may repair the nocive effects of transgressions, it also maintains, through the periodical rites, the world in working order. It is the perfect rite.

This plenitude of meanings is unknown in the sacrificial rites of societies who are not haunted by the paradigm of dying gods. Such is the case of the Nuer. And yet, here also sacrifice seems to revolve around the notions of fault and debt (Chapter I). Let us examine this idea more closely by looking at a few sociological variations of the same theme.

The sacrificial debt paid by the Nuer to the spirits is taken from the very treasure which is supposed to perpetuate life: cattle are in fact bride wealth *par excellence*. They are the basis for the *circulation* of women, for a father's rights over his sons and daughters. A wife is acquired through the transfer of oxen to the wife's kin. Sacrifices thus take a good deal of the medium of exchange out of circulation. We have challenged the concept proposed by Evans-Pritchard that the sacrifier identifies himself with the animal victim. However, other societies do not hesitate to embrace this viewpoint, to transpose, so to speak, the sacrificial debt from the category of 'having' to that of 'being'. This seems to be the case with the Lugbara of Uganda as described by John Middleton (Middleton, 1979). As among the Nuer, sacrifice does not set up an intimacy between men and the spirit world. It intervenes in a crisis. Illness is the typical form of religious communication (Middleton, 1979:179): it is a sign of social tension which must be resolved. Through illness, ancestors or spirits 'show the people what is proper behaviour' (Middleton, 1979:177). Through sacrifice, what the Lugbara really undertake is the healing of the social body, not an individual's illness.

A certain number of acts liable to upset relations of authority within the lineage or the family are defined as *ezata*. This word literally means 'an act that destroys'. Middleton refuses, correctly, to translate it by the word 'sin' (Middleton, 1979:182). It is up to the diviner to assess the situation; certain offences must be atoned for through a sacrifice to the ancestors, guardians of moral order; others require a (non-sacrificial) purification addressed to God, who 'eats' neither the meat nor the blood. As for the spirits of the air, they accept only bloodless offerings: cereals and milk (Middleton, 1979:180–3). Thus, within the ritual space, a sacrificial zone is precisely defined, even though offerings and sacrifices are designated by the same word (*owizu*). The sacrifices to the ancestors (*ori owizu*) are offered to them in 'thanksgiving', in gratitude for inflicting disease upon a member of the group, thus 'showing' him that he did not respect the rules of the social game. Just as in the Nuer system, the illness sign is a reminder of the fearful power of the invisible world, of its regulatory political function.

An ox, a goat or a chicken is 'dedicated' as soon as the cause of the illness has been identified. The animal is led around the patient's house. (If a fowl, it is simply passed around the patient's head.) Then the sick person is 'encircled', given a 'liminal' moral status. He is relegated to a space outside the village. He becomes dependent on the elder of his lineage (Middleton, 1979:188). He is identified with the 'dedicated' animal, which will not be sacrificed until after cure. The animal's remains are distributed among ancestors and living members of the lineage (Middleton, 1979:180). Yet this distribution emphasises the lack of communion. The ancestors receive 'raw meat, raw blood, chyme and chyle, and either unfermented beer or its dregs (both undrinkable); the living consume cooked meat, a cooked mixture of blood, chyme and chyle, and fermented beer' (Middleton, 1979:189). The living and the dead partake of a meal that contains the same elements, but only those going to the living are marked by a cooking fire. This decision can be considered a variant of the Nuer sacrificial system, which decrees that raw elements (chyme, chyle and blood) all belong in full to the spirits but (cooked) meat only to men (see p. 11). Yet in Lugbara thought the sacrificial debt is none other than the guilty person himself, the sacrifier. But here the entire lineage participates in the rite, which marks, so to speak, its liberation, its departure from the 'circle'. Middleton describes this rite of passage in terms used by Hubert and Mauss. It seems to me more relevant to note that the sacrifier undergoes a process of thermal regulation. This, curiously, reverses the Brahman schema. As a result of his offence, the Lugbara sacrifier is in a dangerous state of 'heat'; when he has performed the rite, he recovers the normal state of 'coolness' (Middleton, 1979:189). In Brahman sacrifice, on the contrary, the sacrifier symbolically immolates himself by undergoing a heating process, a 'cooking'.

Lugbara sacrifice thus re-established bodily equilibrium while it restores harmony within the lineage. This 'group therapy', directed by the elder and conducted around an 'encircled' sacrifier, contrasts with the individual sacrifice carried out among the Nuer by one man, proudly brandishing his spear. Even though he is guilty, the Nuer sacrifier pays his debt as if setting his affairs in order. The two rites do present, however, enough points in common to allow me to compare them. Both affirm the impossibility of any positive communication with the invisible world, which manifests itself only through illness and disaster. In both cases, the sacrifice maintains and reaffirms the division between the realm of mankind and that of the spirit. (A Lugbara myth affirms that formerly men could communicate with God by climbing up a rope or scaling a tower that joined the sky and earth. But this bridge was broken, and since then men have lost their understanding of the perfect society; they merely form small, conflicting communities [Middleton, 1979:177]). Although the illness results from an offence, the Lugbara do not consider it a punishment but a reminder of the ideal harmonious order, of God's truth (Middleton, 1979:177).

Let us not give the wrong impression. The Lugbara do indeed, say that illness, like possession, constitutes a means of communication between God and mankind. But sacrifice, which ends social disorder, immediately re-establishes the difference between sky and earth, between the visible and the invisible: it puts God and the Ancestors at a distance. It returns them to their own area. In Nuer as well as in Lugbara thought, an offence entails a discordant conjunction of two universes which must remain separated. In the former, it can be perceived as a breaking of a prohibition, which affects the individual's status (following the untimely intervention of the air spirits); in the latter, the offence is more precisely an anti-social act, a challenge of the elders' authority.

'Being' and 'having'

In the case just cited (and I could add more) the most perfect sacrificial debt is that which a man must pay with his own blood in order to continue to exist. The animal victim is only a substitute. This phenomenon of 'displacement' is problematic. If animal sacrifice has received little attention from anthropologists it is because, more often than not, they perceived it as a banal phenomenon, a form of offering, a mere gift. Yet the 'thing' given must be put to death in order to affect the invisible forces so that life may be perpetuated. This is surely the crux of the matter of sacrifice. Hubert and Mauss were not mistaken.

The sacrifier himself is involved in varying degrees in the animal's destruction. Among the Nuer, the slaughtered ox which is intended to end the sacrifier's state of degradation is deducted from the actual wealth which permits group survival and matrimonial exchanges. When analysing the status of 'sacrifiable' species among the Gurmantche, Cartry notes that goats, sheep, and cattle enter into the circuit of trade exchange (which is not the case among the Nuer). The possession of large and small cattle is a mark of individual wealth. As for chickens, they constitute a potential source of wealth, for the Gurmantche sell them to obtain a goat or a sheep. Thus all the species that are used in sacrifice represent 'an embryonic form of capital' (Cartry, 1976:164), whereas non-'sacrifiable' species (the horse, ass, dog and cat) 'are included in another category of 'having' (Cartry, 1976:165). The Gurmantche show no desire to accumulate these, whereas the animals intended for sacrifice 'can be considered to be pure quantity' (Cartry, 1976:170). It would be wrong, however, to try to reduce the fondness for breeding which these farmers develop to 'an economic undertaking based on a desire for profitability' (Cartry, 1976:171). As we have seen, the animal victim possesses an additional symbolic value: the fertile, intact animal designated by divination constitutes a reserve of life—it embodies the future of the species (see p. 191). This potential 'having' is closely associated with the fate of the sacrifier: the latter is 'represented' by a piece of calabash upon which the specific animals destined for sacrifice have been designated by signs. This piece of calabash is destroyed on the altar at the moment when the victims are killed.

Among the Diola in Senegal, rearing livestock cannot be attributed to practical reason. Sacrificial offerings are a destruction of the most valuable possessions: livestock, rice, or palm wine. The most precious is the ox (Journet, 1979:78). Yet sacrifice is the only destiny of the cattle herds owned by the Diola, which they do not use for themselves, except perhaps for manure (Journet, 1979:78). Collective sacrifices often take the form of a potlatch (Journet, 1979:78).

In such societies, breeding is part of that unusual system which Bataille once called 'a consumption economy'. We do not begin to accept the idea that the urge to breed livestock is always somewhat useless. In the aristocratic societies of southeastern Africa (Lovedu, Swazi, etc.) the accumulation of large herds marks differences of rank and status. The principal function of large herds is, however, to circulate in matrimonial exchanges. The pure and simple accumulation of cattle for 'profit' makes no sense for societies who are essentially interested in the accumulation of women. It is because it represents the reproductive force of men, via women, that cattle are the centre of coveting and sociopolitical strategies. These are, first of all, exchange, not production, strategies, with perhaps the exception of the Tswana. The latter practise preferential marriage with the patrilateral cousin, thereby revealing a pronounced taste for closed exchanges, which annul themselves: the cattle, they profess, must return to the house (Kuper, A., 1982:159). The Zulu carry out sacrificial 'punctures' on this exchange value to activate fertility by renewing with the ancestors. However, the Thonga (as well as the Lovedu, apparently) establish a clear distinction between the use-value of the bovines (as elsewhere destined to assure the circulation of the fertilising force of women) and that of the goats, the only ones reserved for the difficult dialogue with the ancestors. By virtue of a purely symbolic decision, the goats constitute a veritable sacrificial reserve here (see Chapter IV). In an even more remarkable practice the Lele disgustedly exclude the goat from the 'territory' of the village (see Chapter II). Domestic or wild, the animal is symbolically classified before being used for social, political, alimentary, or sacrificial purposes. It has no 'economic' value in itself. The Gurmantche strictly exclude the dog from both trade exchange and the sacrificial system (unless it is changed by sorcery) but, on the contrary, it is the perfect sacrificial victim for the Minyanka, who therefore urgently seek it out in the market (see Chapter VII). 'Currently, for most ceremonial cults, ten to thirty dogs (each worth thirty to fifty French francs) are sacrificed at each semi-annual festival' (Jonckers, 1976:103). The flow of the dogs' blood, shed upon Nya's altars, is a hidden debt of human blood debited from the 'having' account. To see it merely as a kind of offering, that is, as a simple exchange between man and the gods concerned, would be to miss the essential point.

Polarities in sacrifice

We have just established that the notion of debt is at the core of many sacrificial systems. It is not my intention in this survey to accept the concept which traditional anthropologists refer to as 'expiatory sacrifice'. The Nuer think that a transgression can occur accidentally, without any evil intention. It is as if the sacrificial debt, a part of the social order, constitutes its regulatory mechanism. In this respect, the Nuer origin myth is very revelatory. Fire and the spear, the major symbols of human culture, were introduced, respectively, by the dog and the fox at the end of an era in which violence did not exist. Men did not know hunger, they did not work, they did not reproduce, and they lived with the animals in mutual understanding.

The first creature to fall victim to the murderous spear was the mother of the ox and the buffalo, species which, until then, had not been differentiated. This event provoked a conflict between men and the descendants of the first animal victim. The buffalo avenged their mother by attacking humans in the bush, and the urge to own cattle caused quarrels, then wars, among men. But the bovine species, the object of these rivalries, was to have a special destiny: it was set apart and dedicated to sacrifice (Evans-Pritchard, 1956:268–9). As the object of strong desire, of cupidity associated with death, cattle also put an end to violence. When a man has been killed, his family and a representative of the murderer, following the customary compensation, join in drinking the immolated animal's bile mixed with water and a little milk (Evans-Pritchard, 1956:269). Speaking more generally, we saw in Chapter I how the sacrifice of the ox mends a tear in the social fabric, sanctioned by the spirits of the air. The murder of the primordial cow has thus been transmuted dialectically into an instrument of pact, of communication, of exchange. Sacrifice ends the violence of men and the spirits. This totality of complex values transcends the purely economic value of the livestock, to which the Nuer, who use milk and drained-off blood for nourishment, are naturally not indifferent.

Yet they cannot imagine that beef can be eaten outside ritual festivities. It would be vain to try to explain Nuer sacrifice by the scapegoat theory. It is even more dangerous to apply it to Brahman metaphysics, which hold that a sacrifier pays a debt to the primordial genie and to death by offering his own body. It is hard to believe that the ancient Hindu religion is characterised by a masochistic reversal of archaic aggressive impulses. Nevertheless one obsessive question remains. Why does the sacrificial debt sometimes, exceptionally, demand a real human life? Let us try to see this more clearly.

It is more particularly when the stakes of a sacrifice are of a collective and cosmological nature that the preferential victim is none other than man himself. The Lugbara decision is most enlightening. Whereas in family sacrifices the sacrifier pays his debt to the ancestors with an animal, in former times an innocent man was disemboweled on top of a hill in order to end a catastrophic drought. Today the rite is carried out with a ram abandoned alive to God by the rain priest after the territory concerned has been 'encircled' by the animal (Middleton, 1979:181). Several times we have noted that the sheep is a substitute for a human life on the sacrificial scene in similar ceremonies. A black sheep is sacrificed for rain among the Zulu, Thonga, Tswana, and Lovedu. There are grounds for believing that this association between sheep and the sky is part of a very ancient African ritual vocabulary, wherein this animal is systematically opposed to the goat. However, the most remarkable fact is doubtless that where the symbolic structures of sacred kingship exist, the king himself is designated as the supreme sacrificial victim. While the rain medications kept by the Lovedu queen must be constantly 'refreshed' through the sacrifice of a sheep, in case of a calamity (and, in any case, before her natural death), the sovereign must sacrifice herself in person.

I have already commented amply on that royal sacrificial function. In the present perspective, I would like to go into the meaning of this supreme debt. More than one African example allows us to identify the sacred king as a body-territory; in this, he is similar to the Lugbara ram which 'encircles' the tribal space in order to conjure away the peril of drought. This last sacrifice is intrinsically linked with world order, with the blood-debt which is inscribed within it.

The royal figure does present, however, a particularity which is lacking in the innocent victim, condemned to death by Lugbara sacrificial law. The king is the place where human territory meets an exterior territory, wherein lie natural and supernatural forces. It is this strange, indeed monstrous character of the royal body that gives him an ambivalent position within the sacrificial system. It over-determines him. It suffices to recall here the Swazi ritual. When a black ox, stolen from a commoner, is immolated instead of the king, the filth accumulated by the sorcerers during the past year is transferred to the animal. The animal's remains are committed to the purifying fire (see Chapter V). Yet only the Swazi king is capable, by virtue of his absolute uniqueness, of 'overtaking the sun in a race', of starting up again the great cosmic clock, even of re-establishing fertility through his own power. Royalty's own magic responsibility is actually regenerated by the rite, just as Nommo's death-resurrection puts a fantastic energy into circulation in Dogon myth. Nommo's sacrifice is the purification of a disorder which goes back to the tearing of the primordial placenta when the world was born; but it is also the guarantor of individual equilibrium, as well as social and cosmic harmony. It is the founding act. Such complexity cannot be explained either by the scapegoat theory or solely by the notion of expiation. If the sacred king is a formidable Janus it is by virtue of an original symbolic structure. This latter at least partially elucidates the great Bambara and Dogon cosmogonical myths. It explains why Nommo is both innocent and guilty by divine decree, just as the Swazi king is by human decree. Nommo assumes Ogo's (his own double's) transgression. It is as if mankind had merely transposed to the sky the virtues attributed to the sacred chief on earth. 'Divine' kingship is not necessarily inspired by an organized mythology. It is its implicit discourse which opens the way of sacrifice of the gods. Doubtlessly Frazer's perspective must be reversed: sacred kings are not dying gods; it is, on the contrary, their tragic fate which constitutes the very web of sacrificial mythologies. If regicide is so often present without a justifying myth, priority must indeed be given to the rite's symbolic structure.

Traditional labels only minimize and oversimplify this problem. Let us try, rather, to set up the structural frameworks that are developed around sacrifice. As the central phenomenon of the royal problematic as well as of the cosmogonic myths, human sacrifice bears a maximum load. It triggers new energies, short-circuiting or destroying dangerous powers which were previously rampant. It often incites horror. The Bambara accept the sacrifice of the albino, the king's substitute, as a necessary evil; it is the 'bad sacrifice' *par excellence*. It is not the result of murderous blind fury as war is. The Aztecs, in implementing the monstrous conjunction of war and human sacrifice, were convinced that they were obeying the relentless laws of the universe. Frazer, too anxious to relegate human sacrifice to a barbarous stage in human evolution, curiously neglected to point out that the drama of the Passion, re-enacted on Christian altars, is a universal theme. Christianity's greatness lies in knowing how to present the political assassination perpetrated in Judea by the Roman coloniser, as the ultimate sacrifice, and in having tried to build on this schema—at the price of a metaphysical illusion—a society of peace and brotherhood. That message can never again be forgotten.

Yet a blind man's soft voice, which would not have been heard outside Dogon country if Griaule had not been so attentive, also deserves to be considered as a profession of sacrificial faith, based on the hope of a more humane, more balanced world than that dreamed of by the solitary Fox: the sacrifice circulates 'a word', destined for all, says the old Ogotémmeli.

It can be argued, if you will, that the absolute supremacy of Christianity lies in its being a religion of love. However, let us not forget Freud's diagnosis: ' . . . a religion, even if it calls itself the religion of love, must be hard and unloving to those who do not belong to it. Fundamentally, indeed, every religion is in this same way a religion of love for all those whom it embraces; while cruelty and intolerance towards those who do not belong to it are natural to every religion' (Freud, 1951:50–1). Let us moderate this rather severe judgement. Intolerance of nonbelievers is evidently the paradoxical privilege of religions said to be 'universal' which consider themselves 'superior'. An 'archaic' ethnic religion, made to measure for a people, does not pretend to impose its truth on neighbouring societies, which seem to take pleasure in upsetting its foundations, in changing it, without risking dangerous reprisals.

We shall borrow from Hubert and Mauss the notion of a 'sacrificial schema' to designate that primary structural pattern which is centred on the death of a king or a god. Frazer had the insight to detect it, but did not completely understand all its complexity. However, we shall be careful not to see it as a historical transformation of an older and more general schema, engendered by a so called development of mythology, as did Hubert and Mauss. Rather, we propose to contrast it with the area of domestic sacrifice which, as we shall show, obeys in its turn a bipolar topological conception.

We have seen that this second schema, not reducible to the first, takes its form through ritual cooking as practised by such different people as the ancient Greeks, the Mofu of Cameroon, the Zulu and the Thonga of southern Africa. The victim is always an animal. It is the point at which men and gods meet, or confront, each other. The social function predominates. However, the cutting up of the animal, the ways of cooking, and the disposition intended for the various parts outline a cosmological space. A human community marks out its territory at a greater or lesser distance from the invisible world. The joyful intimacy of the Zulu or Mofu family, grouped around the domestic hearth with the ancestors invited to share a meal (if only metaphorically) contrasts with the situation of the Greek citizens grouped around the spit and cauldron, facing the distant gods of Olympus, who merely breathe in the smoke. In one case a lineage community tightens its bonds with its dead, who never cease to participate in the circle of life; in the other a city asserts its cohesion by showing its dependence on the immortal gods who do not share man's fate.

The killing of an animal and its ritual cooking establish a division of space just as much as they do a communication. The Thonga's collective sacrifices occupy a remarkable position in this set of homogeneous practices: in a crisis, the extended family can only communicate with its own ancestors, who are excluded from the familial stew, through the intermediary of the uterine nephews, who roast the ancestors' share in a space outside the village (see Chapter IV).

Nuer and Lugbara sacrifices can be integrated with this pattern of culinary rites provided we take into consideration a certain number of transformations. The sacrificial practice of these two societies does not imply any positive communication with the invisible world; the sacrifier is repaying a personal debt to the ancestors or to the spirits of the air. Among the Lugbara, this debt involves his entire lineage. No more than in the case of the Greeks is there a true alimentary sharing. Here ritual cooking contrasts the *raw* part, reserved for the ancestors, and the *cooked* part, reserved for the Lugbara men. The Nuer's decision is even more radical: the air spirits' portion does not include any meat, but only chyme, chyle and blood. All alimentary communion is completely missing. The territory of the ancestors (Lugbara) or of the air spirits (Nuer) is absolutely distinct from human territory. The Lugbara isolate the sacrifier from thecommunity through an encirclement rite, and he undergoes a veritable rite of passage. However, this procedure is far from being intrinsically linked with the sacrificial schema, as Hubert and Mauss thought.

Among the Nuer, chyme is found in the inedible portion reserved for the air spirits, and among the Lugbara, in the raw part intended for the ancestors. In both cases it obviously points up the lack of commensality between mankind and the gods. The Thonga use chyme as an agent of separation, of transformation or expulsion. The Zulu use it to purify the place of sacrifice, to ward off the actions of withcraft that come from without. In highly differing African civilisations, chyme belongs to rawness, to a space exterior to the human area characterised by the cooking of food.

In this respect, the Mofu's ritual cooking occupies a unique position. Though like the Zulu they invite their ancestors to partake in the meal, they also sprinkle chyme over their altars, 'literally encrusted with remains of the preceding sacrifices' (Vincent, 1976:194). Why? One of Vincent's informants replies that not only will the ancestors be in no hurry to demand a new sacrifice, but what is more, sorcerers will hesitate to enter a home where the ancestors are satisfied, and thus very vigilant. This symbolic position of chyme, here considered in the light of its resistance to rot, could be considered a remarkable synthesis of the purifying function attributed to it by the Zulu, and the separating role accorded to it by the Lugbara (to maintain the ancestors at a distance).

We might be criticised for mixing together indiscriminately different sacrificial cuisines belonging to highly different cultural areas. It should be noted, however, that the topology of these rites is situated along one continuous axis, from the alimentary communion to which the Zulu unreservedly abandon themselves, to the absolute separation of raw and cooked meat (characterising the relations of the Lugbara with their ancestors).

Heat or coolness

Sacrifice involves not only the dialectic of the raw and the cooked. It can also develop an opposition of coolness and heat.

The Zulu call on the ancestors to settle themselves at the domestic hearth and there consume their share of the sacrificial feast. But in order for this conjunction of the dead and the living to be realised, all the participants must be in a moral condition of 'coolness'; the fire of discord must be extinguished in their hearts. Coolness is an attribute of social harmony; it constitutes a preliminary to the sacrifice, a procedure in the course of which the ancestors leave their aquatic dwelling in order to come and warm themselves again, to play with the fire, to promote female fertility.

The reverse situation characterises the Lugbara sacrificial system. The sacrifier is accountable for an offence, and he exists in a dangerous state of 'heat' even after the illness which struck him has been cured. The role of the sacrifice is to 'cool him off' and the ancestors are given only the raw part of the sacrificial victim (Middleton, 1979).

I compare these two approaches in Fig. 29.

Fig. 29

	Recipient	*Sacrifier*
Zulu (conjunctive sacrifice)	Close to the fire	Is in a favourable condition of coolness
Lugbara (disjunctive sacrifice)	Kept away from the fire	Is in an inauspicious condition of heat

Let us examine from this perspective a Chad tribe, the Massa, whose rites have been described for us by Fr. Dumas-Champion (Dumas-Champion, 1979). The sacrifice is performed to drive away a threatening spirit. The sacrifier is in an 'overheated' condition. This dangerous heat passes into the body of a victim whose blood is a 'cooling vector' (Dumas-Champion, 1979). The bloody flux allows the escape of the evil which was to be expelled. The Massa world-vision is dramatised: 'the ancestors and the supernatural powers, *fuliana*, feed on blood and seek to make men die so as to satisfy their urges' (Dumas-Champion, 1979). But these voracious ancestors are not exactly vampires; what they want is to force their kin to join them. The Massa thus seem to move the conjunctive point of the spirits and the living into a frightening hereafter. The peaceful finality of the Zulu sacrifice is here reversed: the Massa drive away those dangerous, greedy creatures, the ancestors.

This new sort of relationship with the supernatural world is aggravated in popular Hinduism, which is practised by certain Dravidian societies (Herrenschmidt, 1978). Meat-eating goddesses as opposed to a vegetarian god, demand ceaseless tributes of domestic animals; chiefly male goats and rams. But, 'basically there is only one perfect victim: man himself' (Herrenschmidt, 1978:128). Certain of these goddesses act as sovereigns, ruling a territory. But others are so dangerous and voracious that the sacrificial rite seeks, purely and simply, to drive them away. Their demands keep increasing: they claim the entire range of domestic animals, from the baby chick to the buffalo. In this haunted universe, it is the recipient of the sacrifice who now finds herself in a terrifying state of 'heat'. The meat offering excites the goddess even further; that is why they offer her, immediately afterwards, cooling foods (milk, yogurt, etc.). Thus thermal regulation takes place this time in the course of the sacrificial sequence, thanks to the opposition between the elements of the offering.

One should recall, here, that classic Brahman sacrifice implies the heating up of the sacrifier (by self-cooking), delivering him up to Agni, the god of the devouring fire.

To eat or be eaten

The alimentary/culinary question dominates our second sacrificial schema. The Greeks vigorously rejected the idea that the gods could consume whatever part of the victim they chose. The Nuer and the Lugbara maintain a division between the raw and the cooked. The Zulu and the Mofu invite their ancestors to share cooked meat. Sometimes, as we have just seen, the gods become cannibals. In Massa country, the water genie and the genie of death have a preference for the dog, because of the human qualities of its blood, described as 'bitter'. But such a victim is never eaten by men; it is thrown away, for eating a dog would be a veritable act of anthropophagy (Dumas-Champion, 1979).

The question is reversed, however, when one considers the other sacrificial schema. The dog, as a substitute for a human being, is eaten by the Nya initiates who, in Minyanka country, constitute a kind of collective royal body. This manducation, however, does bring to mind somewhat the sorcerer's transgression (as does the cult as a whole). When the king is the designated sacrificial victim, the substitute animal is handled with infinite precaution. Such is the case among the Swazi, where the young men designated to eat the flesh of the black ox during the annual ritual of Ncwala must undergo a rigorous purification. In Dogon country only the 'impure' can eat the goat, representing the ancestor Lebe during the sowing festival. The absorption of this sacrificial flesh is particularly dangerous for other men because Lebe had transgressed. Yet, at the limit, any animal sacrifice, for the Dogon implies theophagy. Every Dogon animal sacrifice re-enacts the stages of the death and rebirth of the god Nommo. The sacrifier eats the victim's liver, filled with vital energy. Throwing this organ on the altar and sharing the body among the participants re-enacts, respectively, the rebirth and the dismembering of the divine body (see p. 148). A cannibalistic theme runs through the myth, indeed, through Dogon sacrificial practice. The albino, sacrificed three years after the enthronement of the religious chief (the hogon) was eaten. According to one version of the myth the ancestors devoured the body of their seventh sibling, Nommo's terrestial incarnation, after having sacrificed him. When the victim was reborn as a snake, he in turn swallowed the ancestor Lebe and then vomited him (see p. 132). The only source of this mythic or ritual cannibalism, which contrasts sharply with the peaceful, social institutions and their respect for human life, is metaphysical. We must remember that the Dogon consider every birth, every germination, as an 'externalisation' of words. However, this metaphor implies an inverse and complementary representation of ingestion, the eating of seeds, and of sacrificial victims, which are themselves supports for the Word and for humidity. Life is, so to speak, constantly swallowed and spit out. The victim, destroyed and ingested, sets free a life force which constitutes the very denial of death. Theophagy, the absorption of the god's vital force, is based on this illusion. Catholic communion, in which the bread and wine 'are', according to the strictest dogma, the flesh and blood of Christ, the source of immortal life, belongs to the same order of concerns.

Therefore from this point of view, sacrifice seems to offer two alternatives: to be eaten by the god, or to eat him. This opposition, however, is not always so vividly sensed. The Lugbara sacrifier, in debt to the ancestors, does project himself into the animal victim, but the invisible recipients, who receive a raw portion, are in no way cannibalistic, no more than the men who eat its cooked meat. As for the Zulu, they reach an agreement; they join with their ancestors in a 'Great Feed'. No one—not the sacrifier, not the recipient—is identified with a victim that is 'good to eat' from the double viewpoint of gastronomy and metaphysics.

The pleasure principle is not incompatible with the constraints of religious practice. If it is merely a matter of expelling something evil, the cooking is suspended, eating the animal is forbidden, with no further action. However, the expediting system of the scapegoat is peripheral to the sacrificial pattern. It does not constitute the centre of gravity for all sacrifice as René Girard thinks. We found it to be an exception to the Nuer's paradigmatic sacrifice of the ox: a dog with a cut ear takes away the illness, *thiang*, which threatens little children (Chapter I). In the Zulu rite the young girls by means of a goat expel the 'blackness' threatening their statute when one of them has broken a sexual interdiction. However, such a sacrifice has nothing to do with the culinary treatment to which the Zulu submit an animal offered to the ancestors. On the contrary, the victim is abandoned without being eaten, and the only symbolic operator is the purifying chyme (see Chapter III). From a topological point of view, the 'scapegoat-victim' is relegated to an empty space at the limits of human territory. It is in a deserted location that the Rwanda sacrifice black goats and human monsters, signs of 'unproductivity' which threaten the rainfall; in Rwanda as well, these 'scapegoats' may be sent into enemy territory, that is, into a place the Rwanda would like to devastate (Chapter V). Yet here, as elsewhere, these exceptional acts differ radically from the sacrifice of cattle to the royal ancestors or to the god Ryangombe. In most cases, elaborate, complicated relations between men and the supernatural powers are bound up with the animal and the culinary issue. Among the Nuer, the sacrifier's guilt does not take away his appetite once he has paid his debt to the air spirits. After all, the Nuer rarely eat beef except at sacrifices. There is as much enjoyment and feasting in the atonement for an offence (Nuer) as in a communal meal (Zulu).

All this leads us to question, once again, the very reason for raising animals. A certain positivist history would have us believe that the domestication of animals and agriculture are part of the same undertaking. These two 'neolithic' techniques surfaced at almost the same time in the Middle East and a new division of labour developed among peoples, with some providing meat, others cereals. No doubt this schema is generally applicable. It does, however, neglect a number of problems. The populations we have reviewed, a differing mix of farmers and herdsmen, use domestic animals with varying degree of reservation to maintain a sacrificial project. They chose Abel's side against Cain's, even if vegetable offerings sometimes accompany the sacrifice of goats, sheep and oxen. When cattle are used in social life, it is as a matrimonial exchange medium or as a mark of prestige. Barring exceptions, sacrifice is the necessary condition of butchery. It was the absolute rule among those great beef-lovers and sharp merchants, the Greeks. Among the Diola, sacrificial death is the very purpose of breeding. A Brahman adage expresses it just as strongly: 'Meat-eating goes with sacrifice' (Biardeau, 1976:53). It is the 'interiorisation of sacrifice', the asceticism required of the Brahman in a later period that explains the appearance of vegetarianism in classic Hinduism, whereas the warriors (*ksatriya*) continued to be associated with violence and meat-eating (Biardeau, 1976:81). It is not surprising that the cattle's sacrificial function lessens when it is used in politico-economic strategies, when it becomes the stakes of a dominant class, a cumulative capital. This is the case in traditional Rwanda society, where the possession of large herds, distributed in networks of clientships, guarantees the aristocratic status of the Tutsi. The need to maintain and augment the cattle-capital, the instrument of social domination, surely explains why sacrifice was limited, in principle, to steers and sterile cows. The Tutsi boasted of their ability to nourish themselves exclusively on milk (see Chapter V).

Pastoralist societies are careful to exclude or limit the sacrifice of female animals. This is the case among the Nuer, who sacrifice only oxen, with certain exceptions. However, to cause rainfall, the Swazi do not hesitate to sacrifice a pregnant ewe or a black cow in calf (Kuper, 1947:171). Among the Diola cattle raising is pure sacrificial loss. The same can be said of the raising of goats among the Thonga, of dogs and chickens among the Minyanka, of sheep, goats and indeed of cattle among the Gurmantche. It is as if the role of a certain number, if not all, domestic species is to constitute a reserve of wealth for man to draw on so as to tie or untie the ambiguous bonds with the invisible.

The question of 'eating to live' shifts to another focal point, where it is a matter of eating with or without the gods, yet always in accord with them. One sometimes also risks being eaten by them, just as they can be eaten to acquire their life force.

Provisional conclusions

This long meandering is merely a reconnoitring trip. I have not tried to substitute a new overall theory for that of Hubert and Mauss, which I have challenged, but rather to indicate some new perspectives.

The failure of Hubert and Mauss is rooted in two aporia. Their ambition was to reduce all sacrifice to rite of passage schema based on a vague topology contrasting the 'profane' and the 'sacred'. The two end results which they believed could explain the 'sacralisation' and 'desacralisation' of the sacrifier on this universal basis, seemed to me inoperable. For these notions, I prefer to substitute those of the conjunction and the disjunction of spaces, human and nonhuman. I have thus laid out a culinary sacrificial topology. It cannot be reduced to the schema to which are referred all sacrificial practices associated with sacred kingship or with the mythic sovereignty of a god doomed to die in order to be reborn. In this case the sacrificial debt is entirely based on the cosmogonic order upon which, in the last resort, social order depends.

Hubert and Mauss's second aporia consists in placing these two schemas in an evolutionary sequence thereby contradicting their own premises. Indeed, it is incomprehensible how in a certain number of civilisations the god himself could constitute the sacrificial victim when the authors define the latter as a mediator between a 'profane' world and a 'divine' world which differ radically. They should have explained how the sacrificed god himself could belong to both worlds, even at the risk of destroying the fundamental opposition which was postulated.

Now, many examples indicate that the 'sacred' king, whose function is to control both social harmony and cosmological rhythms, incarnates the group as 'body territory' while at the same time belonging to the world of the Elsewhere, of mysterious nature, of the 'bush' or the sky, haunted by the forces governing life and death. Only a consistent theory of sacred or divine kingship permits us to understand why the sovereign is the victim *par excellence* in such a politico-symbolic configuration. The gods who die and are reborn immortal can be understood in the same way. Nommo, humanity's divine ancestor, is both the Dogon social body and the water genie living in the pond.

These two sacrificial models, far from being united by some mysterious law governing the evolution of religious institutions, are perfectly capable of coexisting in the same society. However, a homogeneous symbolic system must then be agreed on. The Lovedu sacrifice only goats to the ancestors in the domestic realm: they keep the sheep (substituting for a human victim) to be used for sacrifices to bring rain, while waiting for the queen to offer her own life. The Zulu maintain the same division between 'sacrifiable' species: the oxen (or goats) are for the ancestors, the sheep for the python genie, the regulator of rainfall.

In all the societies we have examined, the victim is never just any animal. Aside from a determination of a species or sub-species, subtle criteria often play a role in the individual selection. In any case, the possibility of substituting one animal for another (indeed, a vegetable species for an animal species) operates within strict limits. Nowhere does there exist a general system of convertibility for sacrificial values. If the Zulu can choose indifferently between a goat and an ox for a domestic sacrifice, it is because of the common properties of their digestive systems. On the other hand, a goat could never be substituted for a sheep in sacrifices to bring rain except by changing its status: muzzled, it symbolically acquires the docile nature of that silent animal, a token of the sky.

Many questions have not been dealt with. Specifically, the symbolism of the seed in relation to the animal should have been examined. We have seen (all too rapidly, I fear) that among the Zulu the offering of beer is a type of sacrifice (Chapter III). Let us once again refer back to the Dogon. After the harvest, the officiant re-enacts the different steps in Nommo's sacrifice and rebirth when he successively pours on the (family or collective) altar a mixture of water and flour, first raw, then cooked. The fermentation of the drink is 'likened to the resurrection of the seed (killed by the cooking) and at the same time to Nommo's resurrection' (Dieterlen, 1976:49). The purpose of the libations is to return the seeds to Nommo's collarbones. 'It is done, Dieterlen comments, to avoid any loss of substance from the seeds which stay protected in special granaries until the next seedtime' (Dieterlen, 1976:49). The rite performed on this occasion restores their 'souls' to the seeds, through a reverse procedure.

An unavoidable enigma remains: sacrifice plays with death in a completely different way than do war or hunting. It is a third mysterious term: here the annihilation of a life nourishes a phantasmagoria of want. A want that all the victims in the world would not fulfil. There, at a greater or lesser distance from the gods, society displays its fissures, the hole of death left by the sun in the first Dogons' placenta. It is impossible to penetrate this existential emptiness (or to artificially fill it with violence as Girard does). We can only study sacrifice from the exterior, describe it as a symbolic work and analyse the systems of representations linked with the treatment of the victim. This varies greatly. The animal body can be furiously torn apart, transformed in the hope to reach the signs of the beginning (Gurmantche), or it can be calmly cut up and prepared so that the ancestors can re-inject their own aquatic substance into the woman's vagina, a gaping hole open to death (Zulu). Sacrifice burrows into the deepest part of the animal to extract some meaning. The black bull and black goat the Rwandans expel to the edge of human space along with a breastless woman are also full of meaning, this time as monstrous creatures. However, we must not forget that the killing of a victim is often but one episode among others, within a complex ritual. In all the above mentioned cases, and whatever the form, sacrifice does nevertheless appear to be an autonomous rite. I hope to have shown that the study of its multiple facets does not lead to the emptiness of a theoretical illusion.

I will readily grant the reader that the division I propose between a set of royal and cosmogonic sacrificial practices on one hand, and a set of domestic and culinary practices on the other, is too absolute. A sacrifice to the ancestors introduces guidelines into the universe; it already sketches out a topology even a cosmology. And reciprocally the sacrifices formerly carried out in Brahman India can be defined as a cosmic cooking, a 'cooking of the world'. But the Zulu domestic sacrifice does not re-enact the birth of the universe; it no more cooks it than cools it. We are thus justified in distinguishing two sacrificial spheres. Our analysis has pointed up not only differences of emphasis, but indeed different ways of thinking about sacrifice, of organising symbolic systems. However, it is always a matter of establishing a locus, near or distant—in space or in time—where a debt of life is to be paid.

To perform a sacrifice is, primarily, to try to outwit death. Human sacrifice represents the outer limit which many rites—in which the sacrifier is seen to project himself into the animal victim, losing a part of his 'having' in order to preserve the essential—strive to reach. This limit is indeed reached when the king, the epitome of 'having' and 'being', is doomed to immolation for the good of the community. These ritual acts, which are part of a metaphysical calculation of profit and loss, have nothing to do with the violence of war, which undertakes the blind destruction of the 'other'. When war becomes the servant of sacrifice, when a people decides to appropriate the lives of others in order to incessantly feed its gods, the religious system is lost in madness. We know that this issue disturbed the conscience of the ancient Mexicans at a certain moment in their history. Yet, even then, the victims had to change their status: they ceased to be captives and, themselves, became the gods.

In Africa, human sacrifice is most often only a means of deferring the sacrifice of the king. But it can also denote the perversion of royal power, the illicit means by which a king allows himself to perform an evil deed, a transgression. This is the dark side of sacrifice. To acquire the sacred power, the dreaded *wene*, 'emanation of superhuman forces', held by the earth spirits, the Yombe chiefs (Zaire) did not hesitate to carry out a grim procedure: a young girl, captured by the pretender's soldiers, was, while still alive, cut in two with the 'knife of power'. Her liver was torn out and eaten by the chief (Doutreloux, 1967:240). Indeed, the great *nkisi* fetishes draw their efficacy from the vital principle (*kinyumba*) of human victims. In this case, the warriors' violence interferes with the quest of sacred royalty by an act which Bantu morality expressly considers an abuse of power. Yet all power, when it calls itself sacred, also becomes terrifying, steeped in sorcery. This is clearly stated by the Bambara when they assimilate the immolation of the albino, which regenerates the king's vigour, with 'a bad sacrifice'.

Be it the life of an animal, or of a man, that is at stake, the sacrificial rituals form a coherent set when compared with the techniques of the trance; these, through an upsetting conjunction, abolish the distance between the human realm and that of the gods within the very body of the possessed person, without destroying it. Elsewhere I have outlined a structural analysis of these phenomena (de Heusch, 1971,). To be sure, possession and sacrifice can both be parts of the same ritual sequence. Among the Minyanka, for example, it is always a man in a trance who seizes the bags of Nya and brings them into the sacrificial enclosure. Possession here constitutes an 'adorcism'[2] and necessarily precedes an appeal to Nya's efficacious power, which is brought about through a complex symbolic process by the sacrifice of dogs. On the other hand, the Thonga use sacrificial blood to exorcise those possessed by a violent and dangerous spirit coming from a realm foreign to that of the ancestors (see p. 000). In this case it is a matter of driving away a pathogenic spirit that is responsible for a mental disturbance—in short, to effect a disjunction, and not, as in the case of the Minyanka, a positive conjunction.

This brief summary suggests that the two essential means—sacrifice and possession—that men have at their disposal for establishing a communication with the gods in order to survive—or for breaking it in order not to perish—belong to a more general ritual system for which this book, however fragmentary and incomplete, perhaps provides a few new elements.

---

[2] I proposed to use this word, as opposed to 'exorcism', to designate the positive relation between a possessed man and the possessing spirit.

Bibliography

CHAPTER I. Preliminary readings

Benveniste, Emile (1969), *Le vocabulaire des institutions européennes*, I. Economie, parenté, société – II. Pouvoir, droit, religion; Paris.

Detienne, Marcel (1977), *Dionysos mis à mort*, Paris.

Detienne, Marcel (1979), 'Pratiques culinaires et esprit du sacrifice' in Detienne and Vernant. *La cuisine du sacrifice en pays grec*, Paris.

Evans-Pritchard, E.E. (1948), 'Nuer Marriage Ceremonies', *Africa*, XVIII, I, 29-40.

—(1953), 'The Sacrifical Role of Cattle among the Nuer', *Africa*, XXIII, 3, 181-197.

—(1956), *Nuer Religion*, Oxford.

—(1965), *Theories of Primitive Religions*, Oxford.

Girard, René (1972), *La violence et le sacré*, Paris (English ed., *Violence and the Sacred*, Baltimore, 1977).

de Heusch, Luc (1971), Preface to Mary Douglas, *De la souillure. Essais sur les notions de pollution et de tabou*, Paris, 7-20.

Hubert, Henri and Mauss, Marcel (1968), 'Essai sur la nature et les fonctions du sacrifice', in Mauss, Marcel, *Oeuvres*, I, Paris (first published in *L'Année sociologique*, 2, 1899). English ed., *Sacrifice: its nature and function*, London, 1964.

Jespers, Philippe (1976), 'Contribution à l'étude des autels sacrificiels du Nya chez les Minyanka du Mali', *Systèmes de pensée en Afrique noire*, cahier 2, Le sacrifice I, CNRS, Paris, 111-139.

Jonckers, Danielle (1976), 'Contribution à l'étude du sacrifice chez les Minyanka', *Systèmes de pensée en Afrique noire*, cahier 2, Le sacrifice I, CNRS, Paris, 91-110.

Kiggen, Father J. (1948), *Nuer – English Dictionary*, London.

Lévi-Strauss, Claude (1962), *La pensée sauvage*, Paris (English ed., *The Savage Mind*, London, 1966).

—(1971): *L'homme nu*, Paris (English ed., *The Naked Man*, London, 1981).

Vernant, Jean-Pierre (1976), *Religion grecque, religions antiques* (inaugural lecture on taking up the chair in the Comparative Study of Ancient Religions, Collège de France), Paris.

—(1981) 'Le sacrifice. Le mythe grec', in *Dictionnaire des mythologies* ed. Yves Bonnefoy, Paris.

Vincent, Jeanne-Françoise (1976), 'Conception et déroulement du sacrifice chez les Mofu', *Systèmes de pensée en Afrique noire*, cahier 2, Le sacrifice I, CNRS, Paris, 177-203.

CHAPTER II. To each his own

Biebuyck, Daniel (1953), 'Répartition des droits du pangolin chez les Balega', *Zaïre*, VII, 8, 899-934.

—(1973), *Lega Culture. Art, Initiation and Moral Philosophy among a Central African People*, Berkeley, Los Angeles and London.

Douglas, Mary (1954), 'The Lele of the Kasai', in *African Worlds. Studies in the Cosmological Ideas and Social Values of African Peoples*, ed. Daryll Forde, Oxford University Press, London, New York and Toronto, 1-26.

(1955), 'Social and religious symbolism of the Lele of the Kasai', *Zaïre*, IX, 4, 385-402.

(1957), 'Animals in Lele religious symbolism', *Africa*, XXVII, I, 46-58.

(1963), *The Lele of the Kasai*, Oxford University Press.

(1975), *Implicit Meaning. Essays in Anthropology*, London and Boston.

de Heusch, Luc (1954), 'Autorité et prestige dans la société tetela', *Zaïre*, VIII, 10, 1001-1027.

(1971), Preface to Mary Douglas, *De la souillure. Essais sur les notions de pollution et de tabou*, Paris, 7-20.

Krige, J. D. and E. J. (1943), *The Realm of the Rain-Queen. A Study of the Pattern of Lovedu Society*, London, New York and Toronto.

Vansina, Jan (1964), *Le royaume kuba*, Musée Royal de l'Afrique Centrale, Tervuren.

CHAPTER III. A *calao* for the rainbow

Berglund, Axel-Ivar (1975), *Zulu Thought. Patterns and Symbolism*, London.

Doke, C. M. and Vilakazi, B.W. (1948), *Zulu-English Dictionary*, Johannesburg.

de Heusch, Luc (1982), *Rois nés d'un coeur de vache*, Paris.

Krige, E. J. and J. D. (1943), *The Realm of the Rain-Queen. A Study of the Pattern of Lovedu Society*, London, New York and Toronto.

—(1954), 'The Lovedu of the Transvaal', *African Worlds. Studies in the*

Cosmological Ideas and Social Values of African Peoples, London, New York and Toronto, 55-82.

Kuper, Hilda (1973), 'Costume and cosmology: the animal symbolism of the Ncwala', *Man*, 8, 4, 613-630.

Lévi-Strauss, Claude (1964), *Le cru et le cuit*, Paris (English ed., *The Raw and the Cooked*, London, 1970),

—(1971), *L'homme nu*, Paris (English ed., *The Naked Man*, London, 1981).

Ngubane, Harriet (1977), *Body and Mind in Zulu Medicine. An Ethnography of Health and Disease in Nyuswa-Zulu Thought and Practice*, London, New York and San Francisco.

Roumeguere-Eberhardt, J. (1963), *Pensée et société africaine. Essais sur une dialectique de complémentarité antagoniste chez les Bantu du Sud-Est*, Cahiers de l'Homme, Paris and The Hague.

Stayt, H. A. (1968), *The Bavenda*, London (1st ed. 1931).

Vansina, Jan (1964), *Le royaume kuba*, Musée Royal de l'Afrique Centrale, Tervuren.

Vincent, Jeanne-Françoise (1976), 'Conception et déroulement du sacrifice chez les Mofu', *Systèmes de pensée en Afrique noire*, cahier 2, Le sacrifice I, CNRS, Paris, 177-203.

CHAPTER IV. The Thonga's goat

Hamayon, Roberte (1978), 'Marchandage d'âmes entre vivants et morts', *Systèmes de pensée en Afrique noire*, cahier 3, Le sacrifice II, CNRS, Paris, 151-179.

Harris, Marvin (1959), 'Labour migration among the Moçambique Thonga: cultural and political factors', *Africa*, XXIX, 50-65.

Herrenschmidt, Olivier (1978), 'A qui profite le crime? Cherchez le sacrifiant', *L'Homme*, XVIII, 1-2, 7-18.

de Heusch, Luc (1955), 'Valeur, monnaie et structuration sociale chez les Nkutshu (Kasai, Congo Belge)', *Revue de l'Institut de Sociologie*, Brussels, 4, 400-410.

—(1974), 'The debt of the maternal uncle', *Man*, 9, 4, 603-619.

—(1982), *Rois nés d'un coeur de vache*, Paris.

Hunter, Monica (1936), *Reaction to Conquest*, London.

Jacques, A. A. (1929), 'Terms of kinship and corresponding patterns of behaviour among the Thonga', *Bantu Studies*, 3, 327-48.

Junod, H. A. (1910), 'Les conceptions physiologiques des Bantous sud-africains et leurs tabous', *Revue d'ethnographie et de sociologie*, I, 126-169.

—(1927), *The life of a South African Tribe*, London, 2 vols.

—(1936), *Moeurs et coutumes des Bantous. La vie d'une tribu sud-africaine*, Paris, 2 vols.

Krige, E. J. and J. D. (1943), *The Realm of the Rain-Queen. A Study of the Pattern of Lovedu Society*, London, New York and Toronto.

Lévi-Strauss, Claude (1965), 'Le triangle culinaire', *L'Arc*, 26 (issue dedicated to Claude Lévi-Strauss) 19-29.

Schapera, I. (1971), *Rainmaking Rites of Tswana Tribes*, Leiden and Cambridge.

CHAPTER V. The king on the sacrificial stage

Arnoux, A. (1912), 'Le culte de la société secrète des Imandwa au Ruanda', *Anthropos*, VII, 273-295, 529-558, 840-875.

Bataille, Georges (1973), *Théorie de la religion*, Paris.

Beidelman, T. O. (1966), 'Swazi royal ritual', *Africa*, XXXIV, 4, 373-405.

Berglund, Axel-Ivar (1975), *Zulu Thought. Patterns and Symbolism*, London.

Bourgeois, R. (1956), *Banyarwanda et Barundi. T.III. Religion et magie*, Académie Royale des Sciences Coloniales, Brussels.

Coupez, André (1956), 'Deux textes rwanda', *Kongo-Overzee*, XXII, 2-3, 129-151.

Coupez, A. and Kamanzi, Th. (1962), *Récits historiques rwanda*, MRAC (Annales série Sciences Humaines, 43), Tervuren.

—(1970), *Littérature de cour au Rwanda*, Oxford, Clarendon Press.

d'Hertefelt, M. and Coupez A. (1964), *La royauté sacrée de l'ancien Rwanda*, Musée Royal de l'Afrique Centrale, Tervuren.

Girard, René (1972), *La violence et le sacré*, Paris (English ed., *Violence and the sacred*, Baltimore, 1977.

de Heusch, Luc (1958), 'Essais sur le symbolisme de l'inceste royal', Bruxelles.

—(1972), 'Le roi ivre ou l'origine de l'Etat', Paris.

—(1981), 'Nouveaux regards sur la royauté sacrée', *Anthropologie et Societes*, V, 3, 65-84.

—(1982), *Rois nés d'un coeur de vache*, Paris.

Kuper, Hilda (1947), *An African Aristocracy. Rank among the Swazi*, London, New York and Toronto.

de Lacger, L. (1939), *Ruanda I*, Namur.

Lestrade, Arthur (1972), *Notes d'ethnographie du Rwanda*, Archives d'anthropologie 17, Musée Royal de l'Afrique Centrale, Tervuren.

Maquet, Jacques (1954), *Le système des relations sociales dans le Rwanda ancien*, Tervuren.

Muller, Jean-Claude (1975), 'La royauté divine chez les Rukuba. Benue-Plateau State, Nigeria', *L'Homme*, XV, I, 5-27.

—(1977), 'Chefferie, idéologie et mode de production chez les Rukuba (Plateau-State, Nigeria)', *Revue canadienne des études africaines*, XI, I, 3-22.

—(1980), 'Le roi bouc émissaire Pouroir et rituel chez les Rukuba du Nigéria Central', Paris.

Ngubane, Harriet (1977), *Body and Mind in Zulu Medicine. An*

Ethnography of Health and Disease in Nyuswa-Zulu Thought and Practice, London, New York and San Francisco.

Pages, A. (1933), *Un royaume hamite au centre de l'Afrique*, Mémoire de l'Institut Royal Colonial, Section Sciences morales et politiques, Brussels.

Sandrart, G. (1939), *Cours de droit coutumier*, Astrida (Rwanda).

Smith, Pierre (1970), 'La forge de l'intelligence', *L'Homme*, X, 2, 5-21.

—(1975), *Le récit populaire au Rwanda*, Classiques africains, Paris.

—(1979), 'L'efficacité des interdits', *L'Homme*, XIX, I, 5-47.

de Sousberghe, L. (1963), 'Les Pende. Aspects des structures sociales et politiques' in L. de Sousberghe, B. Crine-Mavar, A. Doutreloux and J. de Loose, *Miscellanea ethnographica*, Musée Royal de l'Afrique Centrale, Tervuren, 1-78.

Stayt, H. A. (1968), *The Bavenda*, London (first ed. 1931).

Vansina, Jan (1964), *Le royaume kuba*, Musée Royal de l'Afrique Centrale, Tervuren.

Ziervogel, D (1957) *Swazi Texts*, Pretoria.

CHAPTER VI. Sacrifice as the core of myth

Adler, Alfred and Cartry, Michel (1971), 'La transgression et sa dérision', *L'Homme*, XI, 3, 5-63.

Bettelheim, Bruno (1971), *Les blessures symboliques*, Paris.

Calame-Griaule, Geneviève (1962), 'Le rôle spirituel et social de la femme dans la société soudanaise traditionnelle', *Diogène*, 37, 81-92.

—(1965), *Ethnologie et langage. La parole chez les Dogon*, Paris.

Cissé, Youssouf (1980), Communication to colloquium on sacrifice, Laboratoire associé No. 221, CNRS, Paris, 5-6 June.

Dieterlen, Germaine (1951), *Essai sur la religion bambara*, Paris.

—(1957) 'Parenté et mariage chez les Dogon (Soudan français)', *Africa*, XXVII, 2, 107-148.

—(1971), 'Les cérémonies soixantenaires du Sigui chez les Dogon' *Africa*, XLI, 1, 1-11.

—(1973) 'L'image du corps et les composantes de la personne chez les Dogon', in *La notion de personne en Afrique noire*, Colloquium of the CNRS, Paris.

—(1976a), 'Introduction à de nouvelles recherches sur le sacrifice chez les Dogon', in *Systèmes de pensée en Afrique noire*, cahier 2, Le sacrifice I, Laboratoire associé 221, CNRS, Paris, 43-50.

—(1976b), 'Analyse d'une prière dogon', in *L'Autre et l'Ailleurs. Hommage à Roger Bastide*, Paris, 247-272.

—(1976c), Discussion de l'exposé de Luc de Heusch 'Le sacrifice ou la violence de Dieu', in *Systèmes de pensée en Afrique noire*, cahier 2, Le sacrifice I, CNRS, Paris, 84-89.

—(1978), Observation, 11 May, Laboratoire associé No. 221.

—(1980), Communication to colloquium on sacrifice, Laboratoire associé No. 221, CNRS, Paris, 5-6 June.

—(1981), 'Forgeron', in *Dictionnaire des Mythologies*, ed. Yves Bonnefoy, Paris, 430-33.

—(1982), *Le titre d'honneur des Arou (Dogon, Mali)*, Paris.

Dieterlen, Germaine and Cissé, Youssouf (1972), *Les fondements de la société d'initiation Komo*, Paris and the Hague.

Dieterlen, Germaine, and de Ganay, Solange (1942), 'Le génie des eaux chez les Dogon', *Miscellanea Africana Lebaudy*, cahier no. 5, Paris.

Griaule, Marcel (1938), *Masques dogons*, Institut d'Ethnologie, Musée de l'Homme, Paris.

—(1940), 'Remarques sur le mécanisme du sacrifice dogon (Soudan français)', *Journal de la Société des Africanistes*, Paris, X, 127-130 (reproduced in *Systèmes de pensée en Afrique noire*, cahier 2, Le sacrifice I, Laboratoire associé No. 221, CNRS, Paris, 51-54).

—(1947a), 'Mythe de l'organisation du monde chez les Dogon du Soudan' *Psyché*, 6, Paris, 443-453.

—(1947b), 'Nouvelles recherches sur la notion de personne chez les Dogon', *Journal de psychologie normale et pathologique*, XL, 4, 405-31.

—(1948), *Dieu d'eau. Entretien avec Ogotemmêli*, Paris (English ed., *Conversations with Ogotemmêli: an introduction to Dogon religious ideas*, London, 1965.

—(1954), 'Remarques sur l'oncle utérin au Soudan', *Cahiers internationaux de sociologie*, XVI, 35-49.

—(1955), 'Rôle du silure Clarias Senegalensis dans la procréation au Soudan', Deutsche Akademia der Wissenschaften zu Berlin, Institut für Orientforschung, *Afrikanische Studien*, 26, Berlin, 299-311.

Griaule, Marcel and Dieterlen, Germaine (1954), 'The Dogon', in *African Worlds. Studies in the Cosmological Ideas and Social Values of African Peoples*, ed. Daryll Forde, Oxford University Press, London, New York and Toronto, 83-110.

—(1965), *Le renard pâle*, T.I. *Le mythe cosmogonique*, Institut d'Ethnologie, Paris.

de Heusch, Luc (1971), *Pourquoi l'épouser et autres essais*, Paris (English ed. *Why marry her?*, 1981, Cambridge).

—(1972), *Le roi ivre ou l'origine de l'Etat*, Paris (English ed., *The drunken king or the origin of the State*, 1982, Bloomington).

—(1978), 'Le dette sacrée de l'oncle maternel', in *Systèmes de signes. Textes réunis en hommage à Germaine Dieterlen*, Paris, 271-298.

—(1976), 'Le sacrifice dogon ou la violence de Dieu', in *Systèmes de pensée en Afrique noire*, cahier 2, Le sacrifice I, CNRS, Paris, 67-84.

—(1982), *Rois nés d'un coeur de vache*, Paris.

Hubert, Henri and Mauss, Marcel (1968), 'Essai sur la nature et la fonction du sacrifice', in Mauss Marcel, *Oeuvres*, I, Paris (first published in

L'Année sociologique, 2, 1899, English ed., *Sacrifice: its nature and function*, London, 1964.)

Liberski, Danuta (1978), 'Masculin/féminin ou l'ambiguïté dans la pensée dogon', mimeo, Université Libre de Bruxelles.

CHAPTER VII. The Dogon's neighbours

Calame-Griaule, Geneviève (1965), *Ethnologie et langage, La parole chez les Dogon*, Paris.

Cartry, Michel (1976), 'Le statut de l'animal dans le système sacrificiel des Gourmantché (Haute-Volta)', 1st part, in *Systèmes de pensée en Afrique noire*, cahier 2, Le sacrifice I, CNRS, Paris, 141-175.

—(1978), 'Le statut de l'animal dans le système sacrificiel des Gourmantché', 2nd part, in *Systèmes de pensée en Afrique noire*, cahier 3, Le sacrifice II, CNRS, Paris, 17-58.

—(1979), 'Du village à la brousse ou le retour de la question. A propos des Gourmantché du Gobnangou (Haute-Volta)' in *La fonction symbolique. Essais d'anthropologie* collected by Michel Izard and Pierre Smith, Paris, 265-288.

Cissé, Youssouf (1980), Communication to colloquium on sacrifice, Laboratoire associé No. 221, CNRS, Paris, 5-6 June.

—(1981), 'Le sacrifice chez les Bambara et les Málinke', in *Systèmes de pausée en Afrique noise*, cahier 5, Le sacrifice IV, 22-59.

Dieterlen, Germaine, (1951), *Essai sur la religion bambara*, Paris.

—(1971), 'Les cérémonies soixantenaires du Sigui chez les Dogon' *Africa*, XLI, 1, 1-11.

Dieterlen, Germaine and Cissé, Youssouf (1972), *Les fondements de la société d'initiation Komo*, Paris and the Hague.

de Ganay (1949), 'Notes sur la théodicée bambara', *Revue d'histoire des religions*, CXXXV, 187-213.

Jespers, Philippe (1976), 'Contribution à l'étude des autels sacrificiels du Nya chez les Minyanka du Mali', *Systèmes de pensée en Afrique noire*, cahier 2, Le sacrifice I, CNRS, Paris, 111-139

—(1979), 'Signes graphiques minyanka', *Journal de la société les Africanistes*, 49, 3, 73-102.

Jonckers, Danielle (1976), 'Contribution à l'étude du sacrifice chez les Minyanka' *Systèmes de pensée en Afrique noire*, cahier 2, Le sacrifice I, CNRS, Paris, 91-110.

Smith, Pierre (1979), 'Naissances et destins: les enfants de fer et les enfants de beurre', *Cahiers d'études africaines*, special issue dedicated to Denise Paulme, XIX, 1-4.

Zahan, Dominique (1960), *Sociétés d'initiation bambara. Le N'domo. Le Koré*, Paris and The Hague.

CHAPTER VIII. The sacrificial debt

Bataille, Georges (1973), *Théorie de la religion*, Paris.

Biardeau, Madeleine (1976), 'Le sacrifice dans l'hindouisme', in Biardeau and Malamoud, *Le sacrifice dans l'Inde ancienne*, Paris, 7-154.

Biardeau, Madeleine and Malamoud, Charles (1976), *Le sacrifice dans l'Inde ancienne*, Paris.

Cartry, Michel (1976), 'Le statut de l'animal dans le système sacrificiel des Gourmantché (Haute-Volta)', part I, in *Systèmes de pensée en Afrique noire*, cahier 2, Le sacrifice I, Paris, 141-175.

—(1979), 'Le statut de l'animal dans le système sacrificiel des Gourmantché (Haute-Volta)' part 2, in *Systèmes de pensée en Afrique noire*, cahier 3, Le sacrifice II, Paris, 17-58.

Cross, Fl. (ed.) (1971), *Oxford Dictionary of the Church*.

Douglas, Mary (1969), *Purity and Danger. An Analysis of Concepts of Pollution and Taboo*, London.

Doutreloux, Albert (1967), *A L'ombre des fétiches. Société et culture Yombe*, Louvain and Paris.

Dumas-Champion, Françoise (1979), 'Le sacrifice comme procès rituel chez les Massa (Tchad)' in *Systèmes de pensée en Afrique noire*, cahier 4, Le sacrifice III, Paris, 95-115.

Freud, Sigmund (1951), *Group Psychology and the Analysis of the Ego*, New York (first ed. 1922).

Hamayon, Roberte (1978), 'Marchandages d'âmes entre vivants et morts', in *Systèmes de pensée en Afrique noire*, le sacrifice II, CNRS, Paris, 151-179.

Herrenschmidt, Olivier (1978), 'Les formes sacrificielles de l'hindouisme populaire' in *Systèmes de pensée en Afrique noire*, cahier 3, Le sacrifice II, Paris, CNRS, 115-133.

—(1979), 'Sacrifice symbolique ou sacrifice efficace', in *La fonction symbolique. Essais d'anthropologie*, collected by Michel Izard and Pierre Smith, Paris, 171-192.

de Heusch, Luc (1971), *Pourquoi l'épouser? et autres essais*, Paris (English ed: *Why marry her?*, Cambridge, 1981).

—(1982), *Rois nés d'un coeur de vache*, Paris.

Jonckers, Danielle (1976), 'Contribution à l'étude du sacrifice chez les Minyanka', in *Systèmes de pensée en Afrique noire*, cahier 2, Le sacrifice I, CNRS, Paris, 91-110.

Journet, Odile (1979), 'Questions à propos du sacrifice chez les Diola de Basse-Casamance', in *Systèmes de pensée en afrique noire*, cahier 4, Le sacrifice III, CNRS, Paris, 77-94.

Kristeva, Julie (1980), *Pouvoir de l'horreur. Essai sur l'abjection*, Paris.

Kuper, Adam (1982), *Wives for Cattle*, London.

Kuper, Hilda (1947), *An African Aristocracy. Rank among the Swazi*, Oxford University Press, London, New York and Toronto.

Lévi, Sylvain (1898), *La doctrine du sacrifice dans les brahmanas*, Paris.

Malamoud, Charles (1975), 'Cuire le monde' in *Purusārtha. Recherches de science sociale sur l'Asie du Sud* (Centre d'étude de l'Inde et l'Asie du Sud), 91-135.

—(1976a), 'Terminer le sacrifice. Remarques sur les honoraires rituels dans le brahmanisme', in Biardeau and Malamoud, *Le sacrifice dans l'Inde ancienne*, Paris, 155-204.

—(1976b), 'Village et forêt dans l'idéologie de l'Inde brahmanique', *Archives européennes de sociologie*, XVII, 3-20.

Maritain, Jacques (1946), *Le péché des anges*, Paris.

Masson-Oursel, P. (1948), *La philosophie en Orient*, supplement to E. Brehier, *Histoire de la philosophie*, Paris.

Middleton, John (1979), 'Rites of sacrifice among the Lugbara', in *Systèmes de pensée en Afrique noire*, cahier 4, Le sacrifice III, Paris, 175-192. Erratum, Le sacrifice IV, 1983, p.217.

Soler, Jean (1973), 'Sémiotique de la nourriture dans la Bible', *Annales (Economie, Sociétés, Civilisations)*, 4, Paris, 943-955.

Vincent, Jeanne-Françoise (1976), 'Conception et déroulement du sacrifice chez les Mofu', *Systèmes de pensée en Afrique noire*, cahier 2, Le sacrifice I, CNRS, Paris, 177-203.

ADDENDUM

Chapter II.

Biebuyck, D. (1953b), 'Maternal uncles and sororal nephews among the Lega', *Report of the Second Joint Conference on Research in the Social Sciences in East and Central Africa*, Markerere College, Kampala, Uganda, 122–33.

Chapter III.

Lévi-Strauss, Claude (1965), 'Le triangle culinaire', *L'Arc*, 26 (issue dedicated to Claude Lévi-Strauss), 19-29.

Chapter V.

Adler, Alfred (1978), 'Le pouvoir et l'interdit. Aspects de la royauté sacrée chez les Moundang du Tchad', in *Systèmes de signes. Textes réunis en hommage à G. Dieterlen*, Paris, 22-40.

—(1982), *La mort et le masque du roi. La royauté sacrée des Moundang du Tchad*, Paris.

Chapter VI.

Lifszyc, D. and Paulme, D. (1936), 'Les fêtes des semailles de 1935 chez les Dogon de Sanga', *Journal de la Société des Africanistes*, Paris, VI, 95-110.

Index